WHAT EVERY CHRISTIAN SHOULD KNOW ABOUT SALVATION

Twelve Bible Terms That Describe
God's Work of Redemption

ROB PHILLIPS

Unless otherwise indicated, Scripture quotations are from the Christian Standard Bible (2017).

Unless otherwise indicated, Hebrew and Greek words and phrases are taken from *Mounce's Complete Expository Dictionary of Old & New Testament Words*, and from *Interlinear For The Rest of Us: The Reverse Interlinear For New Testament Word Studies,* both by William D. Mounce.

Executive editor: Dr. John Yeats
Cover design and graphics: Jo Horn
Layout: Brianna Boes
Production management: Jim Thorne
Kindle production: Brianna Boes
Scripture verification: Christie Dowell
Proofreading: Christie Dowell, Nancy Phillips

Contents

Introduction

WHAT DOES IT MEAN TO BE SAVED?

Christ died to make possible the salvation of all men and to make certain the salvation of those who believe.

- Robert Lightner, *The Death Christ Died*

This resource is designed for personal or group study. It explores twelve Bible terms that describe God's work of salvation as He rescues us from sin, returns us to a right relationship with Him, and ultimately restores us — and the fallen world in which we live — to perfection.

People use the words *salvation* and *saved* in a variety of settings, from sporting events to political campaigns to natural disasters. Even within Christian circles, there is disagreement as to what it means to be saved and how salvation is acquired. So, it's critical for us to begin with a definition.

Stated simply, salvation is God's remedy for the sin that has ruined everything and alienated everyone from Him. The Lord reveals this remedy as soon as Adam and Eve rebel against Him. He promises a future Redeemer who crushes the head of Satan (Gen. 3:15). Then, He provides additional promises throughout the Old Testament, granting us more than four hundred prophecies, appearances, or foreshadowings of the Messiah, a King who comes as a virgin-born child in Bethlehem.[1]

This child, Jesus of Nazareth, bursts onto the scene at just the right time (Gal. 4:4). He lives a sinless life and dies on a Roman cross, taking upon Himself our sins and paying the penalty of death for them (2 Cor. 5:21). Then, He rises physically from the dead on the third day, conquering Satan, sin, and death, and freely offering forgiveness of sins and everlasting life by grace through faith in Him. Before ascending into heaven, He promises to return one day to fulfill all things — that is, to complete His work of salvation and to set everything right (Matt. 16:27; 25:31-46; John 14:1-3).

DELIVERANCE FROM DANGER

The word *salvation* has its roots in the Hebrew *yasa*, which means "to be wide or roomy." It's often rendered "to save, rescue, deliver." Thus, words such as *liberation, emancipation, preservation, protection,* and *security* grow out of it. Essentially, salvation means delivering a person or group from distress or danger.

Yasa, and words derived from it, occur more than three hundred fifty times in the Old Testament. The word *yeshuah* (salvation) is first used in Ex. 14:13 to speak of God's deliverance of Israel from Egyptian bondage. Even more important, *yasa* points forward to a great Deliverer, our Savior Jesus Christ. In the New Testament, the verb *sozo* (to save) and the nouns *soter* (Savior) and *soteria* (salvation) carry over the Old Testament concept of deliverance.[2] As we explore God's work of salvation, the focal point is Jesus, "the author and finisher of our faith" (Heb. 12:2 KJV).

Even so, the word *salvation* is used in many ways throughout the Old and New Testaments, and it's important to consider the context to determine the proper application. For example, the words *save* and *salvation* often refer to physical, not spiritual, deliverance. In the Old Testament, people are saved from enemies on the battlefield (Deut. 20:4). Daniel is rescued from the mouth of the lion (Dan. 6:20). And the righteous are delivered from the wicked (Ps. 7:10; 59:2). In the

New Testament, the Lord delivers Paul from shipwreck (Acts 27:20, 31, 34). In other passages, salvation in the physical sense refers to being taken from danger to safety (Phil. 1:19) and from disease to health (James 5:15).

Of course, the greatest type of salvation is spiritual in nature. God sends His Son to be the Savior of the world (1 John 4:14). Jesus comes to seek and to save lost sinners (Luke 19:10). Because of His finished work on the cross, those who call upon the name of the Lord are saved (Rom. 10:13). This salvation comes by the grace of God, through faith in Christ (Eph. 2:8-9). The Lord is working, even now, to save us from sin's power (Rom. 5:10; Heb. 7:25; James 1:21). One day, God's work of salvation is complete, when even the presence of sin is eradicated (Rom. 13:11; 1 Peter 1:9). These wonderful truths prompt the writer of Hebrews to exhort followers of Jesus not to neglect the great salvation given to us (Heb. 2:3).

AN UNBREAKABLE RELATIONSHIP

For followers of Jesus, salvation is experienced as an everlasting, unbreakable relationship with Him. It has both temporal and eternal benefits. In fact, of the twelve terms this book addresses, several cannot be confined to time or expressed in chronological order. Consider, for example, that we are *foreknown*, *elected*, and *predestined* in eternity past. Put another way, we are saved before time began.

Other elements of salvation are experienced personally within our lifetimes as God *calls* us to Himself; *regenerates* us, or makes us spiritually alive; *justifies* us, or declares us in right standing before Him; *indwells* us, or takes up permanent residence in our human spirits; *baptizes* us in the Holy Spirit, or places us positionally into the church; *sanctifies* us, or sets us apart and begins the process of making us more like Christ; *adopts* us into His family; and *seals* us, or places His mark of ownership on us.

One day, the final act of salvation is completed in *glorification*. We are physically resurrected and given incorruptible bodies similar to the resurrected body of our Savior.

Since Christians possess a relationship with Christ, which already has begun and extends out into eternity future, it is biblically faithful to say we *were saved* (from the penalty of sin), *are being saved* (from the power of sin), and *will be saved* (from the presence of sin). The twelve terms we explore in the following pages show how God applies these marvelous elements of salvation to our lives.

It should be noted that there are biblical terms describing salvation not included in this study: redemption, conversion, propitiation, and reconciliation, to name a few. These are important terms and are addressed in various ways throughout the following pages. But the point of focusing on the twelve selected terms is to illustrate as simply as possible God's glorious plan of salvation, woven as a divine tapestry, spanning time and eternity. These are not twelve separate works that God cobbles together. Rather, they are elements of a unified whole.

Ordo salutis

It's tempting to illustrate these twelve components of salvation in a timeline. However, such an effort, no matter how vigorously pursued, proves untenable. That's because the order of salvation (Latin *ordo salutis*) is not always clear in Scripture. Thus, it is much debated among Evangelical Christians.

For example, should we arrange these elements chronologically? If so, how do we order foreknowledge, election, and predestination — all of which occur outside of time and have always been in the mind of God? Should we order the twelve elements causally; that is, did one trigger another? Perhaps we should arrange them legally, according to which elements of salvation set precedents for the others. Maybe we should order them in a Trinitarian model, ascribing certain elements to the Father, Son, or Holy Spirit.

While these approaches offer some help, they all fail at some point to provide a comprehensive model for God's work of salvation. Robert Morey recommends using a "theological model" in which each element is connected directly to a central point: union with Christ. Then, some elements are linked to others in a variety of ways — chronologically, causally, legally, etc. But a single logical connection cannot encompass them all.[3]

So, rather than impose a linear order on these twelve terms, we have chosen to illustrate them as twelve facets in a multi-faceted diamond. When you view a diamond, you see how each facet plays an integral role in revealing the beauty, complexity, and value of the gem. Further, each facet complements the others so that the marring of one diminishes them all.

In a similar manner, we may imagine God's work of salvation as a perfectly sculpted diamond, with its many facets illuminating, in unique ways, the glorious beauty of God's redemptive work. While no mere image does justice to the splendor of salvation, perhaps the recurring image of the diamond throughout this study helps us see that salvation is one, singular, multi-faceted work of God that stretches from eternity past to eternity future. As such, those who by faith are "in Christ" may be assured that He completes the good work He started in us long ago (Phil. 1:6).

BEFORE, IN, AND BEYOND TIME

Each of the following chapters is a glimpse into one facet of salvation. Section One is titled *Before Time* and explores God's work that, from a human perspective, applied to us long before we were born. Three terms help capture this work: foreknowledge, election, and predestination.

Section Two, labeled *In Time*, seeks to express how Christ's finished work on the cross is applied to believing sinners. This work involves calling, regeneration, justification, indwelling, Spirit baptism, sanctification, adoption, and sealing.

Section Three is called *Beyond Time* and features a single, extended chapter on glorification, when Christ finishes the work of redemption in us — and throughout all creation.

At the end of each chapter is a brief summary, along with questions for personal or group study. While the primary audience for this book is Christians, I wholeheartedly invite non-Christians to read and study this resource. May the indescribable gift of Jesus Christ become real to you. And may deliverance from sin and its consequences be yours by hearing and receiving the gospel.

Jesus could not have made the requirements for eternal life any simpler than this: "Truly I tell you, anyone who hears my word and believes him who sent me has eternal life and will not come under judgment but has passed from death to life" (John 5:24). If you don't know Jesus and you read this book, you have made the decision to "hear." May you also "believe" and thus enjoy everlasting fellowship with the one true and living God, who created you, died for you, and bids you to come to Him.

Rob Phillips
2018

Section One

BEFORE TIME

In this section, we examine the work of God in foreknowledge, election, and predestination. While we say these works are *before time*, they really are outside of time, since God created time, and time cannot bind Him. However, from a human perspective, these completed acts of our sovereign Lord are accomplished prior to our existence. We sometimes explain this by saying that God foreknew, elected, and predestined us in eternity past.

In any case, we want to establish that salvation is God's eternal plan. It didn't come into existence as God's "Plan B" after Adam and Eve fell into sin. Neither was it a reaction to Satan's fall and subsequent temptation of the first human beings. We may rejoice in knowing that God has always had us in mind, as well as in His hand. What He accomplishes in time — through the finished work of His Son, His pursuit of us, and our relationship with Him received by faith — is the culmination of an eternal desire to create us in His image and to rescue us from our own ruin.

As we'll see, *foreknowledge* means more than knowing facts beforehand; it means our omniscient God always has known believers and has reckoned us predestined, called, justified, and glorified

(Rom. 8:29-30). This encompasses the unsearchable depths of God's sovereignty and the certainty of a human response in faith to the gospel message.

Election is God's choice of certain individuals to salvation before the foundation of the world. The Reformed (Calvinist) position on election is that it is *unconditional*; that is, God selected specific persons for everlasting life based solely on His divine will and good pleasure, not on foreseen faith. The non-Reformed (Arminian) view is that election is *conditional*; in other words, God selected specific persons for salvation based on foreseeing that they would respond in belief and repentance to the gospel message. We seek a balanced approach as we explore this much-debated doctrine.

Predestination is God's plan from eternity past to complete the work of redemption in every saint, fully conforming us to the image of His Son. Predestination cannot be separated from His other works of redemption before time, in time, or beyond time. From a human standpoint, God's predestination from the farthest reaches of eternity invades time, applies to us, and continues out into eternity future in glorification.

These three facets of salvation *before time* — foreknowledge, election, and predestination — cannot be divorced from human responsibility. God's sovereignty, and the endowed right of people to make decisions for which we are held accountable, are parallel biblical truths. Where they intersect in the mind of God is a wondrous mystery to His creatures.

Chapter One

YOU ARE FOREKNOWN

"I knew this was going to happen."

Type this phrase into an Internet search engine and you're likely to find at least fifty-seven million matches. Really. Among them: A witness to a fatal motorcycle accident tells authorities she saw the crash coming when the cyclist passed her vehicle at a high rate of speed. An entertainment mogul tells reporters he isn't surprised that a British boy band, which just announced a hiatus, was on the verge of breaking up anyway. And a U.S. politician claims he knew a terror attack like the one in New York's Chelsea neighborhood in 2016 was inevitable.

Sometimes the expression, "I knew this was going to happen," is little more than exaggerated hindsight. Or confirmation of a gut feeling. But it can be more than that. With the proper data, statisticians tell us the probability of particular outcomes. Fortune tellers and false prophets, who claim special insight into the future, sometimes get it right. More often than not, however, their divinations fizzle like cheap fireworks.

When it comes to forecasting, no human being always gets it right. We are fallible creatures who lack, among other things, divine omniscience. But there is someone who knows the future with one hundred percent accuracy. His foreknowledge is more than perfect; it's personal. God knows everything that has ever happened or will happen. Even more wonderful, the Lord knows His children, and He always has known us.

If you are a follower of Jesus, it is biblically faithful to declare, "I am foreknown."

WHAT IS FOREKNOWLEDGE?

God knows everything, which means nothing surprises Him. Satan's brash rebellion didn't catch the Creator off guard. Nor did Adam's Fall send the Lord into divine panic, forcing Him to sacrifice His Son in a desperate "Plan B." Every event in time and eternity plays out exactly as God knows it will. But this raises a number of thorny questions:

- If God knows everything in advance, isn't life rigged?
- If God knew that angels and people would rebel against Him, and therefore suffer terrible consequences, why did He create us in the first place?
- If God knows that children are going to suffer, tyrants are going to brutalize their citizens, and some people are going to spend eternity in hell, why doesn't He do something about it?
- Does the existence of evil expose God's lack of knowledge, power, or presence?
- Is it possible to reconcile God's sovereignty with human free will (if there even *is* such a thing)?
- Since time cannot bind God, can we really say He foreknows anything?
- And what does the Bible mean when it says God foreknows certain people? Did they pre-exist? Are there some people He doesn't know at all?

Let's begin with some definitions.

In the Bible, we find the Greek noun *prognosis*, which means "fore-knowledge" or "knowledge beforehand." We derive the English word *prognosis* from it. In a medical context, it means projecting the probable course of an illness, especially the chances of recovery. In a similar manner, meteorologists offer their prognoses, or forecasts, of approaching weather. In most cases, doctors and weather specialists deal in probability, not certainty. Patients often outlive their prognoses, and sometimes it rains on our parades.

But unlike the predictions of doctors and meteorologists, God's foreknowledge is absolute. There is no guesswork. The Bible tells us that God is omniscient, or all-knowing, and from His omniscience flows His foreknowledge of events and people.

The Greek verb *proginosko* also is found in Scripture, and it means "to know beforehand." Scholars vigorously debate whether this word implies choosing, foreordaining, or adopting, as opposed to simply foreknowing on God's part. Early church fathers such as Origen, Chrysostom, and Jerome interpreted the term as signifying foreknowledge rather than foreordination.

Frederick Godet's *Commentary on St. Paul's Epistle to the Romans* devotes more than a page of fine print to this one word, summarizing, "Some have given to the word *foreknow* the meaning of *elect, choose, destine beforehand....* Not only is this meaning arbitrary as being without example in the NT ... but what is still more decidedly opposed to this meaning is what follows: *He also did predestinate.*"[1]

Robert Picirilli, in *Grace, Faith, Free Will*, writes, "God foreknows everything future as certain. That certainty of future events does not lie in their necessity but in their simple factness. They will be the way they will be, and God knows what they will be because He has perfect awareness, in advance, of all facts. But that knowledge *per se*, even though it is *fore*knowledge, has no more causal effect on the facts than our knowledge of certain past facts has on them."[2]

Other scholars, however, say God's foreknowledge cannot be confined to simple prior awareness. Reformation leader John Calvin insisted that God knows all events precisely because He sovereignly determines what is to happen in human history. At the same time, Reformed theologians tend to assert that human beings are nonetheless responsible for their actions, not victims of blind fate.[3]

No matter how one understands the meaning of foreknowledge,

it's clear that our omniscient God always has known believers and has reckoned them predestined, called, justified, and glorified (Rom. 8:29-30). This encompasses the unsearchable depths of His divine sovereignty and the certainty of a human response in faith to the gospel message.

HUMAN VS. DIVINE FOREKNOWLEDGE

On occasion, Scripture refers to human foreknowledge, which comes through prior experience or study, not omniscience. In this way, foreknowledge means to know already, or to be acquainted with, a person or fact beforehand.

For example, in Acts 26:4-5, Paul writes, "All the Jews know my way of life from my youth, which was spent from the beginning among my own people and in Jerusalem. They have known me for a long time (*proginoskontes*) ..." Here, Paul makes it clear that there are plenty of eyewitnesses who can testify to his prior life as a zealous Pharisee and a persecutor of the early church.

In Peter's second epistle, he exhorts readers to "make every effort to be found without spot or blemish in his sight, at peace ..." and to be on guard against those who twist the Scriptures. "Therefore, dear friends, since you know this in advance (*proginoskontes*), be on your guard, so that you are not led away by the error of lawless people and fall from your own stable position" (2 Peter 3:14-17). Some translations, like the New International Version and the New English Translation, render it, "since you have been *forewarned*," punctuating the responsibility Peter's audience bears for staying true to what they have learned.

But when Scripture speaks of God's foreknowledge, it does not mean things God *learned* in advance through observation or experience. Rather, it includes "all that He has considered and purposed to do prior to human history. In the language of Scripture, something foreknown is not simply that which God was aware of prior to a certain point. Rather, it is presented as that which God gave prior consent to, that which received His favorable or special recognition. Hence, this term is reserved for those matters which God favorably, deliberately and freely chose and ordained."[4]

FOREKNOWLEDGE OF EVENTS AND PERSONS

In Scripture, God reveals His foreknowledge of events and persons.

FOREKNOWLEDGE OF EVENTS

The Bible reveals God's foreknowledge of events, not only in declaring things to come, but in delivering messages to mankind through the prophets. For example, we may note the test of a true prophet in Deut. 18:21-22: "You may say to yourself, 'How can we recognize a message the Lord has not spoken?' When a prophet speaks in the Lord's name, and the message does not come true or is not fulfilled, that is a message the Lord has not spoken. The prophet has spoken it presumptuously. Do not be afraid of him."

A true prophet carries God's Word in his heart and on his lips. When he predicts a future event, God's supernatural insight ensures that it happens exactly as prophesied. If the prediction fails, the prophet is proved false. As theologian John Frame writes, "Knowledge of the future is not only the test of a true prophet. It is also the test of a true God."[5]

This does not mean false prophets are always wrong. In fact, the Lord may allow their predictions to come true as a means of testing His people. On one occasion, He tells the Israelites, "If a prophet or someone who has dreams rises among you and proclaims a sign or wonder to you, and that sign or wonder he has promised you comes about, but he says, 'Let us follow other gods,' which you have not known, 'and let us worship them,' do not listen to that prophet's words or to that dreamer. For the Lord your God is testing you to know whether you love the Lord your God with all your heart and all your soul" (Deut. 13:1-3). The Israelites are to follow the Lord and fear Him. And the false prophet or dreamer "must be put to death" (v. 5).

God's foreknowledge even includes conditional prophecies. For example, the Lord announces the destruction of Nineveh but then suspends punishment when the Ninevites repent (Jonah 3:4-10). Further, He knows what *would* happen under certain circumstances, even though the foreknown possibility doesn't materialize. In 1 Sam. 23:12-14, God tells David that if he stays in Keilah, the citizens will turn him over to Saul. David flees with his men, and they escape the capture God knows they would have experienced.

The apostle Peter reminds us that God foreknew the most pivotal event in human history — the death of Jesus on the cross. Jesus was "foreknown before the foundation of the world but was revealed in these last times for you" (1 Peter 1:20). The Greek word *proegnosmenou* is rendered "foreordained" or "chosen" rather than "foreknown" in some translations. In any case, it means the Son of God always existed, and it was always known that He would be the Redeemer of mankind. "It is not merely that God knew ahead of time that Christ would so come and die; God's foreknowledge is given here as the cause for His Son's sacrifice — because He planned and decreed it."[6]

FOREKNOWLEDGE OF PERSONS

Many times, however, God's foreknowledge is personal. He knows, chooses, and approves of individuals before they come into existence. For example, the Lord tells the prophet Jeremiah, "I chose you before I formed you in the womb; I set you apart before you were born. I appointed you a prophet to the nations" (Jer. 1:5). For God to choose, set apart, and appoint Jeremiah, He has to foreknow him.

The same is true of the apostle Paul, who writes to the Galatians, "But when God, who from my mother's womb set me apart and called me by his grace, was pleased to reveal His Son in me, so that I could preach him among the Gentiles ..." (Gal. 1:15-16).

God's foreknowledge is even the basis of His election of the Jewish people. In assuring his Roman readers that God's rejection of Israel is neither total nor permanent, Paul writes, "God has not rejected his people whom he foreknew" (Rom. 11:2). The Lord chooses the Israelites as the people through whom Messiah is to come. They also produce the Scriptures and bear testimony of the one true God in a world that idolatry has brought to the brink of ruin.

Even so, God's election of Israel is not based on His foreknowledge of the people's meritorious lives. Quite the contrary, as Moses reminds his fellow Israelites, "The Lord had his heart set on you and chose you, not because you were more numerous than all people, for you were the fewest of all peoples. But because the Lord loved you and kept the oath he swore to your fathers, he brought you out with a strong hand and redeemed you from the place of slavery, from the power of Pharaoh king of Egypt. Know that the Lord your God is God, the faithful God who keeps his gracious covenant loyalty for a thousand generations with those who love him and keep his commands" (Deut. 7:7-9).

There is something about God's foreknowledge that frees Him of any obligation to save us based on foreseen faith or meritorious works. Yet it is clear that God is fully aware of how we as individuals exercise the human freedom He has entrusted to us. Further, He holds us accountable for our thoughts, words, and deeds so that His foreknowledge cannot be considered synonymous with fatalistic determinism. More about this in the coming chapters.

But before moving on, we should raise one caution: In seeking to understand God's foreknowledge of certain people, we may be tempted to wrongly conclude that human beings pre-existed, and thus were known in an intimate, face-to-face way with God prior to physical birth. This is a doctrine of the Church of Jesus Christ of Latter-day Saints, which explains that God "has a plan for our eternal salvation, and it began in our premortal life, where we learned, matured, and developed the spirit we each have today. Just as we are individuals now, with distinct personalities, genders, and aptitudes, so were we there."[7]

This is a false teaching that extends even further in the LDS Church to include the belief that all people are eternal, uncreated, and potentially divine. It should be rejected as unbiblical. More to the point, we should remember that God exercises His foreknowledge outside of time. To say that God foreknew us in eternity past is an attempt to explain something eternal from a time-bound human perspective. In reality, God's foreknowledge of us is not predicated on our pre-existence; rather, it is an unsearchable quality of His omniscience.

FOREKNOWLEDGE AND RESPONSIBILITY

But what about God's foreknowledge of us with respect to salvation? *Proginosko* — to know beforehand — involves God's gracious determination to extend fellowship to certain undeserving sinners long before their birth. It is sometimes described as God befriending us beforehand. As we will see in the chapters on election and predestination, the Lord foreordains unto salvation those He knows intimately in eternity past.

Jesus expresses this truth in John 10:14-15 when He declares, "I am the good shepherd. I know my own, and my own know me, just as the Father knows me, and I know the Father." He continues in verses 27-28: "My sheep hear my voice, I know them, and they follow me. I give them eternal life, and they will never perish. No one will snatch them out of my hand."

Such divine foreknowledge is not fatalistic determinism, however. In Acts 2:23, Peter declares about Jesus, "Though he was delivered up according to God's determined plan and foreknowledge, you used lawless people to nail him to a cross and kill him." In this single verse, Peter offers evidence both of God's foreknowledge and human responsibility. God freely delivers His Son. Yet, rather than worship Him, wicked people choose to crucify Him, leaving them with the responsibility for their actions.

For followers of Jesus, God's foreknowledge is an unfathomable blessing. It brings us comfort in times of doubt to know that He is aware of our struggles, hears our prayers, and stays true to His promises. To those who reject Christ, however, His foreknowledge casts an ominous shadow over their lives. They may think their wicked deeds are hidden from God, when in fact they are recorded for the day of judgment. Or, they may deceive themselves into thinking their good deeds are sufficient to tip the scales of justice in their favor. What really counts, however, is whether a person's name is written in the book of life: "And anyone whose name was not found written in the book of life was thrown into the lake of fire" (Rev. 20:15).

Some scholars question whether God truly possesses exhaustive knowledge of the future. This is nothing new. The so-called Socinian doctrine — named after Lelio and Fausto Socinus, an uncle and nephew who lived in the sixteenth century — denies that God has foreordained the free decisions of human beings. Further, it rejects the notion that God foreknows what those decisions will be. The Socinian doctrine supposes either that God voluntarily determines not to foresee people's free choices, or that His omniscience is restricted to that which is knowable. Therefore, since the free acts of human beings are by nature uncertain and unknowable, God cannot foreknow everything.[8]

A similar view is taken by today's "open theists," who hold that God does not have exhaustive knowledge of the future. Open theists argue that if God knows the future completely, the future must be fixed, and therefore man cannot be free. Generally, open theism posits that God has granted people free will to such an extent that He does not know their future free choices.

Open theists believe that God could have known every future event if He had created a fully determined universe. However, God decided instead to create a world in which the future is not entirely knowable, even to Him. Open theists make a case for a personal God who may be influenced through prayer, decisions, and human action. While God is able to anticipate the future, He remains fluid to respond to decisions and actions made contrary to or consistent with His plan.[9]

In response, it's important to note that Scripture does not represent God as a mere onlooker, seeing the future course of events but having little or no part in it. The New Testament in particular regards all history as the unfolding of God's eternal purpose (Acts 4:28), which includes man's salvation (Eph. 1:4-5; 2 Tim. 1:9), the provision of Christ as Savior (1 Peter 1:20), and the good works of Christians (Eph. 2:10). At the same time, Scripture is clear that human beings are responsible for their actions and are destined to give an account one day before Him, either at the judgment seat of Christ or before the great white throne (2 Cor. 5:10; Rev. 20:11-15).

FOREKNOWLEDGE IN KEY VERSES

Now, let's look at several New Testament passages in which God's foreknowledge is applied to Jesus, Israel, and Christians.

REGARDING JESUS

Acts 2:23. In Peter's sermon on the Day of Pentecost, he declares, "Though he [Jesus] was delivered up according to God's determined plan and foreknowledge (*prognosei*), you used lawless people to nail him to a cross and kill him." Peter ties God's foreknowledge to His plan of redemption. This implies that God's foreknowledge is more than seeing the future with perfect clarity; it means He planned (outside of time) the finished work of His Son at Calvary.

CSB	KJV	NIV	NASB	ESV
Foreknowledge	Foreknowledge	Foreknowledge	Foreknowledge	Foreknowledge

Comparing English translations of *prognosei* in Acts 2:23

1 Peter 1:20. In calling followers of Jesus to holy living, Peter writes, "He was foreknown (*proegnosmenou*) before the foundation of the world but was revealed in these last times for you." This indicates the deity and eternality of Jesus, who was with the Father in eternity past (John 1:1; 8:58; 17:5) and who came into time and space as the visible manifestation of deity in human skin (John 1:18; 14:9; Col. 2:9).

CSB	KJV	NIV	NASB	ESV
Foreknown	Foreordained	Chosen	Foreknown	Foreknown

Comparing English translations of *proegnosmenou* in 1 Peter 1:20

REGARDING ISRAEL

Rom. 11:2. Paul seeks to assure his readers that God has not completely rejected Israel, even though the nation, for the most part, has rejected His Son. Paul writes, "God has not rejected the people whom He foreknew (*proegno*) ..."

He goes on to explain, "Or don't you know what the Scripture says in the passage about Elijah — how he pleads with God against Israel? **Lord, they have killed your prophets and torn down your altars. I am the only one left, and they are trying to take my life!** But what was God's answer to him? **I have left seven thousand for myself who have not bowed down to Baal.** In the same way, then, there is also at the present time a remnant chosen by grace. Now if by grace, then it is not by works; otherwise grace ceases to be grace" (Rom. 11:2b-6).

Verse 2 is an obvious reference to God's election of Israel. The key is not Israel's merit, but God's sovereign choice. "God is faithful to His promises because of who He is, not because of Israel's performance."[10] God's election of Israel, and His choosing of a faithful remnant, are grounded in His foreknowledge.

CSB	KJV	NIV	NASB	ESV
Foreknew	Foreknew	Foreknew	Foreknew	Foreknew

Comparing English translations of *proegno* in Rom. 11:2

REGARDING CHRISTIANS

Rom. 8:29-30. Paul assures followers of Jesus that our salvation is secure because God has guaranteed it from eternity past (in foreknowledge) to eternity future (in glorification). He writes, "For those he foreknew (*proegno*) he also predestined to be conformed to the image of his Son, so that he would be the firstborn among many brothers and sisters. And those he predestined, he also called; and those he called, he also justified; and those he justified, he also glorified."

What does Paul say that God foreknew? Our decision to trust in Christ? No, although He certainly saw that coming. Rather, Paul says God foreknew *us*. Personally. What a contrast with those who reject God's gracious offer of salvation. They may proclaim to know Jesus, and even to have done great deeds in His name, but Christ's response on judgment day is, "I never knew you. Depart from me, you lawbreakers!" (Matt. 7:23).

Simply put, God does not foreknow those who reject His Son. Certainly, an omniscient God knows *about* unbelievers, fashions them in their mothers' wombs, showers them with grace, reveals Himself to them in creation and conscience (Romans 1), and perhaps provides further evidence in the story of Christ and the canon of Scripture. Yet He does not know them, in a personal and intimate way, in eternity past, and thus He does not predestine, call, justify, or glorify them.

Yet, this is not fatalistic determinism. Jesus calls them "lawbreakers" who knowingly and defiantly reject the light God has given them. Their departure into hell is on their own heads.

Rom. 8:29-30 has puzzled theologians for centuries. Some leaders of the early church denied that foreknowledge implied any determination of events. Justin Martyr, for example, said, "What we say about future events being foretold, we do not say it as though they come about by fatal necessity."[11]

Reformer John Calvin, however, insisted that God knows all events precisely because He sovereignly determines what is to happen in human history. To be fair, Reformed theologians tend to assert that human beings are nonetheless responsible for their choices — not victims of a blind fate.

Jacobus Arminius, the Dutch theologian for whom Arminianism is named, distinguished foreknowledge from foreordination. While God's plan of salvation is predetermined in a broad way, Arminius argued that each person's response to God is not predetermined because each person has free will. Yet God knows us intimately, so He can foreknow an event, or even a person, without fatalistically decreeing the decisions that person makes.[12]

CSB	KJV	NIV	NASB	ESV
Foreknew	Did foreknow	Foreknew	Foreknew	Foreknew

Comparing English translations of *proegno* in Rom. 8:29

1 Peter 1:1-2. Peter addresses "those chosen, living as exiles dispersed abroad in Pontus, Galatia, Cappadocia, Asia, and Bithynia, chosen according to the foreknowledge (*prognosin*) of God the Father, through the sanctifying work of the Spirit, to be obedient and to be sprinkled with the blood of Jesus Christ."

Peter wonderfully lays out the work of the Trinity in our redemption. He states that believers are chosen, or elected, according to the foreknowledge of God the Father. They are sanctified, or set apart and made holy, through the work of the Holy Spirit. And they are sprinkled with the blood of Jesus, and thus cleansed from all sin.

Peter ties our being chosen to the Father's foreknowledge. We will explore this more fully in the next chapter. But it's important to note that none of the elements of salvation — those before time, in time, or beyond time — may be separated from God's eternal plan of redemption. Yet here, Peter specifically links foreknowledge and election.

CSB	KJV	NIV	NASB	ESV
Foreknowledge	Foreknowledge	Foreknowledge	Foreknowledge	Foreknowledge

Comparing English translations of *prognosin* in 1 Peter 1:2

SUMMARY

Foreknowledge means more than knowing facts beforehand. As the Greek noun *prognosis* and the verb *proginosko* are applied in the New Testament, they reveal that our omniscient God always has known believers and has reckoned us predestined, called, justified, and glorified (Rom. 8:29-30). This encompasses the unsearchable depths of God's sovereignty and the certainty of a human response in faith to the gospel message.

In Scripture, we see that God's foreknowledge applies to Jesus, Israel, and Christians as the Lord foreknows both events and people.

We should be careful to avoid extremes in seeking to understand God's omniscience. His foreknowledge does not mean He has fatalistically determined all things, so that human beings are little more than pawns on a divine chess board. But neither does it mean that God is restricted in His foreknowledge, as open theists suggest.

Finally, as we consider that God always has known us and loved us, we should not embrace the false doctrine of human pre-existence. Speculation should never fill the gaps between what God knows and what He has chosen to reveal to us at this time.

So, let's consider these summary statements about God's foreknowledge:

- God's foreknowledge is an expression of His omniscience. Because God knows everything, He is fully aware of all that happens — and all that will happen.

- In Scripture, God reveals His foreknowledge of *events* and *persons*. Often, His foreknowledge is revealed through the words of His prophets.
- God's foreknowledge, with respect to salvation, is personal. God doesn't just know about us; He knows *us*.
- God's foreknowledge of believers is foundational to His work of redemption. Those He foreknows, He predestines, calls, justifies, and glorifies (Rom. 8:29-30).
- God's foreknowledge of His sheep (John 10:27-28) cannot be separated from His work before time, in time, or beyond time with respect to salvation. From a human standpoint, God's foreknowledge begins in eternity past, intersects with time, and continues into eternity future — with glorification as the capstone of His redemptive work.
- Only God has unrestricted foreknowledge because only God is eternal, sovereign, and omniscient.
- God's foreknowledge is specifically applied to those who inherit eternal life. Jesus tells unbelievers on the day of judgment, "I never knew you" (Matt. 7:23a).
- In many ways, God's foreknowledge is unfathomable. It is infinite, unsearchable, and sublime. We should study the Scriptures to understand what they plainly teach us about God's foreknowledge, but we should be careful not to draw conclusions that assume things God's Word does not say.

THINK
Questions for personal or group study

We raised challenging questions at the start of this chapter. Let's revisit several of them now.

(1) If God knows everything in advance, isn't life rigged? Which of the following answers is most biblically faithful, in your opinion:

- Not rigged, so much, but fatalistically determined down to the smallest detail. There is no such thing as free will. For God to foreknow something means He already has decided it will go a certain way.

- No, God's foreknowledge simply refers to His prior awareness of human acts of free will.
- It's complicated. God is sovereign and human beings are free, which means God has entrusted people with the ability to make choices for which He holds them accountable.

(2) How would you answer the person who says, "If God knew that angels and people would rebel against Him, and therefore suffer terrible consequences, why did He create us in the first place?

(3) Some people argue that if God truly has foreknowledge, He lacks compassion, power, or both. Otherwise, He would do something about suffering children, brutal tyrants, and hell. What might you say in response to this charge?

(4) Since most people — including atheists — believe that evil exists, how might we explain that the reality of evil does not argue against the existence of a God who is sovereign, loving, and just?

(5) *Libertarian free will* says that people are autonomous creatures who may freely choose from more than one possible outcome; without this ability, people are not truly free and cannot be held morally responsible for their actions. *Hard determinism*, on the other hand, essentially denies free will and argues that all decisions are fatalistically determined. These are two extreme positions. *Soft determinism*, or compatibilism, lies in the middle, expressing the view that God grants people a certain amount of freedom, which operates within the boundaries of God's sovereignty.

Consider the following passages of Scripture and note what they say about this issue:

- Ps. 24:1. What is the sphere of God's sovereignty? That is, how much does He control?
- Prov. 16:9. How do human beings operate within the sphere of God's sovereign authority?
- Isa. 46:9-10. How does God involve Himself in human history?
- Isa. 55:8-9. How do God's thoughts and ways compare with ours?

(6) On judgment day, when Jesus tells false disciples, "I never knew you" (Matt. 7:23a), is He denying His own omniscience? How can God know everything — and presumably everyone — yet deny He ever knew some people?

(7) In what ways should followers of Jesus take comfort in God's foreknowledge? That is, how does divine foreknowledge relate to the other elements of salvation, such as election, justification, and glorification?

Chapter Two

YOU ARE ELECTED

In the third installment of the *Mad Max* trilogy starring Mel Gibson, Max squares off against a masked bodyguard named Blaster in Thunderdome, a caged orb in which the only rule is: "Two men enter ... one man leaves." It's a fight to the death. Pass the popcorn.

Sometimes it seems that Christians favor the Thunderdome approach when it comes to the doctrine of divine election. Let's pit Augustine against Pelagius, Calvin against Arminius, or Whitefield against Wesley. Toss them into Thunderdome. Two men enter ... one man leaves.

But does it have to be this way? Is this doctrine a zero-sum game? While followers of Jesus may disagree about the manner in which God's sovereignty and human responsibility intersect in the doctrine of election, we *should* find common ground — for example, in the essential truths of the person and work of Christ, the necessity of proclaiming the gospel, and the need to pray for those outside the kingdom of heaven.

There are many excellent resources that address both the Reformed and Arminian positions, many of which carefully examine key differences and similarities.[1] That's not our primary goal here, however. Our aim is to survey key passages of Scripture that address God's election, or choosing, of certain people to salvation in the context of His fore-knowledge and predestination.

Every Christian should readily acknowledge that the Bible teaches divine election. Differences arise with respect to how this doctrine is defined, and how it's applied to Christians — and even to non-Christians who face an eternity apart from Christ in reprobation, which we also discuss in this chapter.

In any case, if you are a follower of Jesus, it is biblically faithful to say, "I am elected."

WHAT IS ELECTION?

According to *The Baptist Faith & Message*, "Election is the gracious purpose of God, according to which He regenerates, justifies, sanctifies, and glorifies sinners. It is consistent with the free agency of man, and comprehends all the means in connection with the end. It is the glorious display of God's sovereign goodness, and is infinitely wise, holy, and unchangeable. It excludes boasting and promotes humility."[2]

Put more simply, election is God's choice of certain individuals to salvation before the foundation of the world. The Reformed (Calvinist) position on election is that it is *unconditional*; that is, God selected specific persons for everlasting life based solely on His divine will and good pleasure, not on foreseen faith. Put another way, God foreknows all future events — including responses to the gospel message — because He first ordained them.

The non-Reformed (Arminian) position is that God's election is *conditional*; that is, God selected specific persons for salvation based on foreseeing that they would respond in belief and repentance to the gospel message. As taught by Jacobus Arminius, after whom Arminianism is named, God's election to salvation is the election of *believers*, which means that election is conditioned on faith. He also insisted that God's foreknowledge of people's choices did not cause those choices or make them necessary.[3]

In the *Declaration of Sentiments*, Arminius argued that God's decree of election was to save those sinners who repent and believe in Christ. The decree to save and damn particular persons was based on

God's foreknowledge of their faith or unbelief.[4] Therefore, foreknowledge is the basis of election, not the other way around.

Between Calvinism and Arminianism is Molinism. Named for Luis Molina, a sixteenth-century Jesuit priest, Molinism argues that God perfectly accomplishes His will in free creatures through the use of His omniscience. Molinism seeks to reconcile two biblical truths: (1) God exercises sovereign control over all His creation, and (2) human beings make free choices for which they must give an account. As Kenneth Keathley explains, "Molinism simultaneously holds to a Calvinistic view of a comprehensive divine sovereignty and to a version of free will (called *libertarianism*) generally associated with Arminianism."[5]

Molinism teaches that God exercises His sovereignty primarily through His omniscience, and that He infallibly knows what free creatures would do in any given situation. In this way, the Lord sovereignly controls all things, while humans also are genuinely free. Put another way, God is entirely responsible for salvation; human beings are entirely responsible for sin.

Some theologians hold to a fourth view: God's election is *corporate*; that is, according to Eph. 1:4-6, God chose believers *in Christ* before the foundation of the world. Jesus is the "elect one," and the church is an "empty set" to be filled by people who freely choose to receive Christ. However, this is something Arminius never taught. While he emphasized the *Christocentric* nature of divine election — Jesus is the foundation of the church, salvation is by Him, and the gospel is about Him — he insisted that election is personal and individual, not corporate.[6]

The word "election" in Scripture is derived from the Greek *eklegomai*, which means "to choose something for oneself." The Bible also uses words such as "choose," "predestine," "foreordain," and "call" to indicate that God has entered into a special relationship with certain individuals and groups through whom He has decided to fulfill His purposes.

The Bible teaches that certain people are chosen "for salvation" (2 Thess. 2:13), to receive the "adoption as sons" (Gal. 4:5), and "to be holy and blameless in love before him" (Eph. 1:4). The ultimate end of election is the "praise of His glorious grace" (Eph. 1:6).

If all of this seems confusing, perhaps the explanation of Charles Spurgeon, in a sermon delivered Aug. 1, 1858, may help:

> I see in one place, God presiding over all in providence; and yet I see, and I cannot help seeing, that man acts as he pleases, and that God has left his actions to his own will, in a great measure.
>
> Now, if I were to declare that man was so free to act, that there was no presidence of God over his actions, I should be driven very near to Atheism; and if, on the other hand I declare that God so overrules all things, as that man is not free enough to be responsible, I am driven at once into Antinomianism [the belief that there are no moral laws God expects Christians to obey] or fatalism.
>
> That God predestines, and that man is responsible, are two things that few can see. They are believed to be inconsistent and contradictory; but they are not. It is just the fault of our weak judgment. Two truths cannot be contradictory to each other.
>
> If, then, I find taught in one place that everything is fore-ordained, that is true; and if I find in another place that man is responsible for all his actions, that is true; and it is my folly that leads me to imagine that two truths can ever contradict each other.
>
> These two truths, I do not believe, can ever be welded into one upon any human anvil, but one they shall be in eternity: they are two lines that are so nearly parallel, that the mind that shall pursue them farthest, will never discover that they converge; but they do converge, and they will meet somewhere in eternity, close to the throne of God, whence all truth doth spring.[7]

The tension between divine sovereignty and human responsibility elevates these two complementary biblical truths without resolving what the Spirit has revealed to us as divine mystery. While Spurgeon acknowledged this tension, and proclaimed it without apology, he denied the doctrine of unconditional reprobation.[8]

WHAT IS REPROBATION?

Reprobation is a term that describes those who are left in their sinful and fallen states and thus are eternally damned. Wayne Grudem defines reprobation as "the sovereign decision of God before creation to pass over some persons, in sorrow deciding not to save them, and to punish them for their sins, thereby to manifest his justice."[9]

Generally, those who embrace Reformed theology argue that reprobation is *unconditional,* meaning that God's decree of damnation for certain people results in their unbelief. There are two main parts of this doctrine: (1) *preterition,* or God's sovereign decision not to regenerate certain people, for reasons known only to Him; and (2) *condemnation,* or the decree to punish these same people for their sins. To contrast election and reprobation from a Reformed perspective, then, is to say that election is God's direct action on the human will, resulting in salvation, while reprobation is an exercise of His permissive will, resulting in damnation.

Those who hold a more moderate view of Reformed theology, as well as Arminians, contend for *conditional* reprobation. This means that God foresees the unbelief of certain individuals and thereby decrees their damnation. However, as with the Arminian view of election, God's foreknowledge doesn't cause their unbelief, or make it necessary. Thus, election and reprobation are essentially parallel:

- Election is gracious and eternal; reprobation is just and eternal.
- Election is established in Christ; reprobation is declared by Christ.
- Election is conditioned on faith and repentance; reprobation is conditioned on unbelief and rebellion.
- Election is personal in its application; so is reprobation.

Several passages of Scripture address reprobation and thus are the focal points of debate. For example, Paul refers to unbelieving Jews as vessels of dishonor, whom God endures with much patience, but who, nevertheless, are "objects of wrath prepared for destruction" (Rom. 9:22). Peter writes that those who disobey the message of salvation are "destined for this" (1 Peter 2:8). Jude writes that certain false teachers are "designated for this judgment long ago" (Jude 4). John describes those who worship the beast as people "whose names have not been written in the book of life from the foundation of the world" (Rev. 17:8; see also 13:8).

Do these verses mean that God fatalistically condemns some people to hell? Among those who answer with a resounding "yes" are so-called *hyper-Calvinists*. They argue that evangelism is, at best, an exercise in futility since the eternal destiny of all people is fixed. As a result, they say, there is no need to share the gospel or pray for the lost to come to faith in Christ. In essence, they declare that God's sovereignty negates human responsibility. Thus, "the gospel of the hyper-Calvinist is a declaration of God's salvation of the elect and His damnation of the lost."[10]

Critics refer to this skewed doctrine of reprobation as "double predestination," charging hyper-Calvinists with worshipping a God who is capricious, arbitrary, and lacking in redeeming love for all mankind. In some cases, they ride the pendulum of protest too far in the opposite direction, exalting human free will above divine sovereignty. This attempt to defend God's loving nature ends up diminishing His knowledge, power, and will. It may also lead to open theism or universalism.

When considering the Scriptures that address reprobation, it's best to allow God's Word to speak for itself. This means embracing both the clarity and the mystery with respect to election and reprobation. We might say something like this: Of all possible worlds, God decided to create a world in which human beings, entrusted with freedom, rebel against Him and fall into depravity. In genuine love for all, and to manifest His divine attributes, God provides redemption through the finished work of His Son and graciously saves all who respond in belief and repentance. No one goes to heaven on human merit or is fatalistically banished to hell.

While election and reprobation are two sides of the same coin, the Bible presents key differences between them. Election to salvation delights God and results in our thanksgiving and praise; reprobation brings God sorrow (see Ezek. 33:11). The credit for election lies completely with God, while the blame for condemnation is on the people or angels who rebel (John 3:18-19; 5:40). The cause of election lies in God, and the cause of reprobation lies in the sinner. Finally, "the ground of election is God's grace, whereas the ground of reprobation is God's justice.... Our salvation is totally due to grace alone. Our only appropriate response is to give God eternal praise."[11]

ELECTION IN THE OLD TESTAMENT

The Old Testament uses the Hebrew verb *bahar* to describe how one may choose, select, or prefer one thing over another. In some cases, it refers to choices regarding wives (Gen. 6:2), towns in which to live (Deut. 23:16), bulls for a sacrifice (1 Kings 18:23), and soldiers (Ex. 17:9; 1 Sam. 13:2; 24:2; 1 Chron. 19:10).

In religious settings, the psalmist states he would rather stand at the threshold of the house of God than live in the tents of wicked people (Ps. 84:10). The writer of Proverbs says he would prefer to get understanding rather than silver (Prov. 16:16) and a good name over great wealth (Prov. 22:1).

Nevertheless, God is the subject of about sixty percent of the uses of *bahar* in the Old Testament.[12] Prior to Israel's entry into Canaan, the Lord indicates He will choose a place to put His name (Deut. 12:5; 14:23-25; 16:6-7, 11). Jerusalem is that city (2 Chron. 12:13).

God also chooses individuals, such as Israel's first king, Saul (1 Sam. 10:24). Then, He takes David from his father's sheep pens and places him on the throne (Ps. 78:70). Later, as Solomon dedicates the temple, he recalls the Lord's choice of his father to rule Israel (1 Kings 8:16; 2 Chron. 6:6).

However, the main use of *bahar* in the Old Testament is God's choice of Israel as His elect nation. He chooses them, not because of foreseen merit, but because of His abundant love and His faithfulness to the promises He made to Abraham, Isaac, and Jacob (Deut. 7:6-7).

Throughout the psalms and the writings of the prophets, the Lord reaffirms His election of Israel (Ps. 47:4; 135:4; Isa. 41:8; 44:1-2).

One purpose in Yahweh's election of Israel is so His people become a light to the nations (Gen. 12:1-3; Isa. 43:10), a purpose which Peter affirms as applying to the new Israel, the church (1 Peter 2:9-10).

ELECTION IN THE NEW TESTAMENT

In the New Testament, the verb *eklegomai* appears in various forms twenty-two times and means "to choose, set apart, elect." Sometimes, it refers to human decisions. For example, by sitting at the feet of Jesus rather than busying herself with household matters, Mary makes a better choice than does Martha (Luke 10:42). Jesus notes that guests at a Pharisee's home choose the seats of honor (Luke 14:7). And the early church chooses people for service (Acts 1:24; 6:5; 15:22, 25).

But *eklegomai* also signifies God's work of election according to His divine purpose and grace. At Christ's transfiguration, it is clear that He is God's chosen one (Luke 9:35). Jesus chooses the twelve apostles (Luke 6:13; John 6:70; 13:18; 15:16, 19; Acts 1:2). God's sovereign purpose is manifest in His choosing of believers before the foundation of the world (Eph. 1:4) and His preservation of those He has chosen through days of tribulation (Mark 13:20). As William Mounce writes, "His sovereign grace is apparent in that his choosing runs contrary to human wisdom and expectation. He has chosen what is foolish to shame the wise, what is weak to shame the strong, and what is lowly and despised so that no one can boast."[13]

The adjective *eklektos* depicts the quality of being "chosen, elected, set apart," with God as the one choosing. "Many are invited, but few are chosen," says Jesus as He wraps up His parable on the wedding banquet for the king's son. This is a shot across the bow of Israel's religious leaders, who find themselves outside the kingdom while Gentiles are welcomed in (Matt. 22:1-14).

Used as a noun, *eklektos* refers to the body of believers as God's "chosen ones," or "the elect." Mounce comments, "Thus, it has a corporate rather than an individual sense.... The church's experience of salvation rests in the sovereign decision of God from beginning to end. God will indeed 'bring about justice for his chosen ones' (Lk. 18:7), and no one can bring a charge against them (Rom. 8:33). They will display God's praise for bringing them out of darkness into light (1 Peter 2:9)."[14]

God's call to the church to be holy is based on His divine election (Col. 3:12). Further, Matthew and Mark emphasize that election provides the assurance of surviving the coming tribulation — whether understood as the destruction of Jerusalem in A.D. 70, or the end times, or both. The days of tribulation will be cut short so the elect survive (Matt. 24:22). False Christs and false prophets try, but fail, to deceive the elect (v. 24). At the very end, Jesus returns to gather His elect to Himself (v. 31). Even the apostle Paul writes about his ministry for the sake of the elect (Titus 1:2; 2 Tim. 2:10).

These words offer assurance of God's sovereignty, care, and faithfulness, even though His called-out ones may suffer times of intense persecution.

Diverse application

Let's look at selected Scriptures that show the diverse ways "election" is applied in the Old and New Testaments.

People elected for salvation

Eph. 1:4. About God the Father, Paul writes, "For he *chose* us in him [Christ], before the foundation of the world, to be holy and blameless in love before him" (emphasis added).

From this, we may draw the twin truths that the Father is the one who elects, and the Son is the one through whom election is realized. Jesus — the way, the truth, and the life — ensures that all those given to Him are never lost.

2 Thess. 2:13 - "But we ought to thank God always for you, brothers and sisters loved by the Lord, because from the beginning God has *chosen* you for salvation through sanctification by the Spirit and through belief in the truth" (emphasis added).

The apostle uses a different Greek word here, which comes from *aihreomai* and means "to take for oneself," that is, to choose, elect, or prefer. God has determined to take a chosen people for Himself. As they believe the truth — their appropriate response to the gospel — the Lord sets them apart and marks them as His own through the divine work of the Holy Spirit.

An elect Savior

1 Peter 2:6 - "For it stands in Scripture: **See, I lay a stone in Zion, a chosen and honored cornerstone, and the one who believes in him will never be put to shame.**"

Peter quotes Isa. 28:16. The word "chosen" is *eklekton* and means selected, or precious, in reference to Christ. He is the elect one — Messiah, Savior, King of kings and Lord of lords.

Elect angels

1 Tim. 5:21 - "I solemnly charge you before God and Christ Jesus and the *elect* angels to observe these things without prejudice, doing nothing out of favoritism" (emphasis added).

The angels who remain faithful are called *eklekton,* or elect, chosen.

An elect nation

Deut. 7:6-8. Moses tells the Israelites, "For you are a holy people belonging to the Lord your God. The Lord your God has *chosen* you to be his own possession out of all the peoples on the face of the earth. The Lord had his heart set on you and *chose* you, not because you were more numerous than all peoples, for you were the fewest of all peoples. But because the Lord loved you and kept the oath he swore to your fathers, he brought you out with a strong hand and redeemed you from the place of slavery, from the power of Pharaoh king of Egypt" (emphasis added).

The words "chosen" and "chose" come from the Hebrew *bahar*, a verb whose meaning is "to take a keen look at, to prove, to choose. It denotes a choice, which is based on a thorough examination of the situation and not an arbitrary whim."[15] The emphasis in this passage is on God's free and sovereign choice of Israel, and not on any real or foreseen merit.

Isa. 45:3b-4 - "I am the God of Israel, who calls you by your name. I call you by your name, for the sake [of] my servant Jacob and Israel my *chosen* one. I give a name to you though you do not know me" (emphasis added). In Isa. 45:1-8, written at least one hundred forty years before it is fulfilled, God speaks to Persia's Cyrus the Great and announces how He intends to use the king as His agent of redemption. As in other passages in Isaiah (Isa. 41:8-9, for example), the Lord identifies Israel as His chosen people.

Elect servants

Luke 6:13. Luke writes about Christ's selection of the apostles, "When daylight came, he summoned his disciples, and he *chose* [Greek *eklexamenos*] twelve of them, whom he also named apostles" (emphasis added).

John 15:16. Jesus tells the apostles, "You did not *choose* me, but I *chose* you. I *appointed* you to go and produce fruit and that your fruit should remain, so that whatever you ask the Father in my name, he will give you" (emphasis added).

The English verb "chose" here is derived from the Greek *eklegomai* and means to choose or select as recipients of special favor. The word "appointed" comes from the Greek *tithemi* and means to appoint, plant, or place one into a position of privilege or ministry.

Acts 9:15. The Lord speaks to Ananias in a vision regarding Saul of Tarsus, "Go, for this man is my *chosen* [Greek *ekloges*] instrument to take my name to Gentiles, kings, and Israelites" (emphasis added).

Elect churches

In closing out his first epistle, Peter writes concerning the church (possibly in Rome), "She who is in Babylon, *chosen* together [Greek *suneklekte*] with you, sends you greetings, as does Mark, my son" (1 Peter 5:13, emphasis added).

Other passages could be cited, but these should suffice to show the variety of ways in which God's sovereign choices are spelled out in Scripture. Our focus now turns to several key verses that reveal the Lord's election of Israel and individuals.

ELECTION IN KEY VERSES

Rom. 9:11-13 - "For though her [Rebekah's] sons had not been born yet or done anything good or bad, so that God's purpose according to election (*eklogen*) might stand — not from works but from the one who calls — she was told, **The older will serve the younger.** As it is written: **I have loved Jacob, but I have hated Esau.**"

God's choice of the younger twin before the birth of Jacob and Esau shows God's gracious election and indicates that God's blessings are His to give, not a human entitlement. As the *CSB Study Bible* notes, "The divine purpose was revealed from the beginning of the Hebrew nation when God chose one twin over the other. The prophet Malachi traced God's differing treatment of two nations to this divine choice (Mal. 1:1-5). Both nations were punished for their sins, but only one received grace. **I have loved Jacob** means God chose or elected his descendants (the nation of Israel), whereas **I have hated Esau** means that God rejected the nation that stemmed from him (Edom)."[16]

While there is much debate over Paul's intended application of election in Romans 9-11, we may glean the following general observations:

- Paul's over-arching point in these three chapters is that God's present rejection of Israel is righteous. He never promised, unconditionally, to save every descendant of Abraham, Isaac, and Jacob (9:6-13). Further, He made it clear in prophecy that not all "Israel" would be saved (9:25-29).
- God has rejected Israel because Israel has rejected salvation by faith in favor of salvation by works (9:30 - 10:21).
- The Lord has not finally rejected Israel after all. Any who desire may come to God by faith (11:1-10). The present rejection of Israel opens the doors of salvation for all nations (11:11-22). A believing remnant of Israel will yet be saved (11:23-32).

As Robert Picirilli summarizes, "Paul is, in fact, arguing against the

Jewish concept of 'unconditional' election (of all Jews by birth) and establishing, in its place, conditional election — election of believers. He does not 'blame' the rejection of unbelieving Jews on the fact that God arbitrarily rejects whomever He pleases, but blames it on their own unbelief, which amounts to a rejection of His sovereign decision to ordain salvation by faith in Jesus."[17]

CSB	KJV	NIV	NASB	ESV
Election	Election	Election	Choice	Election

Comparing English translations of *eklogen* in Rom. 9:11

Rom. 11:5, 7 - "In the same way, then, there is also at the present time a remnant chosen (*eklogen*) by grace.... What then? Israel did not find what it was looking for, but the elect (*ekloge*) did find it. The rest were hardened."

Paul continues to write about the nation of Israel, whose blindness is not total; the Lord continues to work with His covenant people (vv. 1-4). In the days of Samuel, the people reject God as their King and embrace a human king. Still, "The Lord will not abandon his people, because of his great name and because he has determined to make you his own people" (1 Sam. 12:22). Later, the people reject the King of kings as the leaders declare, "We have no king but Caesar!" (John 19:15). Even so, God is not finished with Israel — a truth to which Paul attests. The remnant of believing Jews is chosen by grace, not works (Rom. 11:5-10).

CSB	KJV	NIV	NASB	ESV
Chosen	According to the election	Chosen	According to *God's* gracious choice	Chosen

Comparing English translations of *eklogen* in Rom. 11:5

CSB	KJV	NIV	NASB	ESV
The elect	The election	The elect	Those ... chosen	The elect

Comparing English translations of *ekloge* in Rom. 11:7

Rom. 11:28 - "Regarding the gospel, they are enemies for your advantage, but regarding election (*eklogen*), they are loved because of the patriarchs ..."

Paul continues his line of argument that Israel's current unbelief does not negate the truth of the gospel. Thomas Schreiner comments, "The reason that Israel is beloved because of the fathers is that God's saving gifts and effectual calling can never be withdrawn, since he freely made saving promises to the fathers."[18]

CSB	KJV	NIV	NASB	ESV
Election	The election	Election	*God's* choice	Election

Comparing English translations of *eklogen* in Rom. 11:28

1 Thess. 1:4 - "For we know, brothers and sisters loved by God, that he has chosen (*eklogen*) you ..."

Paul, Silas, and Timothy begin this epistle with a standard greeting of grace and peace. They relay their thankfulness to the Lord for the Thessalonian believers and ensure them of their constant prayers on the church's behalf. Then, they commend their fellow believers for their work produced by faith, their labor motivated by love, and their endurance inspired by the hope in the Lord Jesus (vv. 1-3).

While the Thessalonians are commended for their work, Paul reminds them that they are the recipients of God's love and the focus of His divine election. It is clear in this context that Paul refers to election unto salvation, because he reminds them that "our gospel did not come to you in word only, but also in power in the Holy Spirit, and with full assurance" (v. 5).

CSB	KJV	NIV	NASB	ESV
Chosen	Election	Chosen	*His* choice	Chosen

Comparing English translations of *eklogen* in 1 Thess. 1:4

2 Peter 1:10 - "Therefore, brothers and sisters, make every effort to confirm your calling and election (*eklogen*), because if you do these things you will never stumble."

Peter is not telling the elect that they risk losing their salvation if they slack off. As we've already noted, there is an unbroken chain that links foreknowledge to glorification. Elect believers persevere because God ensures it — by predestining, calling, justifying, and ultimately glorifying all those He foreknows and elects.

At the same time, Peter notes that those who live ungodly lives show no evidence that they truly belong to God. So, he exhorts his readers to be diligent to *confirm* their calling and election. The KJV renders it, "give diligence to make your calling and election sure." In other words, believers' lives should be consistent with the godly virtues laid out in verses 5-7.

CSB	KJV	NIV	NASB	ESV
Election	Election	Election	Choosing	Election

Comparing English translations of *eklogen* in 2 Peter 1:10

SUMMARY

The doctrine of divine election is one of the most vigorously debated teachings in Christianity today, and it has been for hundreds of years. The Remonstrants, who embraced Jacobus Arminius' Reformation theology in the early 1600s, were officially condemned as heretics. All Arminian pastors in the Dutch Reformed Church, about two hundred of them, were stripped of their offices. Some were banished from the country, while others were imprisoned. The controversy was considered settled.

Even so, Arminian doctrines survived the Canons of Dort in

various forms — not all of them faithful to what Arminius actually believed and taught — and play a role in the beliefs and practices of many local churches and denominations today. The doctrine of election, and the related doctrines of foreknowledge and predestination, continue to serve as flashpoints among Christian fellowships.

That's disheartening, because there is a great deal of common ground to be shared. While followers of Jesus may debate whether election is conditional or unconditional, we all agree that God is the author of salvation. He is sovereign, free, gracious, and just. He withholds salvation from no one and banishes no one to hell without their permission. And He entrusts His highest created beings with an ability to make decisions for which He holds them accountable. We might also agree that it's wise to avoid the extreme fatalism of hyper-Calvinism as well as the Pelagian error that denies the effects of Adam's sin and embraces human potential at the expense of divine aid.[19]

Consider these summary statements:

- While followers of Jesus may disagree about the manner in which God's sovereignty and human responsibility intersect in the doctrine of election, we *should* find common ground — for example, in the essential truths of the person and work of Christ, the necessity of proclaiming the gospel, and the need to pray for those outside the kingdom of heaven.
- Simply put, election is God's choice of certain individuals to salvation before the foundation of the world. "Election" is derived from the Greek word *eklegomai*, which means "to choose something for oneself." The Bible also uses words such as "choose," "predestine," "foreordain," and "call" to indicate that God has entered into a special relationship with certain individuals and groups through whom He has decided to fulfill His purpose.
- Reprobation is a term used to describe those who are left in their sinful and fallen states and thus are destined to be eternally damned. As with election, Christians differ as to whether reprobation is *conditional* (based on foreseen unbelief) or *unconditional* (resulting in future unbelief).

34

- The Old Testament uses the Hebrew word *bahar* to describe how one may choose, select, or prefer one thing over another. God is the subject of about sixty percent of all uses of *bahar* in the Hebrew Scriptures. In the New Testament, the Greek verb *eklegomai* appears twenty-two times and means "to choose, set apart, elect." Sometimes, it refers to human decisions, but most importantly *eklegomai* signifies God's work of election according to His divine purpose and grace.

- In light of various views of divine election, perhaps a biblically faithful case could be stated this way: God's purposes in election — to exalt the Son and to glorify the saints — are beyond full human comprehension, at least for now (Isa. 55:8-9), yet we can rest in the knowledge that God is sovereign, just, gracious, and merciful. Our responsibility is to "confirm" our "calling and election" (2 Peter 1:10) through faith in Christ, trusting Him to complete the good work He began in us (Phil. 1:6), for even the staunchest Calvinist agrees that "everyone who believes in Him will not perish but have eternal life" (John 3:16).

THINK
Questions for personal or group study

(1) How would you explain the similarities and differences between conditional and unconditional election? Which of these concepts appears most biblically faithful to you?

(2) How does a person's definition of divine election affect his or her understanding of reprobation?

(3) What are some examples of election in the Old and New Testaments, depicting choices people make? How do these selections by men and women compare with God's election of people, nations, angels, and churches?

(4) How do you understand the following verses of Scripture in light of the debate between unconditional and conditional election:

- John 3:16
- John 5:24
- 1 Tim. 2:3-4
- 2 Peter 3:9

(5) What do you think Peter means when he encourages his readers to "make every effort to confirm your calling and election" (2 Peter 1:10)?

(6) An apostate is someone who has received the knowledge of the truth but willfully and decisively rejects it. Read 1 Tim. 1:19-20; Heb. 6:1-6; 1 John 2:19; and Jude 4. What do these passages say about apostates? How do apostates fit into your understanding of election and reprobation? How do apostates differ from backslidden Christians? From those who have never heard the gospel?

(7) How would you respond to the following statements about the doctrine of divine election:

- Election means that no one really has a choice whether to accept Jesus as Savior.
- People can't decide for themselves in any meaningful way. God gives us the illusion of free will, but actually He pulls all the strings.
- All Arminians deny the doctrine of divine election.
- All Calvinists are fatalists. By their reckoning, people truly are nothing more than robots.
- If election is true, then people who spend eternity in hell never had a chance for heaven.
- It's not fair for God to choose some people and just ignore the rest.
- The Bible says God wants all people to be saved. God always gets what He wants. Therefore, somehow, all people eventually go to heaven.

Chapter Three

YOU ARE PREDESTINED

I t's the evening of August 8, 1969, and actor Steve McQueen intends to drop by actress Sharon Tate's rented home in Los Angeles. Then, he supposedly gets a better offer from another lady friend and changes plans. Lucky for him. Shortly after midnight, members of the Manson Family enter the Tate home, butchering her, her unborn child, and four others.

McQueen later learns he is on a list of celebrities that cult leader Charles Manson has targeted for death, along with Tom Jones, Frank Sinatra, and Elizabeth Taylor. From then until his death from cancer in 1980, McQueen carries a gun.[1]

That tragic night continues to be the focus of speculation, investigative news stories, and TV documentaries. Is Steve McQueen lucky, or a beneficiary of the invisible hand of fate?[2] Are Sharon Tate and the other victims inescapably destined to die in a cultish bloodbath?

On a wider scale, how much of anyone's life is foreordained? The question gains particular steam when we consider that the Bible refers to some (but not all) people as "predestined." What does that mean? How does predestination fit into God's work of redemption? And if the Bible really teaches fatalistic determination, is there any wiggle room for human freedom?

As we explore these questions from a biblical perspective, it's important to keep in mind one clear truth: For followers of Jesus, it is biblically faithful to say, "I am predestined."

WHAT DOES IT MEAN TO BE PREDESTINED?

Simply put, predestination is God's plan from eternity past to complete the work of redemption in every saint, fully conforming us to the image of His Son.

The Greek word *proorizo* and its variations, found six times in the New Testament, carry the meaning of "predestine," "limit or mark out beforehand," "design definitely beforehand," or "ordain ahead of time." *Proorizo* comes from two Greek words: *pro*, which means "before" or "ahead of," and *horizo*, which means "to appoint, decide, or determine."

It may help to note that in the six New Testament verses where this term appears, God always is the one in focus:

- Those who put Jesus to death do what God decided beforehand (Acts 4:28).
- Believers are "predestined to be conformed to the image of his Son" (Rom. 8:29-30).
- The hidden wisdom of God that Paul preaches was "predestined before the ages for our glory" (1 Cor. 2:7).
- God "predestined us to be adopted as sons through Jesus Christ for himself" (Eph. 1:5).
- And believers receive an inheritance from God because we are "predestined according to the plan of the one who works out everything in agreement with the purpose of his will" (Eph. 1:11).

As William Mounce writes, "These eternal purposes of God for every Christian are a foregone conclusion because they are grounded in his predetermined will. This is why the eighteenth-century theologian Jonathan Edwards referred to God's predestining of believers along with his other saving acts listed in Rom. 8:29-30 as links in the 'inviolable chain of redemption.'"[3]

The *CSB Study Bible* offers several helpful notes:

- "Predestined means that God planned from eternity that 'those [whom] he foreknew' would become like Christ through spiritual rebirth" (Rom. 8:29-30).
- "All of God's blessings are in accord with sovereign predestination, which is purposeful and grounded in love. Predestination refers to the consistent and coherent intention of God's will, an eternal decision rendering certain that which will come to pass" (Eph. 1:5).
- "Christians have been predestined according to God's plan. They come to faith in Christ not by chance, coercion, or unaided choice, but by the enabling of God's Spirit" (Eph. 1:11).[4]

Some theologians, like Wayne Grudem, use the term "predestination" as a synonym for "election," but with a caveat. Grudem writes that "in Reformed theology generally, predestination is a broader term and includes the two aspects of election (for believers) and reprobation (for unbelievers)."[5]

For our purposes, we are dealing with predestination and election as separate but closely related saving works of God. Paul's specific use of the term "predestination," as we see in the Scriptures to follow, goes beyond God's sovereign choice of certain people for salvation, to describe the benefits of being elected, most notably the ultimate joy of being conformed to the image of Christ.

Foreknowledge, election, and predestination may be distinguished but not separated. As eternal decrees of God, they cannot be lined up chronologically since they exist outside of time. Even so, the New Testament writers seem to use foreknowledge as the hinge on which election and predestination swing. The interconnectedness of these three works of God may spur many questions in our minds. But they also should produce great joy. Followers of Jesus may rest assured that God's work of redemption is secure because it is grounded in His unchanging nature and sovereign decrees.

There are additional considerations we should keep in mind. The doctrine of predestination: (1) exalts the majesty of God, who befriends us in eternity past and plans an awesome (and everlasting) life for us; (2) illustrates the riches of His grace, as well as His determination to do something about sin before it even comes into existence; (3) underscores the essential truth that salvation is totally of grace, apart from human effort; (4) confronts us with our sinfulness, which is remedied only in the person and work of Christ; and (5) condemns our pride and deepens our humility.

God's sovereignty and human responsibility

Before we examine passages of Scripture that specifically address predestination, it may help to note the tension that exists between God's sovereignty and human responsibility, which we encountered in our study of foreknowledge and election. While the six verses under consideration in this chapter emphasize God's priority in grace, there are many other biblical texts that affirm the necessity of repentance and faith.

For example, on the Day of Pentecost, Peter makes an emphatic call to follow the Lord: "Repent and be baptized, each of you, in the name of Jesus Christ for the forgiveness of your sins, and you will receive the gift of the Holy Spirit" (Acts 2:38). Read on and discover how God's sovereignty and human freedom are intertwined: "'For the promise is for you and for your children, and for all who are far off, *as many as the Lord our God will call.*' With many other words he testified and strongly urged them, saying, 'Be saved from this corrupt generation!' So *those who accepted his message* were baptized, and that day about three thousand people were added to them" (Acts 2:39-41, emphasis added).

Another example is found in Rom. 10:9-13. The apostle Paul, who writes vigorously about the sovereign hand of God in foreknowledge, election, and predestination, nevertheless stresses the responsibility of human beings to respond positively to the gospel call: "If you confess with your mouth, 'Jesus is Lord,' and believe in your heart that God raised him from the dead, you will be saved. One believes with the heart, resulting in righteousness, and one confesses with the mouth, resulting in salvation. For the Scripture says, **Everyone who believes on him will not be put to shame**, since there is no distinction between Jew and Greek, because the same Lord of all richly blesses all who call on him. For **everyone who calls on the name of the Lord will be saved**."

One more passage should prove sufficient to illustrate the point. In the closing verses of Revelation, the apostle John offers this invitation: "Both the Spirit and the bride say, 'Come!' Let anyone who hears, say, 'Come!' Let the one who is thirsty come. Let the one who desires take the water of life freely" (Rev. 22:17).

In the parables of Jesus and the writings of the apostles, we see a divinely revealed tension between God's sovereignty and human responsibility. Both are true. And both align perfectly in God's plan of salvation. Even so, sinful and fallen human beings cannot fully comprehend these truths or completely resolve the tension between them. These truths are *revealed* to us in Scripture, but their unfathomable depths are *concealed* from us.

Chad Brand writes, "Though the concept of predestination seems to conflict with the responsibility of the individual to answer the Gospel call, the two must be compatible, since the same inspired teachers in Scripture emphasize both."[6]

Scripture teaches the complementary truths of divine sovereignty and human freedom. God does as He pleases, always acting in accordance with His nature and character as revealed in His Word. He has every right to act in any way He chooses with respect to the salvation of mankind.

At the same time, God created human beings in His image, which, among other things, means He entrusted people with an ability to make real decisions for which He holds us accountable. How these divine truths intersect in the doctrines of foreknowledge, election, and predestination is a mystery that sinful and fallen people cannot fully comprehend at this time. That makes them no less true.

Our response should be to thank God for His sovereign work of redemption and to joyfully embrace eternal life through faith in Jesus Christ.

PREDESTINATION IN KEY VERSES

Now, let's look at six verses in the New Testament that specifically address predestination.

Acts 4:27-28 - "For, in fact, in this city both Herod and Pontius Pilate, with the Gentiles and the people of Israel, assembled together against your holy servant Jesus, whom you anointed, to do whatever your hand and your will had predestined (*proorisen*) to take place."

Peter and John have been arrested for preaching, particularly for proclaiming in Jesus the resurrection from the dead (v. 2). The two apostles are summoned before the Jewish rulers, elders, and scribes, along with Annas the high priest, Caiaphas, John, Alexander, and all the members of the high-priestly family. They are questioned, then threatened and released. Peter and John rejoin their fellow believers, reporting everything that has taken place. Together, they raise their voices to God in prayer. In the midst of this, they acknowledge that the acts of Herod and Pontius Pilate in crucifying Jesus are "predestined" by the will of God (v. 28).

This harks back to the Day of Pentecost, when Peter declares to his fellow countrymen, "Though he [Jesus] was delivered up according to God's determined plan and foreknowledge, you used lawless people to nail him to a cross and kill him" (Acts 2:23). As we see from Scripture, God foreknew the crucifixion, planned it, and determined it would happen. Foreknowledge and predestination are two sides of the same coin. Yet, this is not fatalistic determinism, for Peter makes it clear that those who nailed Jesus to the cross were "lawless people" acting in knowing rebellion against God.

CSB	KJV	NIV	NASB	ESV
Predestined	Determined before	Decided beforehand	Predestined	Predestined

Comparing English translations of *proorisen* in Acts 4:28

Rom. 8:29-30 - "For those he foreknew he also predestined (*proorisen*) to be conformed to the image of his Son, so that he would

42

be the firstborn among many brothers and sisters. And those he predestined (*proorisen*), he also called; and those he called, he also justified; and those he justified, he also glorified."

Paul twice uses the word "predestined" in the context of God's eternal plan of salvation. Note that all of the work of God is in the past tense, including our future glorification. That seems to be because, in the mind of God, our full redemption is as good as completed. It is a package deal, embracing God's work before, in, and outside of time — or from a human perspective, from eternity past to eternity future.

Equally important, note that Paul's use of "predestined" refers both to the objects of salvation ("those he predestined") and the goal of His salvation ("predestined to be conformed to the image of his Son").

What does it mean to be conformed to the image of His Son? In simple terms, it means that God is working in us now to make us more like Jesus, and that ultimately (in glorification) He restores us to the sinless perfection in which Adam and Eve were created. What God starts in us, He promises to complete, as Paul notes in Phil. 1:6, "I am sure of this, that he who started a good work in you will carry it on to completion until the day of Christ Jesus."

This complete makeover begins when God's Spirit regenerates us and God the Father declares us righteous through His resulting work of justification. The righteousness of Christ is reckoned to our account, as our sin is transferred to His account and marked "paid in full."

But we're not yet able to live perfectly holy lives. We continue to live in a sinful and fallen world, and we still battle with the flesh — our inclinations to live independently of God. So, the lifelong work of sanctification begins as the indwelling Spirit strengthens our new desires for God and gives us the ability to resist temptation.

Through reading God's Word, praying, worshipping, fellowshipping with other believers, and in countless other ways, "the Holy Spirit polishes the mirror, enabling God's people to 'bring holiness to completion' (2 Cor. 7:1), just as it was in Jesus Christ," according to Greg Bailey. "Of course, God could bring about actual holiness in us in a moment if He chose. But in His wisdom He has ordained that this process should take place gradually over the entire course of our lives."[7]

This process ends when God brings about our glorification. At death, our souls/spirits are taken to heaven to await the restoration of our bodies in resurrection. When that day comes, we are fully conformed to the image of Christ. We see Him as He is and are like Him in every way — not little gods, but perfected in body, soul, and spirit.

CSB	KJV	NIV	NASB	ESV
Predestined	Did predestinate	Predestined	Predestined	Predestined

Comparing English translations of *proorisen* in Rom. 8:29-30

1 Cor. 2:7 - "On the contrary, we speak God's hidden wisdom in a mystery, a wisdom God predestined (*proorisen*) before the ages for our glory."

The message Paul proclaims is God's secret wisdom, which exists eternally and thus is unknowable to human beings apart from divine revelation. At the core of this wisdom is God's plan of salvation, determined before time and revealed to us most clearly in the person of Jesus Christ. He sets aside His privileged position at the Father's right hand, adds sinless humanity to His deity via the miracle of the virgin birth, and lives a parable-teaching, miracle-performing, prophecy-fulfilling life. As deity in human skin, He shows us the Father (John 14:9), proclaims Himself the way to the Father (John 14:6), and restores those who believe in Him to a right relationship with the Father through faith in Jesus.

The glorious benefits of salvation, stretching from eternity past to eternity future, are decreed long before the creation of the universe. While pagan mysteries in Paul's day are (allegedly) revealed to a select few, the gospel mystery is made known to all who obey the truth. People are not left to guess about God's existence, or His care and concern for sinful and fallen humanity; we simply perceive His revelation in creation and conscience (Romans 1), receive His Son (John 1:12), and believe the gospel for everlasting life (John 5:24).

Warren Wiersbe notes the characteristics of this divine wisdom. First, it originates in God, not in human beings; the wisest of the princes of this age could not invent or discover this marvelous wisdom that resides in God and is shared with Paul. Second, this wisdom has been hidden in ages past but now is revealed through Paul and the apostles. Third, this wisdom involves God's ordination. "The great plan of redemption was not a hasty afterthought on the part of God after He saw what man had done."

Fourth, Wiersbe writes, this wisdom results in the glory of God's people. What a staggering thought that one day we will see Him as He is and be like Him. Fifth, this wisdom is hidden from the unsaved world. Paul writes in 2 Cor. 4:3-4, "But if our gospel is veiled, it is veiled to those who are perishing. In their case, the god of this age has blinded the minds of the unbelievers to keep them from seeing the light of the gospel of the glory of Christ." Finally, this wisdom applies to believers' lives today. Eternal life is not merely a treasure laid up in heaven; it is a divine reality now.

The believers at Corinth have taken their eyes off the cross. Getting their perspective right once again enables them to experience the joy of knowing Christ and the fruitfulness of a life lived for Him.[8]

CSB	KJV	NIV	NASB	ESV
Predestined	Ordained	Destined	Predestined	Decreed

Comparing English translations of *proorisen* in 1 Cor. 2:7

Eph. 1:5, 11 - "He predestined (*proorisas*) us to be adopted as sons through Jesus Christ for himself, according to the good pleasure of his will ... In him we have also received an inheritance, because we were predestined (*prooristhentes*) according to the plan of the one who works out everything in agreement with the purpose of his will ..."

In the context of this passage, Paul makes several points about God's sovereign work of predestination, tying it to election, adoption, and inheritance:

- God chose us before the foundation of the world (v. 4). His foreknowledge, predestination, and election are conceived, and reckoned as complete, even before our existence.
- God chose us in Christ (v. 4). There is salvation in no one

else, and it is only through Christ, the chosen one of God the Father, that we find everlasting life (John 14:6; Acts 4:12).

- God's purpose in predestination is to make us holy and blameless before Him (v. 4).
- Predestination flows out of God's love (v. 4), good pleasure (vv. 5, 9), lavish grace (vv. 6-7), wisdom and understanding (v. 8), mystery of His will (v. 9), and plan (v. 11).
- The Lord predestines believers to be adopted children who receive an inheritance (vv. 5, 11). The Greek word for "adoption to sonship" is a legal term referring to the full legal standing of an adopted male heir in Roman culture.[9]
- Predestination should produce in us "the praise of his glorious grace that he lavished on us in the Beloved One" (v. 6).

CSB	KJV	NIV	NASB	ESV
Predestined (v. 5)	Having predestinated (v. 5)	Predestined (v. 5)	Predestined / having predestined (v. 5)	Predestined / having predestined (v. 5)
Were predestined (v. 11)	Being predestinated (v. 11)	Having been predestined (v. 11)	Having been predestined (v. 11)	Having been predestined (v. 11)

Comparing English translations of *proorisas* and *prooristhentes* in Eph. 1:5, 11

SUMMARY

Foreknowledge, election, and predestination form the three-legged stool upon which rests God's work of salvation in time. Forever in the mind and plan of our eternal Lord, these gleaming facets of redemption shine into human history and produce benefits that carry out into eternity future. God, who knew us and elected us before time, also predestined us to be conformed to the image of His Son — long before the Lamb of God burst onto the scene to take away the sin of the world (John 1:29; Rom. 8:29). None of these marvelous works of God excuses the sinner from a responsibility to believe on the Lord

Jesus Christ in order to appropriate everlasting life (John 5:24; Acts 2:38).

While followers of Jesus may rest confidently in our secure position in Christ, we should resist the twin temptations of arrogance and complacency. Our predestination is by God's grace and acquired by faith; it is not granted due to foreseen merit or inherent virtue. This excludes boasting because salvation is fully of the Lord. Further, while He sets the secure borders of our lives, we should always seek to point those outside the sheepfold to the Good Shepherd (John 10:11).

Consider these summary statements about predestination:

- Predestination is solely the work of God and is tied inextricably to His foreknowledge and election in eternity past.
- God predestines believers to become His adopted children, who are joint heirs with Jesus, and who become conformed to the image of Christ.
- God's predestination of believers cannot be separated from His other work of redemption before time, in time, or beyond time. From a human standpoint, God's predestination from the farthest reaches of eternity extends through time, applies to us, and continues out into eternity future in glorification.
- Predestination is personal. God doesn't just predestine His purposes; He predestines *us*.
- While human beings may create and execute plans for themselves and others, only God ultimately predestines human history because only God is eternal, sovereign, and omniscient.
- Predestination is specifically applied to those who inherit eternal life (Eph. 1:11).
- Predestination of people and purposes does not excuse anyone from the responsibility for their thoughts, words, and actions. Further, it does not let anyone off the hook for rejecting the revelation of God in creation, conscience, Christ, and the canon of Scripture.
- Predestination and human responsibility may best be

considered as complementary. That is, God's sovereign decrees and the ability of people to make choices for which we are held accountable are parallel truths from a human perspective; where they intersect in the mind of God is currently a mystery to His creatures.

THINK
Questions for personal or group study

(1) How might you explain to someone that God's predestination of people is certain but not fatalistically determined?

(2) What is God's purpose in predestination?

(3) How is predestination distinguished from foreknowledge and election? In what ways are they related?

(4) Read Jesus' parable of the wedding banquet (Matt. 22:1-14). How does Jesus maintain the tension between predestination and human responsibility in this parable (pay particular attention to verse 14)? This is a great opportunity for Jesus to clear up the issue, yet He doesn't. Why?

(5) If predestination ensures glorification, why do you think so many Christians have doubts about their salvation?

(6) Read Matt. 7:21-23. Why do you think some people are surprised on judgment day when Jesus sends them away?

(7) Hyper-Calvinism is an extreme branch of Reformed theology, which teaches that everyone's eternal destiny is so fatalistically determined that evangelism is unnecessary, and that God delights in the damnation of lost sinners. In what ways does this view of predestination distort the character of God? His genuine offer of salvation to all? The Great Commission (Matt. 28:19-20)?

Section Two

IN TIME

We explored God's work of salvation *before time* in Section One, including foreknowledge, election, and predestination. We move now to God's work of salvation *in time*, specifically those facets of redemption that followers of Jesus experience in our lifetimes.

Our focus is on eight such acts of God:

Calling involves both a general call as the gospel is proclaimed, and an effectual call in which those whom God foreknew, elected, and predestined are drawn to Christ, resulting in belief and repentance. God's sovereignty and human responsibility are bound together mysteriously in calling.

Regeneration is the work of the Holy Spirit that brings a sinner from spiritual death to spiritual life; it often is referred to as being "born again" or "born from above."

Justification is a legal declaration in heaven. There, Christ's perfect righteousness is transferred to the account of believing sinners, while our sin debt is transferred to His account, so that we are acquitted before the Father's holy bench.

Indwelling is a divine act in which the Holy Spirit takes up permanent residence in the body of a believer in Jesus Christ. Followers of Jesus are indwelt once, and permanently.

Baptism in the Holy Spirit is the means by which God places new believers into the body of Christ. Thus, all Christians — whom the Holy Spirit has regenerated and indwelt — share the common bond of the Spirit as members of the universal, or invisible, church.

Sanctification is the work of God making followers of Jesus more like our Savior. It may be understood in two ways, both of which relate to holiness. First, there is *positional* sanctification, the state of being set apart for God. Second, there is *practical* sanctification, the lifelong process by which the Holy Spirit makes us more like Jesus.

Adoption is the Father's gracious act of making new Christians members of His family. Having been born again, we are adopted by the Father as His sons and daughters. And, incredibly, this makes us coheirs with Jesus, the eternal Son of God — a sharing of spiritual wealth and privilege that prompts Jesus to burst with joy, not jealousy.

Sealing is part of the gift of the Holy Spirit granted to new believers as God places His divine mark of ownership on us, thus ensuring His everlasting presence and our eternal security.

Many of these facets of salvation are applied instantaneously as one-time, non-repeatable acts of God, with benefits extending throughout our lifetimes and into eternity future. Sanctification is different in that it is both a singular act and an ongoing process that meets its apex in glorification, the subject of our final chapter in Section Three. In any case, all eight of these works of redemption *in time* are permanent and irrevocable.

Chapter Four

YOU ARE CALLED

Growing up in a working-class neighborhood of small homes packed tightly together, my friends and I discovered the efficiency of communicating through open windows and across fenceless back yards. When it was time to walk to school, play kick the can, or hustle a game of boot hockey on snow-packed streets, we'd just open the window and summon our pals living a few feet away. If that didn't work, we walked to their back doors and called their names in a sing-song manner.

If I wanted to play with my friend Dennis, I'd approach the back door of his house and crow, "Deh-uh-niss! Deh-uh-niss!" If Dennis was home, he'd answer the door. Then we'd make our plans, which usually included our mutual buddy in the VanBoxel house across the street, where we'd warble, "Tim-uh-thee! Tim-uh-thee!" You get the idea.

In that bygone era, most homes had only one phone line (often a "party line" shared by two or more subscribers), which was to be kept open for important calls. The very idea of communicating with friends via social media or texting was the stuff of futuristic comic books, if it was imagined at all. So, we called our friends personally with lilting voices. By name. There was no mistaking the call, and the one called was responsible for answering.

How similar this is to the call of God in salvation. While there is a general call to everyone to trust in Christ through the proclamation of the gospel, the Bible tells us that God also extends an effectual call to those He foreknew, elected, and predestined. For every child of God, there is a time when the Holy Spirit calls him or her personally to faith in Christ, resulting in belief and repentance that lead to everlasting life.

Believers may disagree about the timing and nature of this call. Nevertheless, if you are a follower of Jesus, it is biblically faithful to say, "I am called."

WHAT DOES IT MEAN TO BE CALLED?

The words "call," "called," and "calling" in Scripture are derived from several Hebrew and Greek words and are applied in various ways. In the Old Testament, the verb *qara* is used more than seven hundred times and is the most common verb in Hebrew that means "to call, summon, proclaim." The basic meaning is to draw attention to oneself by using one's voice.[1]

In the New Testament, the verb *boao* means "to cry out, call loudly." John the Baptist is a voice of one *calling* in the desert, "Prepare the way for the Lord" (Matt. 3:3; Mark 1:3; Luke 3:4; cf. Isa. 40:3; John 1:23). Evil spirits *shriek* as they come out of many people (Acts 8:7 NIV). Citizens *call out* or *complain* to a public official (Acts 17:6; 25:24). In some instances, *boao* is used to describe begging or pleading, either to Jesus or to the Father. Jesus *cries out* on the cross, "My God, my God, why have you abandoned me?" (Mark 15:34). In Luke 9:38 and 18:38, Jesus hears the *cry* of a person and responds with a miracle. And in Luke 18:7, Jesus says God hears the elect who *cry out* to Him.

The verb *kaleo* is used quite often in the New Testament. It means "to call, invite, summon," and it's applied in three primary ways:

- To call someone to get his or her attention. For example, Herod *summons* the Magi (Matt. 2:7). Jesus' mother and brothers *call* to Jesus to meet with Him (Mark 3:31). A Pharisee *invites* Jesus to dine with him (Luke 7:36, 39).

- To name someone or something. An angel tells Zechariah that his son is to be *named* John (Luke 1:13). Gabriel tells Mary that her baby is to be *named* Jesus (Luke 1:31).
- To call in a spiritual sense. "This moves from the simple idea of inviting or summoning to a more theological meaning of *kaleo*."[2] We first see this in Matt. 2:15, where Matthew quotes Hosea 11:1. God says, "Out of Egypt I called my son." When Jesus begins His ministry, He *calls* James and John to follow Him (Matt. 4:21; Mark 1:20). This spiritual sense is seen in Jesus' statement, "I didn't come to call the righteous, but sinners" (Mark 2:17; cf. Luke 5:32).

William Mounce comments, "While the idea of spiritual calling is not prevalent in the gospels and Acts, it is highly developed in Paul's writings. When God calls, it is a call that roots in predestination and ends in glorification (Rom. 8:29-30). God calls us by his grace (Gal. 1:6). But his calling is not only to salvation; it is also to a life of serving him and our fellow believers (Eph. 4:1, 4; 1 Thess. 2:12; 4:7; 2 Tim. 1:9)."[3]

The compound verb *epikaleo* — from *epi*, meaning "on, upon," and *kaleo*, meaning "to call" — is used to depict those who call on someone, or to appeal for help. Peter declares on the Day of Pentecost, "Then everyone who calls on the name of the Lord will be saved" (Acts 2:21). Paul repeats this truth in Rom. 10:13. The verb also describes Jesus as the object of prayers as Stephen calls on Him (Acts 7:59). And Paul uses this verb when he appeals to Caesar (Acts 25:11).

The adjective *kletos* is used ten times in the New Testament and denotes someone or something that has been called. All of its uses in the New Testament denote someone who has been called by God.[4] For example, Paul writes to "you who also are called by Jesus Christ" (Rom. 1:6). Jude writes to "those who are the called" (Jude 1). And John notes that those with Christ are "called, chosen, and faithful" (Rev. 17:14).

The noun *klesis* refers to the action God takes to summon people to Himself. Paul writes about the calling of God (Rom. 11:29; Phil. 3:14); the hope of His calling (Eph. 1:18); and a holy calling (2 Tim. 1:9). Elsewhere, *klesis* is used to describe God's calling in the life of a Christian. "Let each of you remain in the situation in which he was called," writes Paul in 1 Cor. 7:20. And, "live worthy of the calling you have received" (Eph. 4:1).

A couple of other Greek words are used to communicate the idea of calling. For example, the verb *lego* usually is translated "say" but sometimes carries the notion "to call."

Finally, the verb *phoneo* means "to call out, call to, make a noise." Sometimes it's used for calling out a question (Acts 10:18) or, more commonly, a statement or command. On the cross Jesus *cries out*, "My God, my God, why have you abandoned me" (Matt. 27:46).[5] Earlier in His earthy ministry, Jesus takes the hand of a dead girl and *calls*, "Child, get up!" (Luke 8:54). *Phoneo* also can mean to summon or invite (e.g., Luke 14:12; Acts 10:7). Last, it can have broad application, describing not only the verbalizations of people but of roosters, who *crow* (Matt. 26:34), and of evil spirits, who *shout* (Mark 1:26).

So, we can see the broad uses and varied applications of the Hebrew and Greek words translated "call," "called," and "calling." As with other terms used to describe God's great salvation, we always should consider context, and compare Scripture with Scripture, to seek the clearest understanding possible of these terms as they relate to God's general call to salvation, and His effectual call that results in everlasting life.

THE GENERAL CALL

Jesus and the New Testament writers describe an invitation God issues to all people to be saved from their sins. God issues this call, and Christ commands His followers to carry this call to the ends of the earth, knowing full well that many reject it, while others die without hearing it. This in no way excuses those who don't specifically hear the gospel from the responsibility for their sins. Paul reminds us that every unbeliever before the great white throne one day stands "without excuse" (Rom. 1:20).

That's because God has revealed Himself to all people in creation and in conscience. No one will be able to say, "I didn't know there was a God," for "the heavens declare the glory of God, and the expanse proclaims the work of his hands" (Ps. 19:1). The psalmist looks up in the dead of night and marvels, "When I observe your heavens, the work of your fingers, the moon and the stars, which you set in place, what is a human being that you remember him, a son of man that you look after him?" (Ps. 8:3-4).

Paul writes that what can be known about God is evident even to those who reject Him, "because God has shown it to them. For his invisible attributes, that is, his eternal power and divine nature, have been clearly seen since the creation of the world, being understood through what he has made" (Rom. 1:19b-20). Further, no one will be able to say, "I didn't know there was an absolute standard of right and wrong," because God has set His moral compass in their hearts (Rom. 2:12-16).

Even so, those who reject God's self-revelation in creation and conscience begin to exalt created things — themselves, or someone or something else — above the one true God, thus engaging in idolatry. In time, their hearts become so hardened that God gives them over in the desires of their hearts to sexual impurity, disgraceful passions, and corrupt minds (Rom. 1:24, 26, 28). Paul concludes, "Although they know God's just sentence — that those who practice such things deserve to die — they not only do them, but even applaud others who practice them" (Rom. 1:32). In short, God allows them to have their way. They pass the point of no return. Judgment and hell await them.

Let's look at a few passages that describe the general call.

Matt. 13:3-9; 18-23. In the parable of the sower, Jesus illustrates the manner in which the "word of the kingdom" is spread widely and indiscriminately. The word falls on some, whose hearts are as hard as the footpaths bordering the fields. For others, the word falls on rocky soil, the hearts that embrace the gospel from a purely emotional or shallow sense of commitment; then, pressures or persecution lead them to abandon the faith they once professed. Others are like soil that sprouts thorns, which choke the word as "the worries of this age and the deceitfulness of wealth" make them unfruitful. But, at last, some seed falls on fertile soil, the tender, broken hearts of true believers who bear much fruit. Like the seed cast broadly, the message of the kingdom goes out across the world, but it only sinks into the hearts of those ready to receive it.

Matt. 22:14 - "For many are invited, but few are chosen." With these words, Jesus ends the parable of the wedding banquet (Matt. 22:1-14). Addressing the chief priests and the Pharisees, Jesus tells them the kingdom of heaven is like a king who gives a wedding banquet for his son. As the time for celebration draws near, the king sends his servants to those who were invited — and who, by the way, had enthusiastically accepted the offer when it was first given. Now, however, they make excuses. Some return to their farms or businesses, too preoccupied with their own worldly concerns to honor their commitment. Others react violently, seizing the king's servants, mistreating them, and killing them.

There is no doubt who these ungrateful rebels are: the leaders of the nation of Israel. Initially embracing a covenant with Yahweh — "We will do all that the Lord has spoken" (Ex. 19:8); "We will do everything that the Lord has commanded" (Ex. 24:3) — they have hardened themselves over the centuries, rebelling against the godly kings and faithful prophets who proclaim the blessings of the covenant and the curses for rejecting it.

Continuing the parable, Jesus says the king is enraged at the treatment of his servants. He sends out his troops, kills the murderers, and burns down their city. This is what the Lord in fact does about forty years after Jesus speaks these words. In A.D. 70, He sends the Roman general Titus and his army to besiege Jerusalem, destroy the temple, kill an estimated one million Jews, and scatter the rest.

Jesus then turns His attention to what the king does next. With the banquet table set, but the invited guests unworthy, he sends his servants out with the command to "invite everyone you find to the banquet." Soon, the banquet hall is filled. This illustrates the gospel call, which goes out broadly and indiscriminately, so that the kingdom has "both evil and good" — a reminder that some who profess to know Christ are in fact pretenders.

The king singles out one such pretender. He is easy to spot, for he is not wearing appropriate attire — likely a simple linen robe the king offers to everyone who enters his banquet hall. This man dishonors the king by refusing to don the required robe, preferring to wear the filthy rags of his own righteousness. For that, he is bound hand and foot and cast into outer darkness, a symbol of what is to come on judgment day for many who profess to know Christ but live inwardly as rebels.

At last, Jesus summarizes by saying, "For many are invited, but few are chosen." God's purpose always has been to fill His banquet hall with people of every tribe, nation, people, and language (see Rev. 5:9). The gospel goes out to the ends of the earth, but only those "chosen" enter into everlasting fellowship with the King and His Son. In this verse, Jesus could have cleared up the tension between divine sovereignty and human responsibility, but instead He appears to let it stand.

However, some scholars argue that "chosen" is not a reference to a decision made in the past but to a judgment that will be made in the future.[6] While many are "invited," only those robed with the righteousness of Christ will be "chosen" (or accepted). As Kenneth Keathley writes, "Rather than being a proof text for an inward call given only to the elect, the saying reinforces the notion of human responsibility for not being chosen."[7]

Matt. 28:19-20 - "Go, therefore, and make disciples of all nations, baptizing them in the name of the Father and of the Son and of the Holy Spirit, teaching them to observe everything I have commanded you. And remember, I am with you always, to the end of the age." After His resurrection and just prior to His ascension, Jesus commands His followers to "make disciples" of all nations — a clear call to spread the gospel message everywhere. Like the seed falling on fertile soil, the gospel will sink into the hearts of those who truly follow the Lord.

Mark 16:15 - "Go into all the world and preach the gospel to all creation." Similar to the Great Commission (Matt. 28:19-20), this command of Jesus to His followers is to spread the good news of the kingdom around the world. Many people hear the gospel, but not all respond in belief and repentance. Nevertheless, our command is to go and to preach the gospel.

It is clear that this general call, as well as the Lord's effectual call, is for Jews and Gentiles alike (see Rom. 9:22-26; Gal. 3:28-29).

John 3:14-21. In this night-time visit with Nicodemus, Jesus explains the necessity of the Son of Man being "lifted up," or crucified, for the redemption of those who believe. This is an expression of God's love for the world and His assurance of salvation to "everyone who believes in him" (v. 16). Jesus makes it clear that those who reject God's provision of everlasting life, found only in His Son, are already condemned (v. 18). They are without excuse, loving darkness rather than light, and doing evil rather than good (vv. 19-20).

John 16:7-11. As Jesus prepares His disciples for the Holy Spirit's ministry, He offers them a preview of the Spirit's work in the unbelieving world. Jesus says, "When he [the Holy Spirit] comes, he will convict the world about sin, righteousness, and judgment" (v. 8). Through the Spirit-filled messengers of the gospel, unbelievers will hear the proclamation of the good news and be convinced of its truth.

Specifically, the Spirit convicts unbelievers of three truths. First, of *sin,* "because they do not believe in me" (v. 9). It is not the sin of murder, adultery, or fraud that keeps people out of the kingdom of heaven; it is their stubborn refusal to admit they are sinners in need of the redemption found only in Jesus.

Second, Jesus says the Spirit convicts unbelievers of *righteousness,* "because I am going to the Father and you will no longer see me" (v. 10). It is not the relative righteousness that people can claim — "I may not be as good as Mother Teresa, but I'm no Adolf Hitler!" — rather, it is the perfect righteousness of Christ that ensures salvation. The one who comes to Jesus claiming good works, while denying the only work sufficient to obtain eternal life (the finished work of Christ), will be told, "I never knew you. Depart from me, you lawbreakers!" (Matt. 7:23).

Finally, the Spirit convicts unbelievers of *judgment,* "because the ruler of this world has been judged" (v. 11). The ruler of this world is none other than Satan, "the prince of the power of the air" (Eph. 2:2 KJV), and "the god of this age" (2 Cor. 4:4). Today, he is free, prowling the earth like a roaring lion, looking for anyone to devour (1 Peter 5:8). But he has been judged. Christ defeated Satan through His finished work on the cross. One day, Satan's sentence of everlasting torment in hell will be carried out (Matt. 25:41; Rev. 20:10). Jesus' words of warning, through the Spirit, are that if a person rejects the gospel and persists in unbelief, he or she will suffer the same judgment decreed for Satan — everlasting banishment to hell.

As the gospel is proclaimed, the Spirit does the necessary work of convicting lost people of their perilous state. While many fall under this conviction and respond in belief and repentance, others do not. Like King Agrippa to Paul, some will say, "Are you going to persuade me to become a Christian so easily?" (Acts 26:28).

We could cite other passages, but these verses should adequately illustrate how the *general call* goes out around the world. For those God foreknew, elected, and predestined, His call becomes effectual, resulting in justification and glorification (Rom. 8:29-30).

THE EFFECTUAL CALL

Within the general call, which goes out broadly and indiscriminately, there is an effectual call in which those whom God foreknew, elected, and predestined are drawn to Christ, resulting in belief and repentance. M.G. Easton writes, "An effectual call is something more than the outward message of the Word of God to men. It is internal and is the result of the enlightening and sanctifying influence of the Holy Spirit, effectually drawing men to Christ, and disposing and enabling them to receive the truth."[8]

All who hear the gospel message and respond in faith are, by definition, objects of the effectual call. This is the crux of the mystery embracing divine sovereignty and human responsibility. Far too often, followers of Jesus try conclusively to solve the mystery, only to deepen it — and often, sadly, to create unnecessary and harmful divisions in the body of Christ.

Does God sovereignly elect some people for salvation? *Yes.* Has God created people with an ability to make choices for which they are held accountable? *Yes.* One statement of biblical truth does not negate the other, even though we can't fully resolve the mystery that envelopes both. So, when overcoming grace meets human freedom, let's welcome both of these biblical truths and thank the Author of salvation that they are no mystery to Him.

As we look at several passages of Scripture that address the call of God to salvation, it's important to understand that we are not describing a fatalistic roll call; rather, we are witnessing the mysterious work of God in redemption. Human beings may claim no part in the work of salvation, yet they are commanded to repent and believe, something that requires an exercise of the human will. Equally important, God is not diminished in His sovereignty by enabling people created in His image to freely accept or reject His offer of salvation.

CALLING IN KEY PASSAGES

John 6:44 - "No one can come to me unless the Father who sent me draws (*helkuse*) him, and I will raise him up on the last day."

Jesus has just fed the five thousand. Many are following Him in His travels around the Sea of Galilee because they're looking for another meal (v. 26). Others hope to make Him king (v. 15). Still others are on the verge of walking away (v. 66). No doubt, Jesus is speaking to a diverse audience that bears a plethora of personal motives. So, He uses this opportunity to sift His disciples. He declares Himself the bread who has come down from heaven (v. 41), and He insists that unless people eat His flesh and drink His blood (that is, receive Him as their only hope of eternal life), they have no part in Him (vv. 53-55). It is in this context that Jesus offers several statements regarding the effectual call.

In verses 37-39, He says, "Everyone the Father gives me will come to me, and the one who comes to me I will never cast out. For I have come down from heaven, not to do my own will, but the will of him who sent me. This is the will of him who sent me: that I should lose none of those he has given me but should raise them up on the last day." Those foreknown, elected, and predestined are certain to be glorified — a truth that the apostle Paul later affirms (Rom. 8:29-30).

In verse 45, Jesus declares, "It is written in the Prophets: **And they will all be taught by God**. Everyone who has listened to and learned from the Father comes to me." Here is the balance between divine sovereignty and human responsibility; those who come to Jesus have listened and learned from the Father by way of the Old Testament prophecies.

The use of "draws" in verse 44 can be translated, "brings," or "leads." Variations of the Greek verb *helkuo* are used in John 12:32;

21:6; Acts 16:19; and James 2:6 and are translated "draw," "haul," "dragged," and "drag," respectively. *Helkuo* is a strong verb that communicates the certainty of an act being accomplished. Those the Father draws to Jesus come to Him without exception. While this illustrates the power of God to call out His elect, it doesn't release those who hear the gospel from the responsibility to respond affirmatively.

Those who refuse to believe are not drawn to Jesus, as the Savior makes plain in verses 64-65: "'But there are some among you who don't believe.' (For Jesus knew from the beginning those who would not believe and the one who would betray him.) He said, 'This is why I told you that no one can come to me unless it is granted to him by the Father.'" This raises a thorny question: Does God decide not to draw some people to Jesus because they refuse to believe, or do they refuse to believe because they are not drawn? More on this in the next chapter, which deals with regeneration.

CSB	KJV	NIV	NASB	ESV
Draws	Draw	Draws	Draws	Draws

Comparing English translations of *helkuse* in John 6:44

Acts 2:39 - "For the promise is for you [Jewish listeners at Pentecost] and for your children, and for all who are far off, as many as the Lord our God will call (*proskalesetai*)."

Those who are far off are Gentiles. They are geographically far away, and they are far away in their knowledge of the one true God. The promise of salvation is for "as many" as the Lord calls. Peter follows this with "many other words" in which he "testified and strongly urged them, saying, 'Be saved from this corrupt generation!'" (v. 40).

But how are they to be saved? Luke provides the answer in the next verse, "So those who accepted his message were baptized, and that day about three thousand people were added to them." God's sovereign call demands a human response.

CSB	KJV	NIV	NASB	ESV
Will call	Shall call	Will call	Will call	Calls

Comparing English translations of *proskalesetai* in Acts 2:39

Acts 13:48. Paul and Barnabas address unbelieving Jews in Antioch, telling them that because they reject the gospel and judge themselves unworthy of eternal life, the apostle and his companion are turning to the Gentiles. They quote Isa. 49:6, "**I have made you a light for the Gentiles to bring salvation to the end of the earth**" (v. 47). Verse 48 reads: "When the Gentiles heard this, they rejoiced and honored the word of the Lord, and all who had been appointed (*tetagmenoi*) to eternal life believed."

The *CSB Study Bible* comments, "This verse expresses one of the great enigmatic truths of Scripture: **all who had been appointed to eternal life believed.** This touches both on God's election ('appointed') and the human responsibility to choose ('believed')."[9]

J.O. Buswell comments, "Actually the words of Acts 13:48-49 do not necessarily have any reference whatever to the doctrine of God's eternal decree of election. The passive participle *tetagmenoi* may simply mean 'ready,' and we might well read, 'as many as were prepared for eternal life, believed.'" He cites English theologian Henry Alford, who commented, "The meaning of this word must be determined by the context. The Jews had *judged themselves unworthy of eternal life* (v. 46); the Gentiles, 'as many as were disposed to eternal life,' believed ... To find in this text preordination to life asserted, is to force both the word and the context to a meaning which they do not contain."[10]

A few verses later, Luke writes, "In Iconium they [Paul and Barnabas] entered the Jewish synagogue, as usual, and spoke in such a way that a great number of both Jews and Greeks believed" (Acts 14:1). Norman Geisler concludes that "there is no contradiction between preordination and persuasion since God preordained the means (persuasion) with the end (eternal life)."[11]

CSB	KJV	NIV	NASB	ESV
Appointed	Ordained	Appointed	Appointed	Appointed

Comparing English translations of *tetagmenoi* in Acts 13:48

Acts 16:14. As Paul and his traveling companions sail into Philippi, they find a place just outside the city on the Sabbath. They sit down and speak to the women gathered there. Luke writes, "A God-fearing woman named Lydia, a dealer in purple cloth from the city of Thyatira, was listening. The Lord opened (*dienoixen*) her heart to respond to what Paul was saying."

Luke addresses both divine and human initiative in his record of Lydia's response to the gospel. The Lord opens this woman's heart, and she — already a God-fearing woman — responds. In the next verse, Luke records that Lydia and her household are baptized, after which she urges the men, "If you consider me a believer in the Lord, come and stay at my house" (v. 15).

While this passage stresses the necessity of the Holy Spirit's work in the heart of unbelievers, it does not negate the responsibility of the hearer to believe. Luke records nothing about the Spirit's wooing of other women, or the people in Lydia's household, yet no doubt many respond to the gospel message.

CSB	KJV	NIV	NASB	ESV
Opened	Opened	Opened	Opened	Opened

Comparing English translations of *dienoixen* in Acts 16:14

Acts 26:16-18. Paul shares his testimony with King Agrippa. He recalls his encounter with Jesus on the road to Damascus, where the Lord says, "But get up and stand on your feet. For I have appeared to you for this purpose, to appoint (*procheirisasthai*) you as a servant and a witness of what you have seen and will see of me. I will rescue you from your people and from the Gentiles. I am sending you to them to open their eyes so that they may turn from darkness to light and from the power of Satan to God, that they may receive forgiveness of sins and a share among those who are sanctified by faith in me."

The means by which God opens the eyes of unbelievers is through Paul's proclamation of the gospel, punctuated with miracles, which are true signs of an apostle (2 Cor. 12:12). Here, we see God appointing, or calling, Paul as an apostle. We also see God's purpose in the call: to open the eyes of Jews and Gentiles through the preaching of God's Word. At the same time, the elect must "*turn* from darkness to light," "*receive* forgiveness of sins," and be "sanctified by *faith*" in Christ.

CSB	KJV	NIV	NASB	ESV
Appoint	Make	Appoint	Appoint	Appoint

Comparing English translations of *procheirisasthai* in Acts 26:16

Rom. 8:28, 30 - "We know that all things work together for the good of those who love God, who are called (*kletois*) according to his purpose.... And those he predestined, he also called; and those he called, he also justified; and those he justified, he also glorified."

We've already examined this passage in some detail, seeing how this *golden chain of salvation* links God's foreknowledge, predestination, calling, justification, and glorification, extending from eternity past to eternity future. There is little doubt here that Paul's use of "called" is a specific reference to believers, for unbelievers are never described in Scripture as foreknown, predestined, justified, or glorified.

Paul does not negate the general call of God to repent and believe, for his life's passion is to preach Christ crucified, even when many who hear his message reject it. However, the apostle's use of "called" illustrates the fact that within the general call to all people is the effectual call that always results in everlasting life.

It also should be kept in mind that God calls the elect "according to his purpose" — a purpose that is two-fold: to exalt Christ as the first-born among many brothers and sisters (Rom. 8:29), and to gather a people for Himself who reflect the glory of the Son now and forevermore (John 11:52; Eph. 1:3-14). A Puritan prayer captures this well:

O God,
Thy main plan, and the end of thy will
is to make Christ glorious and beloved
in heaven
where he is now ascended,
where one day all the elect will behold his glory
and love and glorify him forever.[12]

The *CSB Study Bible* notes, "**Called** is the 'effectual' call in which God opens our heart so we can hear his voice. 'Calling' in Paul's writing never means just an invitation. It is a sovereign summons that draws the sinner from death to life."[13]

At the same time, as Norman Geisler points out, "That these and like texts show the unconditional nature of election from God's point of view is not challenged. But the question is not whether election is unconditional from the vantage point of the *Giver* but whether there are any conditions for the *receiver*.... God is the unconditional source of the election, and that election is done with full foreknowledge of all things. But ... the elect will freely choose to believe. Election is not *based on* or dependent on foreknowledge. Rather, it is merely *in accord with* it."[14]

CSB	KJV	NIV	NASB	ESV
Called	The called	Called	Called	Called

Comparing English translations of *kletois* in Rom. 8:28

2 Thess. 2:13-14 - "But we ought to thank God always for you, brothers and sisters loved by the Lord, because from the beginning God has chosen you for salvation through sanctification by the Spirit and through belief in the truth. He called (*ekalesen*) you to this through our gospel, so that you might obtain the glory of our Lord Jesus Christ."

God's election in eternity past is made real in time through *sanctification*, the work of grace in which the Spirit sets apart the believer as His own, and through *belief in the truth*, the receiving of God's grace into the sinner's life. Once again, we see the consistent work of divine sovereignty in election as well as human responsibility in the response to the gospel. The result is that the Christian obtains the glory of our Lord Jesus Christ, initially through the presence of the indwelling Spirit, and later through the glorification of the body in resurrection.

Geisler states, "In short, we were chosen *but free* — which is directly contrary to the conclusion of the extreme Calvinists.... the error of extreme Calvinism regarding 'unconditional election' is the failure to adhere to an election that is unconditional from the standpoint of the Giver (God), but has one condition for the receiver — faith. This, in turn, is based on the mistaken notion that faith is a gift only to the elect, who have no choice in receiving it"[15]

CSB	KJV	NIV	NASB	ESV
Called	Called	Called	Called	Called

Comparing English translations of *ekalesen* in 2 Thess. 2:14

2 Tim. 1:9-10 - "He has saved us and called us with a holy calling (*hagia klesei*), not according to our works, but according to his own purpose and grace, which was given to us in Christ Jesus before time began. This has now been made evident through the appearing of our Savior Christ Jesus, who has abolished death and has brought life and immortality to light through the gospel."

Paul no doubt is writing about Christians — the "us" whom God has saved and called with a holy calling. God's saving call is in accordance with His purpose and grace, reserved for us in eternity past in Jesus Christ. This illustrates the unbroken chain that links the work of God in time and eternity. Christ's finished work not only fulfills the ancient promises of God, it carries forward into eternity. Those He has called attain immortality when we are resurrected and glorified.

While this is a strong statement of God's effectual call to the elect, it does not rule out His call to those who reject the gospel, or the responsibility of those who hear the gospel to respond in belief and repentance. Salvation is entirely a work of God; the Triune Godhead both initiates and completes it. As Kenneth Keathley notes, "If you are saved, it is because of the sovereign, gracious, and monergistic [sole] work of God. If you are lost, it is your fault. The saved are delivered entirely by grace. The lost are lost entirely by their own rebellion."[16]

CSB	KJV	NIV	NASB	ESV
Holy calling	Holy calling	Holy life	Holy calling	Holy calling

Comparing English translations of *hagia klesei* in 2 Tim. 1:9

1 Peter 2:9 - "But you are **a chosen race, a royal priesthood, a holy nation, a people for his possession, so that you may proclaim the praises** of the one who called (*kalesantos*) you out of darkness into his marvelous light."

The *CSB Study Bible* notes, "The transfer from darkness to light is a common NT description of conversion."[17] Jesus tells Saul He is "sending you to them [the Gentiles] to open their eyes so that they may turn from darkness to light and from the power of Satan to God ..." (Acts 26:17b-18).

This same Saul, now known as Paul, writes to the Corinthian church, "For God who said, 'Let light shine out of darkness,' has shone in our hearts to give the light of the knowledge of God's glory in the face of Jesus Christ" (2 Cor. 4:6). And Paul writes to the Ephesian believers, "For you were once darkness, but now you are light in the Lord. Live as children of light ..." (Eph. 5:8).

Again, the fact that God calls the elect out of darkness into His marvelous light does not necessarily mean He doesn't also call others, who, to their peril, reject Him and His promise of eternal life.

CSB	KJV	NIV	NASB	ESV
Called	Called	Called	Called	Called

Comparing English translations of *kalesantos* in 1 Peter 2:9

DRAWING ALL PEOPLE

Finally, let's consider the issue of God's call to all people. In the

Gospel of John, Jesus offers three "lifted up" sayings that touch on the effectual call to salvation:

John 3:14-15 - "Just as Moses lifted up the snake in the wilderness, so the Son of Man must be lifted up, so that everyone who believes in him may have eternal life."

John 8:28 - "So Jesus said to them [Jewish listeners, particularly the Pharisees], 'When you lift up the Son of Man, then you will know that I am he [light of the world; Son of God], and that I do nothing on my own. But just as the Father taught me, I say these things.'"

John 12:32 - "As for me, if I am lifted up from the earth I will draw all people to myself."

First, it's important to note that the "lifting up" in every case is a reference to Jesus' crucifixion, as John 12:33 makes clear: "He said this to indicate what kind of death he was about to die." It may also help to see the link to Isa. 52:13, which is part of a lengthy passage on the Messiah as Suffering Servant: "See, my servant [the Targum adds, 'the Messiah'] will be successful; he will be raised and lifted up and greatly exalted." This may indicate not only the Messiah's lifting up on the cross, but His resurrection and glorification as He ascends to the Father's right hand.

Next, the word "draw" in John 12:32 is a strong and descriptive verb. It's from the Greek *helkuo* and means to drag, draw, or haul. In John 6:44, this word refers to the necessary drawing by the Father of people to Christ for eternal life, and it carries the meaning of "bringing" or "leading." In John 18:10, it describes the manner in which Peter draws his sword to defend Jesus in the Garden of Gethsemane. In John 21:6 and 11, it depicts the effort of fishermen to haul in a big catch. In Acts 16:19, it describes the owners of a fortune-telling slave girl. These men, having seized Paul and Silas, drag them to the authorities in response to Paul and Silas' casting an evil spirit out of the girl. In Acts 21:30, the "whole city" of Jerusalem is stirred up, resulting in the people seizing Paul and dragging him out of the temple. And in James 2:6, the rich oppress the poor, dragging them into court.

In each of these examples, the action is completed successfully: the sword is drawn, the fish are hauled in, Paul and Silas are delivered to the authorities, Paul is dragged out of the temple and brought before magistrates, and the rich successfully force the unsuspecting poor into unwanted litigation.

So, with respect to salvation, it seems clear that those God foreknew, elected, and predestined must be called, or drawn to Jesus, resulting in eternal life. But what does Jesus mean when He says He will draw "all people" to Himself? Certainly, He is not preaching universalism, for Jesus speaks more of hell, or outer darkness, than He does about heaven. And He tells the religious leaders of His day they are destined to receive "the greater damnation" (Matt. 23:14 KJV) for their hypocrisy. So, what does "all people" mean?

One possibility is that Jesus is speaking of "all" the elect. While the word "all" certainly encompasses everyone that God has chosen for salvation, it doesn't seem to be the best application of Jesus' words here. Perhaps a better interpretation of "all" is "all kinds of people," Jews and Gentiles alike. This is clear in other New Testament passages. In John 10:16, for example, Jesus says He has "other sheep," a reference to Gentile believers. In John 11:52, we are told that Jesus' death will "unite the scattered children of God," a family that extends beyond Jewish people of faith. And in John 12:20-21, we learn that Greeks came up to Jerusalem to worship during one of the feasts, seeking Jesus.

We also know that in Rev. 5:9-10 John sees the four living creatures and the twenty-four elders falling down before the Lamb and singing a new song. Because Jesus was "slaughtered" (lifted up on the cross), the living creatures and elders declare: "you purchased people for God by your blood from every tribe and language and people and nation. You made them a kingdom and priests to our God, and they will reign on the earth."

So, perhaps it's best to understand these "lifted up" passages as referring to the necessity of the cross to secure the redemption of the elect; the promise that the elect are effectually drawn to Jesus; and the fact that people of every ethnicity, language, and nation are brought into the kingdom as they hear the gospel message and respond in belief and repentance.

Summary

God's call to sinners for salvation is expressed in two ways in the New Testament: A *general call* to everyone through creation, conscience, the canon of Scripture, and the gospel of Christ; and an *effectual call* that connects believers with God's work outside of time (foreknowledge, election, predestination, and glorification). God chooses His people unconditionally, yet eternal life is conditioned on faith in Christ.

The tension between divine sovereignty and human responsibility gets no easier to resolve by understanding the theological terms that describe God's work in time, as distinguished from His work in eternity. Nevertheless, these truths are affirmed in Scripture as God issues both a general call and an effectual call, and as all people are urged to repent and believe the gospel. Those who respond affirmatively are foreknown, elect, predestined, and called. They also are justified, sanctified, and glorified.

This is not a mechanistic process by which God fatalistically picks some for eternal life and, with equal passion, morbidly chooses others for outer darkness. Rather, it is a mysterious working of the Triune God as the Father, Son, and Holy Spirit call upon all people to repent, while enabling those who receive the call to enter God's kingdom.

Consider these summary statements:

- The words "call," "called," and "calling" appear hundreds of times in the New Testament. Often, these words apply to God's call to people for salvation and service. As with other terms used to depict His work of redemption, we should consider context, and compare Scripture with Scripture, to seek the clearest understanding possible of these terms as they relate to God's general call to salvation, and His effectual call that results in everlasting life.
- Jesus and the New Testament writers describe an invitation God issues to all people to be saved from their sins. This is known as the general call. Christ commands His followers

to carry this call to the ends of the earth (Matt. 28:19-20; Mark 16:15).

- Many people reject the general call to salvation, while others die without hearing it. This in no way excuses them from the responsibility for their sins because God has revealed Himself, specifically His eternal power and divine nature, to all people in creation and conscience. As a result, "people are without excuse" (Rom. 1:20b).

- Within the general call, which goes out broadly and indiscriminately, there is an effectual call in which those God foreknew, elected, and predestined are drawn to Christ, resulting in belief and repentance that lead to everlasting life.

- All who hear the gospel message and respond in faith are by definition objects of the effectual call. This is the crux of the mystery embracing divine sovereignty and human responsibility. Far too often, followers of Jesus try conclusively to solve the mystery, building theological systems to articulate their perspectives. In the process, they only deepen the divide — and often, sadly, create unnecessary and harmful divisions in the body of Christ.

- When overcoming grace meets human freedom, let's welcome both of these biblical truths and thank the Author of salvation that they are no mystery to Him.

- Human beings may claim no part in the work of salvation, yet they are commanded to repent and believe, something that requires an exercise of the human will. Equally important, God is not diminished in His sovereignty by enabling people created in His image to freely accept or reject His offer of salvation.

THINK
Questions for personal or group study

(1) How would you explain, to someone who doesn't know Jesus, the difference between God's general call and God's effectual call? Would you explain it the same way to a Christian? Why or why not?

(2) What is it that most troubles you about the tension between divine sovereignty and human responsibility?

(3) If the lost (non-elect) are totally depraved and incapable of responding positively to the gospel — unless God intervenes with an effectual call — how do we explain the fact that God holds them responsible for their sins?

(4) Look up the following New Testament passages and consider: What means does God use to call us? And what are the primary purposes for which He calls us?

- Gal. 1:6
- Eph. 4:1, 4
- 1 Thess. 2:12; 4:7
- 2 Tim. 1:9

(5) Jesus closes the parable of the wedding banquet with these words, "For many are invited, but few are chosen" (Matt. 22:14). This is a perfect opportunity for Christ to clear up the tension between divine sovereignty and human responsibility, but He doesn't. Why do you think He lets the tension stand? What are some other great doctrines of Scripture that remain shrouded in mystery?

(6) What is the motivation for sharing the gospel when God already knows everyone who will be saved?

(7) Look up the three "lifted up" proclamations of Jesus: John 3:14-15; 8:28; 12:32. Consider:

- To what singular event do all of these passages refer?
- What makes the word "draw" in John 12:32 such a strong term?
- Which of the following do you believe is the best application of "all" in Jesus' statement, "As for me, if I am lifted up from the earth I will draw *all* people to myself" (emphasis added):
    ____ All people; everyone
    ____ All of the elect
    ____ All kinds of people (Jews and Gentiles)

Chapter Five

YOU ARE REGENERATED

While working in the petroleum industry early in my career, I had the privilege of visiting an oil workers' camp at El Alamein in Egypt's Western Desert. The camp stood among the remains of a World War II battle between two legendary field marshals: Germany's Erwin Rommel and Britain's Bernard Montgomery. You could still explore the ruins of an underground hospital at the edge of the site. It wasn't hard to find medicine bottles, ammo shells, and an occasional button or boot. The combination of arid climate and restricted access to the Western Desert keeps many of the sand-blown war relics intact.

A long, narrow plateau rose over the camp and made the perfect perch for shooting video, which I decided to do the next morning. Rising before dawn, I shouldered my gear, walked down the rock-lined street that led into and out of the camp, passed a sleeping soldier with a rifle spanning his bent knees, and clawed to the summit of the plateau, where I spent the next couple of hours meandering over the rocky ridge and capturing images for our company's video magazine. As the sun rose above the horizon and began its scorching ascent into the cloudless sky, I smelled breakfast cooking in the mess quarters below, packed my gear, and headed back to camp.

Reaching the plateau's edge, I instantly became the center of attention. The soldier, now wide awake and clearly agitated, paced along the rock-lined street and waved his rifle — not exactly *at* me, but in a menacing enough way to let me know I was in trouble. He shouted brusquely in Arabic, raising his voice with each command so I would grasp his meaning, if not his words. At last, my English-speaking escort appeared beside the soldier. He cupped his hands around his mouth and blurted, "Sir, the soldier says you must come down at once!"

"Got it," I replied, watching as more workers streamed down Main Street and gathered curiously around the soldier. I couldn't help but ask, "Why do I need to come down? What's the problem?"

"Sir," my interpreter said in muted urgency, "you must come down because ... you're standing in a minefield!"

Little did I know that much of the Western Desert was still littered with unexploded World War II land mines. The only safe place was where the mine sweepers had been — the paths marked off with rocks.

I didn't move for what seemed an eternity. Finally, I mustered the courage to put one foot gingerly in front of the other, grimacing with each tentative step. At last, having descended the slope, I stepped across the row of rocks onto Main Street and into security, and vowed never again to venture out without an escort — or a mine sweeper.

My, how quickly my perspective changed at the edge of that plateau. As I wolfed down a celebratory breakfast, I thought about how, just a few hours earlier, I felt carefree and in control, unaware of the danger beneath my feet, and oblivious to the fact that I was one false step away from passing into eternity. While my antics caused my hosts a great deal of anxiety, I was grateful for their vigilance and their genuine concern for my safety.

Often, I think of that day in the Western Desert as an apt analogy of the work of the Holy Spirit in regeneration. As unbelievers go cheerily along, zig-zagging through the minefield of a life without Christ, God's Word and the Holy Spirit move swiftly and decisively, convincing them of their precarious journey, and drawing them into the security of the kingdom of heaven. As my experience at El Alamein reminded me, unbelievers cannot fully embrace the joy of life without realizing the proximity of their death.

While Christians may disagree about such issues as the relationship between regeneration and baptism, or whether regeneration precedes faith, it is biblically faithful for a follower of Jesus to say, "I am regenerated."

WHAT DOES IT MEAN TO BE REGENERATED?

The Greek noun *palingenesia* appears only twice in the New Testament (Matt. 19:28; Titus 3:5), but the concept of regeneration goes beyond this single word, embracing the ideas of being "born again" (John 3:3; 1 Peter 1:23), "born of the Spirit" (John 3:5), becoming a "new creation" (2 Cor. 5:17; Gal. 6:15), and experiencing a "new birth" (1 Peter 1:3).

In common Greek usage in ancient times, *palingenesia* meant "a recovery, a restoration, a revival."[1] The word is a compound of *palin* ("again") and *ginomai* ("to become"). As it's used in the New Testament, *palingenesia* means "regeneration," "renewal," or "recreation." In Matt. 19:28, it refers to God's ultimate renovation of the cosmos, and in Titus 3:5, it speaks of the work of the Holy Spirit, bringing back to life a dead human spirit — "a radical change of heart and mind resulting in renewed devotion to God and Christ."[2]

Put simply, regeneration is the work of the Holy Spirit that brings a sinner from spiritual death into spiritual life. Our spirits — our innermost beings created for intimacy with God — are dead in trespasses and sins (Eph. 2:1), and they remain so unless and until the Holy Spirit breathes new life into them. John Frame writes, "The new birth brings life out of that [spiritual] death. Without this new birth, we cannot even see the kingdom of God, because our spiritual eyes are dead. Paul teaches in Romans 1 that sinners suppress the truth and exchange it for a lie. So the new birth marks the beginning of spiritual understanding, as well as the beginning of obedient discipleship."[3]

Regeneration is a one-time, non-repeatable act by which the Holy Spirit enters the dead human spirit of a sinner and makes him or her spiritually alive. Regeneration also is permanent. That is, a person whom God foreknows, predestines, calls, justifies, and glorifies cannot lose the gift of regeneration without losing all of the associated links in God's golden chain of redemption. Every person is born physically, but only the elect are regenerated, or born again. Just as a person cannot be born physically multiple times, a believer cannot be born again repeatedly. The whole of salvation is the work of God. He doesn't need a mulligan when the Spirit regenerates His own.

The phenomenon of regeneration in the New Testament mirrors that of "heart circumcision," or the receiving of a "new heart" or "new spirit" in the Old Testament. For example, in Deut. 10:16 and 30:6, we read about circumcision of the heart, a spiritual transformation that God both commands and carries out. Further, God promises this renewal to coming generations. He will remove their "heart of stone" and replace it with a "heart of flesh" (Ezek. 36:24ff). In like manner, God vows to establish a "new covenant" with His people, one featuring the renewal of people's hearts and minds (Jer. 31:31ff).

The apostle Paul picks up this theme in his letter to the Colossians, in which he speaks of the transformation wrought in the hearts of people by the saving work of Christ. This work is described as "a circumcision not done with hands ... the circumcision of Christ" (Col. 2:11).[4]

Two-thirds alive

It may help our understanding to consider the three-fold nature of people.[5] God created us with body, soul, and spirit. The body, of course, is the physical part of us. Through our five senses, we relate to the natural world in which we live. Next, there is the soul, which is the unseen, conscious life consisting of mind, emotion, and will. Finally comes the spirit, the innermost part of us with which we relate to God, who is Spirit.

The "natural man" (KJV), or "person without the Spirit" (CSB, NIV), certainly is alive in body and soul, but is spiritually dead (1 Cor. 2:14; Eph. 2:1). That is, he can think, emote, and make decisions. But because he has rejected Christ, the Holy Spirit does not inhabit his human spirit. Therefore, his life is directed by what he experiences through his five senses, what he thinks about, and what he reasons from a mind that Satan has blinded and the Spirit has not renewed (Rom. 12:2; 2 Cor. 4:4).

In essence, the "natural man" is only two-thirds alive. Being spiritually dead, he cannot know God or benefit from God's presence in his life. It takes the regeneration of the Holy Spirit to make a person fully alive and able to live in a manner pleasing to God (John 3:3, 5; Rom. 8:9; 1 John 3:24; 4:13). Paul makes a distinction between believers and unregenerate persons in Titus 1:15-16: "To the pure, everything is pure, but to those who are defiled and unbelieving nothing is pure; in fact, both their mind and conscience are defiled. They claim to know God, but they deny him by their works. They are detestable, disobedient, and unfit for any good work."

THE WALKING DEAD

To get a proper perspective on regeneration, it may prove helpful to consider what the Bible teaches about the state of those who don't know Christ. Let's look at eight ways the Word of God describes unregenerate people, regardless of their religious views or experiences.

1. **Natural / without the Spirit.** The apostle Paul writes that "the person without the Spirit does not receive what comes from God's Spirit, because it is foolishness to him; he is not able to understand it since it is evaluated spiritually" (1 Cor. 2:14). Unlike the "spiritual person" (v. 15) who has "the mind of Christ" (v. 16), unbelievers see God's revealed truth through the lens of their fallen natures and thus declare it foolishness.

2. **Blind.** Paul tells the Corinthians the gospel is "veiled to those who are perishing" because "the god of this age has blinded the minds of the unbelievers to keep them from seeing the light of the gospel of the glory of Christ, who is the image of God" (2 Cor. 4:4). Satan often blinds the lost with half-truths. For example, many counterfeit forms of Christianity emphasize salvation through a combination of faith and works rather than by faith alone in Christ alone.

3. **Bound.** Timothy, a young pastor, is urged to instruct his opponents with gentleness, trusting God to grant them repentance to know the truth. "Then they may come to

their senses and escape the trap of the devil, who has taken them captive to do his will" (2 Tim. 2:26).

4. **Alienated.** Unbelievers, who walk "in the futility of their thoughts" and are "darkened in their understanding," are therefore "excluded from the life of God" (Eph. 4:17-18). Paul goes on to say that unbelievers become callous as they give themselves over to ungodly practices, a state he calls "the old self ... corrupted by deceitful desires" (v. 22).

5. **Enemies.** Christians should remember that we once were helpless "enemies" of God — a situation God remedied through the death of His Son (Rom. 5:6-11). Though once "alienated and hostile in your minds expressed in your evil actions," believers have been reconciled to God by Christ's body through His death (Col. 1:21-22).

6. **Condemned.** God sent His Son so that the world might be saved through Him. "Anyone who believes in him is not condemned," says Jesus, "but anyone who does not believe is already condemned, because he has not believed in the name of the one and only Son of God" (John 3:18).

7. **In darkness.** Jesus sends Paul to the Gentiles "to open their eyes so that they may turn from darkness to light and from the power of Satan to God" (Acts 26:18). Believers once were "darkness, but now [they are] light in the Lord" (Eph. 5:8). Christ came to rescue us from "the domain of darkness" (Col. 1:13), and He calls us "out of darkness into his marvelous light" (1 Peter 2:9).

8. **Spiritually dead.** Paul reminds the Ephesian believers that they once were "dead in [their] trespasses and sins" (Eph. 2:1). That is, while alive in body and soul, unbelievers are dead in their spirits — their innermost beings God created for His habitation via the indwelling Holy Spirit.

So, what hope possibly exists for any lost person? Perhaps these spiritual maladies help set the stage for us to see the necessity of the Spirit's work of regeneration.

KEY PASSAGES ON REGENERATION

Let's survey several Bible verses that address regeneration. Then, we'll turn our attention to the thorny issues of *baptismal regeneration* and *monergism/synergism*.

RENEWAL / REGENERATION

Matt. 19:28 - "Jesus said to them, 'Truly I tell you, in the renewal (*palingenesia*) of all things, when the Son of Man sits on his glorious throne, you who have followed me will also sit on twelve thrones, judging the twelve tribes of Israel.'"

The word translated "renewal" in the CSB is rendered "regeneration," "new world," or "Messianic Age" in other versions. Jesus is coming back one day to set things right as He reigns over the new heavens and new earth (2 Peter 3:10-13; Revelation 21-22). The *CSB Study Bible* notes, "The reign of the twelve disciples over Israel demonstrates that Jesus's disciples constitute the new Israel, the chosen people of God who will benefit from his covenant with Abraham. In a great divine reversal in which the first become last and the last become first, those who made personal sacrifices for Christ will enjoy enormous blessings, and those like the rich young ruler, who loved wealth more than Christ, will be punished."[6]

When Jesus speaks here of the "renewal" (*palingenesia*), He is not referring to individual regeneration, in which the Holy Spirit makes us spiritually alive, but of the refurbishment of the created order, including our corruptible bodies. The prophet Isaiah alludes to it (Isaiah 65-66), and the apostle Paul describes the creation's anticipation of it: "For the creation eagerly waits with anticipation for God's sons to be revealed. For the creation was subjected to futility — not willingly, but because of him who subjected it — in the hope that the creation itself will also be set free from the bondage to decay into the glorious freedom of God's children. For we know that the whole creation has been groaning together with labor pains until now. Not only that, but we ourselves who have the Spirit as the Firstfruits — we also groan within ourselves, eagerly waiting for adoption, the redemption of our bodies" (Rom. 8:19-23).

One other note: In Revelation 21, John uses the Greek word *kainos* for "new" in describing the new heavens and new earth. This means "different from the usual," "better than the old," or "superior in value or attraction." In other words, God does not simply annihilate the old order of things and start from scratch. He purges the sinful and fallen cosmos and restores it to its pristine beauty. It could be said that Yahweh is the ultimate craftsman, and the *palingenesia* is His masterpiece.

CSB	KJV	NIV	NASB	ESV
Renewal	Regeneration	Renewal	Regeneration	New world

Comparing English translations of *palingenesia* in Matt. 19:28

Titus 3:5 - "... he saved us — not by works of righteousness that we had done, but according to his mercy — through the washing of regeneration (*palingenesias*) and renewal by the Holy Spirit."

Paul denies the meritorious value of human deeds, stressing instead divine action in God's merciful work of salvation. Nevertheless, some commentators see the phrase "washing of regeneration" as a reference to water baptism, which we examine shortly. The errant doctrine of baptismal regeneration was developed early in church history, and it persists in many Christian denominations today.

However, the washing that Paul describes is the Holy Spirit's ministry of spiritual cleansing. New believers in Christ signify God's work of regeneration through the ordinance of water baptism, which testifies to the death, burial, and resurrection of Jesus. In addition, water baptism depicts believers' identity with their Savior, and pictures the death of their old lives and resurrection to new lives in Christ.

It should be noted that Paul does not mention faith or repentance here. Likely, this is because he desires to focus completely on God's kindness toward people, or what Matthew Henry calls "the divine philanthropy."[7]

Warren Wiersbe adds, "'Washing' here means 'bathed all over.' When a sinner trusts Christ, he is cleansed from all his sins, and he is made 'a new person' by the indwelling Holy Spirit. Paul related this same cleansing experience to the Word of God (Eph. 5:26). Salvation comes to a sinner when he trusts Christ, when the Spirit of God uses the Word of God to bring about the new birth."[8]

CSB	KJV	NIV	NASB	ESV
Regeneration	Regeneration	Rebirth	Regeneration	Regeneration

Comparing English translations of *palingenesias* in Titus 3:5

BORN AGAIN / BORN FROM ABOVE

John 3:3, 7 - "Jesus replied, 'Truly I tell you, unless someone is born again (*gennethe anothen*), he cannot see the kingdom of God.... Do not be amazed that I told you that you must be born again.'"

Jesus tells Nicodemus that a person who is not "born again" may neither see the kingdom of God nor enter it (vv. 3, 5). The Greek term *anothen* can mean "again" or "from above," and perhaps Jesus uses this word to stress both. Nicodemus misunderstands Jesus and thinks he must enter his mother's womb a second time and be born physically. But Jesus makes it clear that, while everyone is born "of the flesh," not everyone is born "of the Spirit." For a person to enter the realm of God's divine authority, that person must experience a second birth — one that is not physical, but spiritual; one that the Holy Spirit initiates and comes from above.

The much-disputed phrase, "born of water and the Spirit" (v. 5), perhaps is best understood as two ways of saying the same thing. Jesus equates being "born of water" with the "washing of water by the Word" (Eph. 5:26) and the "washing of regeneration" (Titus 3:5), which is the same as being born of the Spirit. The work of the Spirit in regeneration is in view here, which ties Jesus' words with the writings of Paul, Peter, and other New Testament writers.

CSB	KJV	NIV	NASB	ESV
Born again / from above	Born again	Born again / from above	Born again / from above	Born again / from above

Comparing English translations of *gennethe anothen* in John 3:3

New birth

1 Peter 1:3, 23 - "Blessed be the God and Father of our Lord Jesus Christ. Because of his great mercy he has given us new birth (*anagennesas*) into a living hope through the resurrection of Jesus Christ from the dead ... because you have been born again (*anagegennemenoi*) — not of perishable seed but of imperishable — through the living and enduring word of God."

In verses 1-2, Peter reviews the work of the three persons of the Godhead in providing salvation for us. We are *chosen* according to the *foreknowledge* of God the Father; *sprinkled* with the blood of Jesus Christ; and *sanctified* by the Holy Spirit. To place this work in order from a human perspective, the Father saved us in eternity past by marking us as His own. The Son saved us two thousand years ago by dying a sacrificial and substitutionary death on the cross; and the Spirit saved us when He drew us to Christ, revived our dead human spirits, and set us apart as children of God.

The apostle builds on this stunning, panoramic view of salvation in verse 3, reminding us that our salvation is an act of an infinitely merciful Father, who sent His Son to die and rise from the dead so that we could receive His gift of "new birth into a living hope." The result of the new birth is an indestructible inheritance, one that is "imperishable, undefiled, and unfading, kept in heaven for you" (v. 4). It is "ready to be revealed in the last time," a reminder that our salvation extends unbroken into eternity future (v. 5; see Rom. 13:11; Phil. 3:20-21; Heb. 9:28).

This "living hope" naturally should result in holy living, a point Peter picks up in verse 13 and carries through the end of the chapter. Our "sincere brotherly love for each other" comes from a pure heart because we have been "born again — not of perishable seed but of imperishable — through the living and enduring word of God" (vv. 22-23).

The word "imperishable" in verse 23 (*aphthartou*) is from the same Greek word used in verse 4 to describe the believer's inheritance (*aphtharton*). Here, it depicts the Word of God. Peter supports the indestructible nature of the gospel by quoting Isa. 40:6-8, which says in part, "The grass withers, and the flower falls, but the word of the

Lord endures forever" (vv. 24b-25; cf. Isa. 40:8). Just as God's Word stands for all eternity, His promise to save us, and to keep our birthright intact, endures without fail — and without end.

CSB	KJV	NIV	NASB	ESV
New birth	Begotten us again	New birth	Born again	Born again

Comparing English translations of *anagennesas* in 1 Peter 1:3

CSB	KJV	NIV	NASB	ESV
Born again	Born again	Born again	Born again	Born again

Comparing English translations of *anagegennemenoi* in 1 Peter 1:23

NEW CREATION

2 Cor. 5:17 - "Therefore, if anyone is in Christ, he is a new creation *(kaine ktisis)*; the old has passed away, and see, the new has come!"

Paul often uses the phrase "in Christ" in his epistles to speak of a believer's spiritual relationship with Jesus.[9] Placing us "in Christ" is the Father's way of reconciling us to Himself and thus committing to us the ministry of reconciliation as we proclaim the gospel to others who need Jesus (vv. 18-20). We are united with Christ by faith, just as the branch is united with the "true vine" (John 15:1-8).

Those who have been born again are new creations as a result of the Spirit's work of regeneration. The old life of slavery to sin is gone. The new life of devotion to Christ means that new attitudes and actions spill over from the indwelling presence of the Holy Spirit. It's important to note that the agent of regeneration, the Holy Spirit, doesn't just impart new life to us in the new birth; He keeps that flame burning forever as He indwells us and equips us to serve our Lord and Master.

The permanence of the new birth is made clear in Paul's use of verb tenses. The phrase, "the old has passed away," is in the aorist tense, referring to a completed act in past time. In contrast, "the new has come" is in the perfect tense, indicating a past, completed act with continuing results.[10]

The rabbis used the idea of new creation to depict a person converted from idolatry. As the saying went, "He who brings a foreigner and makes him a proselyte is as if he created him."[11]

CSB	KJV	NIV	NASB	ESV
New creation	New creature	New creation	New creature / new creation	New creation / new creature

Comparing English translations of *kaine ktisis* in 2 Cor. 5:17

Gal. 6:15 - "For both circumcision and uncircumcision mean nothing; what matters instead is a new creation (*kaine ktisis*)."

Paul uses the same term, *kaine ktisis*, in this passage that he employs in 2 Cor. 5:17 to describe the person who has been born again, or regenerated, by the Holy Spirit. In this case, he stresses the importance of believers' common bond in the new birth over issues such as circumcision, which false teachers use to divide the body of Christ.

Matthew Henry writes, "The false teachers were very zealous for circumcision; yea, to such a degree as to represent it as necessary to salvation, and therefore they did all they could to constrain the Gentile Christians to submit to it.... But what they laid so great a stress upon Paul made very little account of.... Here he instructs us both wherein real religion does not and wherein it does consist. It does not consist in circumcision or uncircumcision, in our being in this or the other denomination of Christians; but it consists in our being new creatures; not in having a new name, or putting on a new face, but in our being renewed in the spirit of our minds and having Christ formed in us: this is of the greatest account with God, and so it is with the apostle."[12]

CSB	KJV	NIV	NASB	ESV
New creation	New creature	New creation	New creation	New creation

Comparing English translations of *kaine ktisis* in Gal. 6:15

BAPTISMAL REGENERATION

We should address the doctrine of *baptismal regeneration*, the belief that water baptism is necessary for salvation. Proponents of this view, ranging from Roman Catholics to Lutherans to those in the Church of Christ, differ in their understanding of this doctrine. However, they uniformly agree that water baptism plays an essential role in obtaining everlasting life. For many, baptism is a necessary element — in addition to belief, confession, and repentance — that completes the work of salvation.

One of the earliest church fathers to articulate the doctrine of baptismal regeneration was Cyprian, who lived in the third century. "While he attributed all the saving energy to the grace of God, he considered the 'laver of saving water' the instrument of God that makes a person 'born again', receiving a new life and putting off what he had previously been. The 'water of new birth' animated him to new life by the Spirit of holiness working through it."[13]

Those who contend for baptismal regeneration do not view belief, confession, repentance, and/or baptism as meritorious works that earn salvation. Rather, these are "works of obedience" that must be accomplished so that God may grant salvation to the sinner.[14] Nevertheless, the addition of anything to faith as a requirement for receiving everlasting life runs contrary to the New Testament teaching on salvation by grace alone through faith alone.

Let's look at several passages of Scripture used to support the doctrine of baptismal regeneration, followed by brief responses.

Mark 16:16 - "Whoever believes and is baptized will be saved, but whoever does not believe will be condemned."[15]

To contend that this verse teaches the necessity of water baptism for salvation is to commit a fallacy known as negative inference. Put simply, if a certain proposition is true, it does not necessarily follow that a negative inference from the proposition is true. For example, the statement, "I was born in the United States; therefore, I'm a U.S. citizen," is true. However, that doesn't mean if I were born in another country, I could not be a U.S. citizen.

In the same way, "Whoever believes and is baptized will be saved," is true. However, this does not mean that the one who believes and is not baptized cannot be saved. Yet, this is the argument from those who embrace baptismal regeneration. For Mark 16:16 to mean what they say, the verse would have to read, "Whoever believes and is baptized will be saved, but whoever does not believe *and is not baptized* will be condemned."

The second part of this verse is key, for it lays out the conditions by which a person is condemned: by refusing to believe. Further, this verse must be seen in the context of numerous, consistent verses where *only* belief is mentioned as a requirement for everlasting life (for example, John 3:18; 5:24; 12:44; 20:31; Rom. 4:4-5; Eph. 2:8-9; Titus 3:5; 1 John 5:13).

Jesus mentions an act related to salvation — namely, baptism — in Mark 16:16. But a related act should not be confused with a requirement. "For example, having a fever is *related* to being ill, but a fever is not *required* for illness to be present. Nowhere in the Bible do we find a statement such as 'whoever is not baptized will be condemned.' Therefore, we cannot say that baptism is necessary for salvation based on Mark 16:16 or any other verse."[16]

John 3:5 - "Jesus answered, 'Truly I tell you, unless someone is born of water and the Spirit, he cannot enter the kingdom of God.'"

Those who hold to baptismal regeneration point to the phrase "born of water" to mean baptism, making it a requirement for entrance into God's kingdom. However, Jesus does not use the word "baptism" in this passage. Further, Christian baptism is not yet instituted at the time of this evening encounter with Nicodemus. The interpretation that best fits the context of this passage, and proves consistent with the rest of the Scriptures in their instruction about salvation, is that the phrase "born of water and the Spirit" describes two aspects of the same event — what it means to be "born again" or "born from above" (v. 3). Throughout the Old and New Testaments, water, or washing, often is used symbolically of spiritual cleansing or regeneration (see, for example, Ps. 51:2, 7; Ezek. 36:25; John 13:10; 15:3; 1 Cor. 6:11; Eph. 5:26; Titus 3:5).

Thus, the water mentioned in John 3:5 is neither baptismal water, nor amniotic fluid (as some suggest, contending that "born of water" means physical birth). Rather, it is the living water Jesus promises the woman at the well and those to whom He speaks at the festival (John 4:10; 7:37-39). Jesus makes this clear in John 3:5-8 when He says this new life is the work of the Holy Spirit.

Acts 2:38 - "Peter replied, 'Repent and be baptized, each of you, in the name of Jesus Christ for the forgiveness of your sins and you will receive the gift of the Holy Spirit.'"

Proponents of baptismal regeneration argue that this passage teaches that baptism, and perhaps repentance, enable a person to receive forgiveness of sins. A key is the little word "for." It is *eis* in the Greek and is found more than one thousand seven hundred times in the New Testament. Like the English word "for," *eis* can carry several different meanings. Noted Greek scholars such as A.T. Robertson, Julius Mantey, and Kenneth Wuest write that the Greek preposition *eis* in Acts 2:38 should be translated "because of" or "in view of," and not "in order to," or "for the purpose of."[17]

One oft-cited example of how this preposition is used elsewhere in the New Testament is Matt. 12:41. Here, *eis* describes the result of an action. The people of Nineveh "repented at (*eis*) the preaching of Jonah." Clearly, the people repented as a result of Jonah's preaching.

Besides Acts 2:38, there are three other verses where *eis* is used with the word "baptism" or "baptize." In Matt 3:11, John the Baptist says, "I baptize you with water *for* repentance" (emphasis added). Obviously, his followers could not be baptized *in order to* attain repentance; rather they were baptized *because* they already repented. In Rom. 6:3, Paul writes that "all of us who were baptized *into* Christ Jesus were baptized *into* his death" (emphasis added). Again, this fits the meaning of "because of" or "in regard to." And in 1 Cor. 10:2, we read about the Israelites who "all were baptized *into* Moses in the cloud and in the sea" (emphasis added). The Israelites were not baptized in order to get Moses to be their leader; he already was their leader and led them out of Egypt.

In light of these passages, and the clear teaching throughout the

New Testament that salvation is by grace alone through faith alone, it seems best to conclude that Peter, in Acts 2:38, highlights three aspects of conversion. He calls on his listeners to "repent," or to change their minds about Jesus, since many Jews had conspired to crucify Him as a blasphemer; to "be baptized" in the name of Jesus as a public declaration of their faith; and to "receive the gift of the Holy Spirit," who is given to all believers in Christ (see 1 Cor. 12:13).

No doubt, this is a challenging verse of Scripture, one that's best understood in the company of other Bible passages dealing with salvation and baptism. The preponderance of evidence argues in favor of baptism as a public declaration of God's work of salvation, not a prerequisite for receiving the gift of eternal life.

Acts 22:16 - "And now, why are you delaying? Get up and be baptized, and wash away your sins, calling on his name."

This verse is part of Paul's testimony before the Jerusalem mob. He recounts his dramatic encounter with Christ on the road to Damascus, and later his care under a devout Jewish believer named Ananias. The key questions here are, "When is Paul saved?" and "How are his sins washed away?"

Paul makes it clear that he did not receive the gospel from Ananias, but directly from Christ on the road to Damascus. In Gal. 1:11-12, he recounts, "For I want you to know, brothers and sisters, that the gospel preached by me is not of human origin. For I did not receive it from a human source and I was not taught it, but it came by a revelation of Jesus Christ." So, Paul already had received Christ when he met Ananias.

We also may note that Paul received the Holy Spirit when Ananias prayed for him to receive his sight, and then he was baptized (Acts 9:17-18). GotQuestions.org says, "The events recorded in Acts are not always normative. With regard to receiving the Holy Spirit, the norm is that a person receives and is permanently indwelt by the Holy Spirit at the moment of salvation."[18]

Next, we may see in Acts 22:16 that the phrase translated "calling on his name" is *epikalesamenos*, which refers either to action that is simultaneous with or before that of the main verb, "be baptized." Paul's calling on Christ's name for salvation precedes his water baptism. "The participle may be translated, 'having called on His name,' which makes more sense, as it would clearly indicate the order of events."[19]

It's also interesting that when Paul recounts this event again later (Acts 26:12-18), there is no mention of Ananias or his words to Paul. A.T. Robertson notes, "Baptism can be a picture of death, burial and resurrection (cf. Rom. 6:4-6). So here baptism pictures the change that had already taken place when Paul surrendered to Jesus on the way. Baptism here pictures the washing away of sins by the blood of Christ."[20]

Gal. 3:27 - "For those of you who were baptized into Christ have been clothed with Christ."

Does this verse teach that water baptism equals being saved, or "clothed with Christ"? No. The overarching point of Paul's letter to the Galatians is that some of them are turning from the true gospel to a false gospel that is unable to save them (Gal. 1:6-10). The false gospel preached in Galatia is a mixture of grace and works of the law, including circumcision. In a similar manner, it may be said that adding water baptism to faith as a necessary ingredient for salvation is a false gospel, for it undermines the doctrine of salvation by grace alone through faith alone in Christ alone.

Paul's message is crystal clear: We are justified, not by works of the law, but by faith in Jesus Christ (Gal. 2:16). Further, he writes that we are all sons of God in Christ Jesus through faith (Gal. 3:26). While baptism is an important way of publicly proclaiming our identification with Jesus, it only has meaning as a symbol of Christ's finished work on the cross and our identification with Him by faith as He gives us new life.

When the Holy Spirit regenerates us, we are baptized with the Spirit, or placed positionally into the body of Christ (1 Cor. 12:13) so that every believer has the Spirit in common (Rom. 8:9). John the Baptist wants his followers to know that he is sent to baptize with water, but Jesus will baptize with the Holy Spirit (Matt. 3:11).

1 Peter 3:21 - "Baptism, which corresponds to this, now saves you (not as the removal of dirt from the body, but the pledge of a good conscience toward God) through the resurrection of Jesus Christ ..."

Does this verse mean that water baptism saves us? If so, it contradicts many other passages of Scripture that state salvation is God's gift of grace received by faith. The normal pattern we see in the New Testament is faith in Christ, which results in receiving the Holy Spirit, and is publicly proclaimed through water baptism. Peter does not seek to twist the biblical standard in this single verse, which must be viewed in context.

We don't have to guess what Peter means, because he clarifies it with the phrase, "not as the removal of dirt from the body, but the pledge of a good conscience toward God." While he connects baptism with salvation, he connects it as a demonstration of the results of a sinner's appeal to God for forgiveness, based on the resurrection of Christ. The appeal to God comes first, then water baptism follows as a testimony of God's work of regeneration.

Kenneth Wuest writes, "Water baptism is clearly in the apostle's mind, not the baptism by the Holy Spirit, for he speaks of the waters of the flood as saving the inmates of the ark, and in this verse, of baptism saving believers. But he says that it saves them only as a counterpart. That is, water baptism is the counterpart of the reality, salvation. It can only save as a counterpart, not actually.... Water baptism is the outward testimony of the believer's inward faith. The person is saved the moment he places his faith in the Lord Jesus. Water baptism is his visible testimony to his faith and the salvation he was given in answer to that faith."[21]

In summary, there are several reasons to deny the doctrine of baptismal regeneration:

1. The Bible is clear that we are saved by grace alone through faith alone in Christ alone (John 1:12; 3:16; 5:24; 6:47; 20:31; Acts 4:11-12; 10:43; 13:39; 16:31; Rom. 4:4-5; Gal. 2:16; 3:6-26; Eph. 2:8-9; Titus 3:5-7). To take away faith in Jesus as the sole requirement for salvation is universalism; to add to it is legalism.
2. Water baptism is an important public testimony of our faith, not an essential element in our salvation. In a first-century context, for Jews embracing Jesus as Messiah, a public declaration of faith might mean their banishment from family, friends, and religious leaders. Water baptism in a first-century Jewish context served as a bold and

unmistakable sign of one's faith in Jesus. It demonstrated that a person was trusting fully in the finished work of Christ on the cross.

3. The Bible says a person is condemned for not believing (John 3:18); it doesn't say a person is condemned for failing to be baptized.

4. Forgiveness of sins and everlasting life are received as gifts from God, by faith, apart from any works, whether considered meritorious or obedient. Water baptism symbolizes the death, burial, and resurrection of Christ, and publicly identifies the new believer with Christ.

5. If water baptism is required for salvation, then no one could be saved without the help of another person, thus limiting who can be saved, and when.

WHICH COMES FIRST: FAITH OR REGENERATION?

We come now to one of the key questions related to this issue: Does faith result in regeneration, or does regeneration trigger faith? This issue has divided Christians for centuries, and it's a question with which the Reformers wrestled.

The Reformed position is that regeneration necessarily precedes faith. Calvinists argue that God does not force sinners to believe against their wills, but through regeneration God changes their wills. Since lost people are spiritually dead, they are totally incapable of coming to faith in Christ. Therefore, the Holy Spirit must regenerate those elected to salvation, awakening them to the truth of the gospel and drawing them irresistibly to Christ.

This is known as *monergistic regeneration*, meaning the Holy Spirit works alone. It stands in contrast to *synergistic regeneration*, which refers to a cooperative effort between the Spirit and the believing sinner. So, when the term *monergism* is linked with regeneration, the phrase describes "an action by which God the Holy Spirit works on a human being without this person's assistance or cooperation," according to R.C. Sproul.[22]

Sproul further explains, "In the Reformation view, the work of regeneration is performed by God and by him alone. The sinner is completely passive in receiving this action. Regeneration is an example of operative grace. Any cooperation we display toward God occurs only *after* the work of regeneration has been completed."[23]

In short, Reformed theology insists that regeneration must precede faith. We cannot exercise saving faith until we have been regenerated, so faith depends on regeneration, not the other way around.

To be fair, we might consider this view a reflection of a "fully Reformed," "strong Calvinist," or "five-point Calvinist" position.[24] To classify everyone who disagrees with this view of regeneration as Arminian is more than an oversimplification; it is inaccurate. Many Christians who consider themselves Reformed in their theology do not embrace a strong Calvinist position when it comes to regeneration. Further, it's important to remember that Dutch theologian Jacobus Arminius, for whom Arminianism is named, played an important role in the Dutch Reformation. That is, he was a Reformer, too.[25]

A leading "moderate Calvinist" is theologian Norman Geisler, who has written a popular response to strong Calvinism in his book, *Chosen But Free: A Balanced View of Divine Election*. Geisler contends that "there are no verses properly understood that teach regeneration is prior to faith. Instead, it is the uniform pattern of Scripture to place faith logically prior to salvation as a condition for receiving it."[26]

Geisler takes issue with the strong Calvinist position on "irresistible grace," extended only to the elect, regenerating them and supplying them with saving faith, which they inevitably exercise by trusting in Christ for salvation. He offers these objections:

- **It is not supported by the Bible.** "There is no biblical support for the extreme Calvinists' view of irresistible grace on the unwilling. The Bible affirms that all can, and some do, resist the grace of God (Matt. 23:37; cf. 2 Peter 3:9)."
- **It is not supported by the church fathers.** "With the explainable exception of the later Augustine, no major church fathers up to the Reformation held to irresistible grace on the unwilling. Even Luther's view, the first major one after the later Augustine, was reversed by his disciple and systematizer, Melanchthon."

- **It is not supported by the attribute of God's omnibenevolence.** "One of the primary problems with extreme Calvinism is the denial of God's essential omnibenevolence. By the admission of this view, God is not all-loving in a redemptive sense. He loves, sent Christ to die for, and attempts to save only the elect. However, this is contrary to Scripture."
- **It is not supported by man's God-given free will.** "Since love is always persuasive but never coercive God cannot force anyone to love Him — which is what irresistible love on the unwilling would be. God's persuasive, but resistible love, goes hand in glove with human free choice. Free will is self-determination. It involves the ability to choose otherwise. One can either accept or reject God's grace."

Geisler summarizes, "God's grace works synergistically on free will. That is, it must be received to be effective. There are no conditions for giving grace, but there is one condition for receiving it — faith. Put in other terms, God's justifying grace works cooperatively, not operatively. Faith is a precondition for receiving God's gift of salvation. Faith is logically prior to regeneration, since we are saved 'through faith' (Eph. 2:8-9) and 'justified by faith' (Rom. 5:1 NASB)."[27]

One other view merits our consideration: the so-called *overcoming grace* model, which affirms both the *monergism* of strong Calvinism and the *resistibility* of moderate Calvinism and Arminianism. It is monergistic because the Holy Spirit alone does the work of drawing unbelievers to Christ, and it is resistible because all that is necessary for lost sinners to remain lost is that they refrain from acting. In other words, unbelievers may reject grace that truly was available. This model seeks to provide a solution to Calvinism's problem of "the well-meant offer" in which the non-elect who hear the gospel could have been saved if only God had not bypassed them. As one author puts it, "To offer salvation while withholding the necessary ability to respond seems like offering healing to any quadriplegic who can get up to receive it."[28] Overcoming grace exalts the sovereign work of God in salvation while holding unbelievers fully responsible for rejecting a genuine offer of everlasting life.

Is there any way to reconcile these different views of regeneration? As we wrestle with the issue, it may help to consider that regeneration and faith are, in a sense, inseparable. Whether regeneration precedes faith, or faith results in regeneration, every adopted child of God experiences both. Every saved person has heard the gospel and responded in faith; likewise, he or she has been born again. While the matter pertaining to the order of regeneration and faith is important, it should not divide Christians in our common fellowship, nor should it keep any of us from an obedient response to Christ's command to "Go, therefore, and make disciples of all nations" (Matt. 28:19a).

Summary

While the Greek noun *palingenesia* appears sparingly in the New Testament, the concept of regeneration, or new birth, is a consistent theme of Jesus and the New Testament writers. Jesus makes it clear that people must be "born again," or "born from above," if they are to see the kingdom of heaven. The work of the Holy Spirit, making an individual a "new creation" (2 Cor. 5:17), prepares that person for the future work of Christ as He creates "new heavens and a new earth" (2 Peter 3:13). All those the Spirit regenerates are assured a place with Christ when He refurbishes the cosmos, purging it completely of sin and its stain.

Consider these summary statements about regeneration:

- Regeneration is the work of the Holy Spirit that brings a sinner from spiritual death to spiritual life. Our spirits — that is, our innermost beings created for intimacy with God — are dead in trespasses and sins (Eph. 2:1), and they remain so unless and until the Holy Spirit breathes new life into them.
- Regeneration is a one-time, non-repeatable act by which the Holy Spirit enters the dead human spirit of a sinner and makes him or her spiritually alive. Regeneration also is permanent. That is, a person God foreknows, predestines, calls, justifies, and glorifies cannot lose the gift of

regeneration without losing all of the associated links in God's golden chain of redemption.

- The Bible describes unbelievers as the walking dead. Not only are they spiritually dead (Eph. 2:1), but they are depicted as natural / without the Spirit (1 Cor. 2:14); blinded in their minds (2 Cor. 4:4); bound by Satan (2 Tim. 2:26); alienated from God (Eph. 4:17-18); enemies of the Lord (Rom. 5:6-11; Col. 1:21-22); condemned in their unbelief (John 3:18); and in spiritual darkness (Acts 26:18; Eph. 5:8; Col. 1:13; 1 Peter 2:9). These spiritual realities set the stage for the necessity of God's work of regeneration.

- Proponents of *baptismal regeneration* believe that water baptism plays an essential role in obtaining everlasting life. In response to verses of Scripture often quoted to support this view, we should carefully consider the context of each passage, as well as the historical audience being addressed. While water baptism is *related* to salvation, it should not be confused with a *requirement* for everlasting life. Nowhere does God's Word state that if a person is not baptized, he or she is not saved.

- In fully Reformed theology, regeneration precedes faith, with the Holy Spirit acting alone (*monergism*). In contrast, moderate Calvinists and Arminians contend that the Bible places faith before regeneration as the Holy Spirit works in concert with human freedom (*synergism*). A third view, the overcoming grace model, falls somewhere in between. While these doctrinal differences often lead to contentious debates, it's important to keep in mind a central point of agreement: For those who willingly place their trust in Jesus Christ for eternal life, the golden chain of redemption holds us secure. God foreknows, elects, predestines, calls, justifies, and ultimately glorifies every person the Spirit regenerates.

- As with other issues related to God's gracious work of salvation, the doctrine of regeneration reminds us of the mysterious ways God's sovereignty and human responsibility interact. We must embrace *both* biblical truths, and be contented with seeing, now, "through a glass, darkly," but one day "face to face" (1 Cor. 13:12 KJV).

THINK
Questions for personal or group study

(1) How does Jesus' depiction of "renewal" in Matt. 19:28 differ from Paul's use of "regeneration" in Titus 3:5? How are these different applications of the Greek noun *palingenesia* related to one another?

(2) Read John 1:11-13 and John 3:3, 5-8. Who takes the initiative in regeneration? How does one become a true child of God according to John 3:16; 8:41-47?

(3) Why is regeneration impossible from a human perspective without the work of the Holy Spirit? Consider John 3:18; Acts 26:18; Rom. 5:6-11; 1 Cor. 2:14; 2 Cor. 4:4; Eph. 2:1; 4:17-18; 5:8; Col. 1:13, 21-22; 2 Tim. 2:26; 1 Peter 2:9.

(4) How would you explain Jesus' words about being "born again" to someone who holds a Far Eastern worldview, such as a Hindu (who believes in reincarnation of the soul) or a Buddhist (who believes in rebirth but denies the existence of the soul)? What questions could you ask your Hindu and Buddhist friends — who acknowledge Jesus — so you may understand their beliefs before sharing your Christian convictions?

(5) How are the following passages of Scripture used to support the belief in baptismal regeneration? What is a biblically faithful response, taking into consideration context, historical audience, comparison with other Scriptures, and other principles of biblical interpretation?

- Mark 16:16
- John 3:5
- Acts 2:38
- Acts 22:16
- Gal. 3:27
- 1 Peter 3:21

(6) Which do you believe comes first: regeneration or faith? Why is this an important question in our study of salvation? Why shouldn't we allow this question to divide followers of Jesus, even though we may debate it vigorously?

(7) Consider the passages in the table below and determine whether they support a strong Calvinist position, or a moderate Calvinist position (or perhaps both). How might you reconcile these "proof texts"?

SCRIPTURE	STRONG CALVINIST	MODERATE CALVINIST
Ezek. 36:26		
Luke 13:13		
John 3:6-7		
John 3:16		
Acts 13:48		
Acts 16:31		
Rom. 3:24-25		
Rom. 5:1		
Eph. 2:1		
Eph. 2:8-9		
Titus 3:5-7		
2 Peter 3:9		

Every human being needs God's declaration of righteousness because no one possesses the righteousness necessary to enter God's presence.

Chapter Six

YOU ARE JUSTIFIED

One of the first times I heard the word "justify" was, of all places, in shop class in junior high school. Yes, we learned to use jigsaws, discovered the difference between a rasp-cut file and a wood-chuck, and heard repeatedly the threats of expulsion if we used the acetylene torch for anything other than soldering. But we also practiced the art of typesetting — a painstaking process when done by hand. While newspapers of that era used Linotype machines to produce *slugs*, or lines of type from hot metal, many small-shop operators, as well as purists, preferred to test their dexterity (and patience) by setting type one letter at a time.

Drawing the appropriate letter, number, or symbol from the type case, we filled our hand-held *sticks* by arranging the metal pieces upside-down and backwards. The all-important *en space* was a small piece of metal used to separate words. And if the printed piece was to be neither centered, ragged left, nor ragged right, we were instructed to insert *en spaces* to *justify* the type, making sure the first letter of each line aligned with the left margin, and the last letter of each line aligned with the right margin. Take a look at the pages of this book and you'll see that the left and right margins form straight vertical lines — thanks to modern computer software we take for granted.

After all these years, the lesson from shop class still comes to mind when I think about God's work of justification. Just as typesetters align their letters with the left and right margins so that readers see an orderly page, Christ ensures, through His finished work on the cross, that the Father sees us in right standing before Him.

Justification does not make us holy; that is the ongoing work of sanctification, along with the final salvific act of God in glorification. Rather, justification is the transfer of Christ's perfect righteousness to our account, while our sin debt is transferred to His account, so that we are acquitted before the Father's holy bench. Just as the *en space* is inserted to make words line up with the margins on a printed page, Christ's righteousness comes to our aid so the demands of the Father for perfect holiness are met.

In justification, God *declares* us righteous. In sanctification and glorification, He *makes* us so. One day, then, we are fully conformed to the image of Christ. We'll look at these elements of salvation in later chapters. But for now, let's explore the great work of God in justification. As we do, let's keep in mind that it is biblically faithful for followers of Jesus to say, "I am justified."

WHAT DOES IT MEAN TO BE JUSTIFIED?

The Greek verb *dikaioo* is a legal term meaning "acquit" or "declare righteous." It is the opposite of "condemn." Used in various New Testament contexts, "justify" means to make right, act with justice, vindicate, hold as guiltless, accept as righteous, and approve. In this sense, God issues a legal declaration about us. This is why theologians refer to justification as *forensic*, which means "having to do with legal proceedings."

This legal declaration does not change our internal character. A judge does not make defendants guilty or innocent; he simply declares them to be one or the other. Regeneration, indwelling, and sanctification are ways God works salvation *in* us, making us spiritually alive, taking up permanent residence in our spirits, and conforming us to the image of Christ. But justification occurs *outside* of us. Put another way, the location of justification is heaven, where God declares believing sinners in right standing before Him. It may be said that regeneration precedes justification, which results in sanctification.

John Murray puts it well: "Regeneration is an act of God in us; justification is a judgment of God with respect to us. The distinction is like that of the distinction between the act of a surgeon and the act of a judge. The surgeon, when he removes an inward cancer, does something in us. That is not what a judge does — he gives a verdict regarding our judicial status."[1]

It should be noted that "justify" sometimes is used in Scripture in non-forensic contexts. For example, people are said to justify God, or declare Him righteous (Luke 7:29). Obviously, God does not need to be made righteous; He *is* righteous. Rather, people acknowledge Him as such. In another non-forensic usage, people occasionally seek to justify themselves by claiming to be righteous. Jesus chastens the Pharisees, who are lovers of money, by saying, "You are the ones who justify yourselves in the sight of others, but God knows your hearts. For what is highly admired by people is revolting in God's sight" (Luke 16:15). Context is key in determining the proper meaning of this term.

For this study, we focus primarily on the manner in which the apostle Paul uses the word *dikaioo*. Out of the thirty-nine occurrences of the verb "justify" in the New Testament, twenty-nine are found either in Paul's epistles or in his words as recorded in other New Testament books. Another two occurrences of the corresponding noun *dikaiosis* are found in Romans (4:25; 5:18).[2]

We may envision a courtroom setting, with God presiding as Judge. Scripture makes it clear that He is the Judge of the whole earth (Gen. 18:25). His law reflects His holiness and reveals how people created in His image should behave. He requires righteousness, or conformity to the law, and He demonstrates His own righteousness in exercising wrath on those who fail the test (cf. Ps. 7:11; Isa. 5:16; Acts 17:31; Rom. 2:5; 3:5ff). "There is no hope for anyone if God's verdict goes against him," writes J.I. Packer.[3]

A guilty judgment is assumed, of course, because no one is righteous (Rom. 3:10). God's law is not designed to acquit us, but to expose our sinfulness. We are doomed.

But then, the Judge provides a star witness: His Son, who speaks on our behalf. Because Jesus lived a sinless life, upheld and fulfilled the law, and because He paid the penalty for our lawbreaking on the cross, those who trust in Him may rightly be declared "not guilty" before the Father. "In this way, God demonstrates that He is both a righteous Judge and the One who declares us righteous, our Justifier (Rom. 3:26)."[4]

Warren Wiersbe writes, *"Justification is the act of God whereby He declares the believing sinner righteous in Jesus Christ.* Every word of this definition is important. Justification is *an act* and not a process. No Christian is 'more justified' than another Christian. 'Having therefore been once-and-for-all justified by faith, we have peace with God' (Rom. 5:1, literal translation). Since we are justified by faith, it is an instant and immediate transaction between the believing sinner and God. If we were justified by works, then it would have to be a gradual process."[5]

WHY DO WE NEED TO BE JUSTIFIED?

In some respects, justification is the lynch pin in God's great work of salvation. It is His fundamental act of blessing by which He saves us from the past and secures us for the future. Paul places justification in the golden chain of redemption in Rom. 8:29-30. Those whom God foreknows, He predestines, calls, *justifies*, and glorifies. Followers of Jesus may look backward at God's foreknowledge, predestination, and calling. But from the standpoint of justification, we also look forward, knowing God will complete the work He began in us by conforming His adopted children to the image of Christ in glorification (see Phil. 1:6).

At the same time, we should grasp the sublime importance of justification, apart from which a person cannot be saved. The disobedience of the first man, Adam, brought condemnation and death upon the entire human race. From that time forward, death reigned universally. The sin nature — that natural tendency to live independently of God — has been passed on to everyone.

Not that we can blame Adam for our sinful acts of rebellion against God and thus justify ourselves. We should distinguish between being born with a tendency to sin, and sinning. It's true that we sin because we are natural-born sinners. But every sin — whether in thought, word, or deed — is a conscious act of rebellion against God and the testimony He has written on the heart of every human being (see Rom. 1:18-25).

Paul argues in Rom. 1:18 - 3:23 that all people are sinners, rightly condemned before God and without a legitimate defense. Those who know the law of God disobey it. And those without the law reject the revelation of God's eternal power and divine nature in creation and conscience (1:20). In Romans 3, Paul highlights two results of our sin. First, we are rendered unrighteous as persons (vv. 10-18). Second, we are rendered guilty in our standing before God, "so that every mouth may be shut and the whole world may become subject to God's judgment" (v. 19).

Not only is every person a sinner (Rom. 3:10, 23), but our sins place us under condemnation. God's eyes are too pure to look on evil, and He cannot tolerate wrongdoing (Hab. 1:13). He must judge sin. We stand guilty of violating God's perfect and holy standards as expressed in His law, which is not given to us for our salvation, but to expose our sin. "By detecting and provoking transgressions, it [the law] was to teach Israelites their need for justification, thus acting as a *paidagogos* (the household slave who took children to school) to lead them to Christ (Gal. 3:19-24; Rom. 3:20; 5:20; 7:5, 7-13). This epoch of divine preparatory education lasted till the coming of Christ (Gal. 3:23-25; 4:1-5)."[6]

In short, every human being needs God's declaration of righteousness because no one possesses the righteousness necessary to enter God's presence. Our best efforts are but filthy rags (literally, menstrual garments) in the eyes of God (Isa. 64:6). Like the guest who arrogantly shuns the king's offer of a wedding robe, and thus is bound hand and foot and cast into outer darkness (Matt. 22:1-14); like the Pharisee who fasts and pays tithes, yet who leaves the temple unjustified (Luke 18:9-14); and like those who profess to have accomplished much in the name of Jesus, yet are told to depart as lawbreakers (Matt. 7:21-23), we cannot justify ourselves despite our most strenuous efforts.

And yet, God loves us and desires an intimate, everlasting relationship with us. That begs the question: On what grounds can God justify the ungodly without compromising His role as righteous Judge?

Whose idea was justification?

Where does justification come from? Whose idea was it? The Bible is clear that God the Father is the author of justification. Paul is emphatic in declaring this to be the case. Consider these passages:

Rom. 3:30 - "...since there is one God who will justify the circumcised by faith and the uncircumcised through faith." Paul's reference to "God" in verse 29 makes it clear, in context, that he is referring to God the Father.

Rom. 4:5 - "But to the one who does not work, but believes on him who declares the ungodly to be righteous, his faith is credited for righteousness." Paul compares the believing sinner to Abraham, whose faith was credited to him for righteousness by God the Father (see vv. 1-3).

Rom. 8:30 - "And those he predestined, he also called; and those he called, he also justified; and those he justified, he also glorified." The context of verses 28-30 establishes that the "he" is none other than God the Father.

Rom. 8:33 - "Who can bring an accusation against God's elect? God is the one who justifies." Continuing his defense of the believer's triumph, Paul says the Father declares righteous the believing sinner based on the finished work of His Son (see v. 34).

We could consult additional passages, but Paul's point is clear: God the Father is the member of the Triune Godhead who declares the believing sinner righteous.

On what grounds?

But what are the grounds for our acquittal? How can the Father declare sinners righteous — when He knows full well we are wicked — without negating His own holiness? Isn't this cheap grace, or divine contradiction?

Paul supplies an answer: The Father justifies sinners based on the person and work of Christ, who, acting on behalf of helpless sinners, satisfies the claims of God's law on them. Let's think through the process:

- Jesus is born "under the law" (Gal. 4:4). That is, He knows what it's like to live under the Mosaic Law. Subject to the same requirements of holiness as all other people, He is tempted in every way we are tempted, yet He endures a lifetime without sin (Heb. 4:15).

- Having fulfilled the law, Jesus becomes obedient to the point of death — even to death on a cross (Phil. 2:8). He experiences, or "learns," obedience through His faithful suffering (Heb. 5:8), and He offers up His sinless life as a substitute for ours. As Paul writes in Gal. 3:13, "Christ redeemed us from the curse of the law by becoming a curse for us." This fulfills Isaiah's prophecy from seven centuries earlier: "But he was pierced because of our rebellion, crushed because of our iniquities; punishment for our peace was on him, and we are healed by his wounds" (Isa. 53:5; see vv. 4-12).

- Jesus does not merely atone for, or temporarily cover, our sins, as is the case with animal sacrifices under the Mosaic Law. He puts away, once and for all, our sins by His blood (Rom. 3:25-26; 5:9). "For by one offering he has perfected forever those who are sanctified" (Heb. 10:14).

- By His complete obedience to the law, Jesus wins for us the status of law-keepers. Paul writes, "So then, as through one trespass [Adam's] there is condemnation for everyone, so also through one righteous act [Christ's finished work on the cross] there is justification leading to life for everyone. For just as through one man's [Adam's] disobedience the many were made sinners, so also through the one man's [Christ's] obedience the many will be made righteous [in sanctification and glorification]" (Rom. 5:18-19).

- So, the Father maintains His perfect justice, while extending to those who are "in Christ" the gift of justification. As Paul writes about the Father, "He made the one who did not know sin to be sin for us, so that in him we might become the righteousness of God" (2 Cor. 5:21). The apostle further tells his Roman readers, "Therefore, there is now no condemnation for those in

Christ Jesus, because the law of the Spirit of life in Christ
Jesus has set you free from the law of sin and death" (Rom.
8:1-2).

J.I. Packer writes, "So, when God justifies sinners on the ground of
Christ's obedience and death, he acts justly. So far from compromising
his judicial righteousness, this method of justification actually exhibits
it."[7]

How are we justified?

If God is just, and the one who justifies us based on the finished
work of Christ, then how does a sinner receive the gift of justification?
The answer is: by faith. Faith is the *means* by which we receive the offer
of right-standing with God. Paul refers us to the case of Abraham, who
"believed God, and it was credited to him for righteousness" to prove
that a person is justified by faith without works (Rom. 4:3ff; Gal. 3:6).

Our simple trust in Jesus results in God reckoning us in right
standing with Him. And there's more. In justification, our sins are
imputed, or charged, to the account of Christ and paid in full. This is a
one-time act in which the penalty for all sins — past, present, and
future — is cancelled, and we are declared once and forevermore in
right standing with God.

As Paul writes in Gal. 3:13, "Christ redeemed us from the curse of
the law by becoming a curse for us." At the same time, Christ's righteousness is imputed to us, or transferred to our account. In other
words, Jesus takes full responsibility for the sin debt we owe God, and
in exchange we receive His righteousness (Rom. 5:18; 2 Cor. 5:21).

Need proof? Consider Christ's resurrection, which demonstrates
the Father's acceptance of His sacrifice on our behalf. Romans 4:23-25
tells us, "Now **it was credited to him** [that is, Abraham; Gen. 15:6]
was not written for Abraham alone, but also for us. It will be credited
to us who believe in him who raised Jesus our Lord from the dead. He
was delivered up for our trespasses and raised for our justification."

This doesn't negate all consequences of sin. When we are justified,
the *eternal* consequences of sin are canceled, including everlasting separation from God in hell. But the *temporal* effects of sin, both those that

fall on the individual and those that fall collectively on the human race, continue. Thus, we still experience the effects of the Fall, including aging, sickness, and physical death. Ultimately, these are banished in our glorification and in Christ's creation of new heavens and a new earth.

One other thought: Justification is not a synonym for "pardon." Robert Morey comments, "Justification is more than mere pardon, for pardon means 'declared guilty but delivered from punishment,' while justification is God's declaration that we are *not* guilty and therefore *not* worthy of punishment. But, instead, God positively declares that we are *righteous* before Him, and therefore *worthy* to receive all the blessings and privileges of the righteous."[8]

FORGIVENESS AND IMPUTATION

Two inseparable elements come into play in justification: forgiveness and imputation. In forgiveness, God acquits us, or declares that our sins are forgiven based on the finished work of Christ. As Paul puts it, in Christ "we have redemption through his blood, the forgiveness of our trespasses" (Eph. 1:7a). At the same time, our sins are imputed, or transferred, to the account of Christ, in exchange for His righteousness. Without these two important elements occurring together, there can be no justification.

It may help to note three vital imputations in Scripture. First, when Adam sinned, God viewed it as belonging to the entire human race; that is, Adam's sin was imputed to us. Second, when Christ died, the Father counted our sins as belonging to Jesus; in other words, our sin was imputed to Christ. Third, when Jesus fulfilled the law through His sinless life, and then offered Himself on our behalf, the Father reckoned the Son's righteousness as belonging to us; in short, Christ's righteousness was imputed to all who are "in Christ."

So, if justification is an acquittal of the penalty of all sins — even future sins — why do believers need to seek the Lord's ongoing forgiveness as we live our imperfect lives? As Robert Morey explains, justification and forgiveness are related, but not identical: "The forgiveness which comes to us in justification is called judicial forgiveness to distinguish it from parental forgiveness. Judicial forgiveness has in view our relationship as sinners before God the Judge of all the earth. Parental forgiveness has in view our relationship as children before God our heavenly father."[9]

Put another way, judicial forgiveness is once for all and is neither repeatable nor revocable. Parental forgiveness, on the other hand, is needed every day. Judicial forgiveness covers all sins past, present, and future. Parental forgiveness covers only the past and present sins, which we are to confess and forsake. Judicial forgiveness is received once. Parental forgiveness is received as often as we ask our Heavenly Father.

What does justification produce?

While justification is a declaration of the Father in heaven, it produces results in believers' lives on earth.

Justification brings peace:

- "Therefore, since we have been declared righteous by faith, we have peace with God through our Lord Jesus Christ" (Rom. 5:1).
- "For God was pleased to have all his fullness dwell in him [Jesus], and through him to reconcile everything to himself, whether things on earth or things in heaven by making peace through his blood, shed on the cross" (Col. 1:19-20).

Justification results in the righteousness of God:

- "All of us have become like something unclean, and all our righteous acts are like a polluted garment; all of us wither like a leaf, and our iniquities carry us away like the wind" (Isa. 64:6). But ...
- "He made the one who did not know sin to be sin for us, so that in him we might become the righteousness of God" (2 Cor. 5:21).

Justification leads to sanctification, which produces evidence that we are right with God and that His Spirit is working in us to conform us to the image of Christ:

- "What should we say then? Should we continue in sin so that grace may multiply? Absolutely not! How can we who died to sin still live in it?" (Rom. 6:1-2)
- "He gave himself for us to redeem us from all lawlessness and to cleanse for himself a people for his own possession, eager to do good works" (Titus 2:14).

Justification produces works appropriate to the nature of the new creature that has come into being:

- "For you are saved by grace through faith, and this is not from yourselves; it is God's gift — not from works, so that no one can boast. For we are his workmanship, created in Christ Jesus for good works, which God prepared ahead of time for us to do" (Eph. 2:8-10).

Millard Erickson summarizes: "Justification, then, is a three-party, not a two-party, matter. And it is voluntary on the part of all three. Jesus is not an unwilling victim conscripted to the task. He willingly volunteered to give himself and unite with the sinner. There is also a conscious decision on the part of the sinner to enter into this relationship. And the Father willingly accepts it. That no one is constrained means that the whole matter is completely ethical and legal."[10]

KEY PASSAGES ON JUSTIFICATION

Let's survey several Bible verses that address justification.

Rom. 3:20-28 - "For no one will be justified in his sight by the works of the law, because the knowledge of sin comes through the law. But now, apart from the law, the righteousness of God has been revealed, attested by the Law and the Prophets. The righteousness of God is through faith in Jesus Christ to all who believe, since there is no distinction. For all have sinned and fall short of the glory of God. They are justified freely by his grace through the redemption that is in Christ Jesus. God presented him as an atoning sacrifice in his blood, received through faith, to demonstrate his righteousness, because in his restraint God passed over the sins previously committed. God presented him to demonstrate his righteousness at the present time, so that he would be righteous and declare righteous (*dikaiounta*) the one who has faith in Jesus. Where, then, is boasting? It is excluded. By what kind of law? By one of works? No, on the contrary, by a law of faith. For we conclude that a person is justified by faith apart from the works of the law."

Paul establishes that all humanity stands on level ground at the foot of the cross. All of us are sinners, and despite our best efforts, we cannot attain the glory of God — that is, "the honor or approbation which God bestows."[11] An acknowledgement of our unworthiness — and utter helplessness — is key to understanding justification, for it makes this a work of God alone. "Though men differ greatly in the *nature* and *extent* of their sinfulness, there is absolutely no difference between the best and the worst of men, in the *fact* that 'all have sinned,' and so underlie the wrath of God."[12]

Paul tells us the righteousness of God is ours through faith alone in Jesus Christ. God justifies us "freely by his grace through the redemption that is in Christ Jesus." So, grace, or God's unmerited favor, is extended to us by means of Christ's redeeming sacrifice of Himself. That's the offer: an acquittal based on the payment of another, who received our guilt and suffered the consequences in our place.

The Greek word for "redemption" in verse 24 is *apolytrosis*, from *lytron*, "a ransom payment." The death of Christ on the cross is "the price of payment for human sin which secured release from the bondage of Satan and sin for every person who trusts God's promise of forgiveness and salvation."[13]

Paul's reference to God passing over sins previously committed harkens back to the Old Testament sacrificial system in which, by faith, the believing sinner offered a spotless animal sacrifice whose blood *atoned for* — or temporarily covered — his sins. But now, Jesus, the Lamb of God who takes away the sin of the world, has died on the cross — not to cover our sins, but to *take them away*.

In the finished work of Jesus, God demonstrates His righteousness by demanding death as the penalty for sin. He also demonstrates that this penalty is placed on the shoulders of His eternal Son. Therefore, He may declare the one who believes in Jesus as acquitted and in right standing before Him.

All of this excludes boasting. An honest self-appraisal results in the admission of our guilt and shame as sinners who have offended a holy God. It drives us to acknowledge the depths of our depravity, and to grasp the lifeline extended to us in Christ, who did what we could not do: fulfill the law through a sinless and fully obedient life. That's why Paul can conclude that a person is justified by faith apart from the works of the law.

As Warren Wiersbe summarizes, "The swimmer, when he is saved from drowning, does not brag because he trusted the lifeguard. What else could he do? When a believing sinner is justified by faith, he cannot boast of his faith, but he can boast in a wonderful Saviour."[14]

CSB	KJV	NIV	NASB	ESV
Declare righteous / justify, acquit	The justifier	Justifies	The justifier	The justifier

Comparing English translations of *dikaiounta* in Rom. 3:26

Rom. 4:1-5 - "What then will we say that Abraham, our forefather according to the flesh has found? If Abraham was justified (*edikaiothe*) by works, he has something to boast about — but not before God. For what does the Scripture say? **Abraham believed God, and it was credited to him for righteousness.** Now to the one who works, pay is not credited as a gift but as something owed. But to the one who does not work, but believes on him who declares the ungodly to be righteous (*dikaiounta*), his faith is credited for righteousness."

Paul asks us to look back at Abraham, through whom Yahweh raised up the Israelite people. How did the patriarch receive the covenant promises? Certainly, not by works, for God chose Abraham and his offspring based on His own sovereignty, not on any innate worthiness in those He called to be His special people. Abraham had nothing to boast about, for God took the initiative to credit righteousness to his account after he believed in God's promises of a child and descendants.

Next, Paul applies the lesson of Abraham's justification to us. If we may be declared righteous before God based on our merits, then God owes us something. Justification is no longer a gift, but an obligation. Perish the thought, Paul says. God owes us nothing, and our feeble efforts to justify ourselves before Him are little more than footprints in the flowing blood of Christ. So, how can things ever be right between us? We believe on the one who declares the ungodly to be righteous. As a result, our faith is reckoned as righteousness.

The word "credited" in verse 3 is *elogisthe*. It means "to put to one's account." It's a banking term that Paul uses eleven times throughout the chapter. Depending on the English translation and context, the word is variously rendered "credited," "reckoned," "counted," or "imputed." When people work, they earn a salary, which the employer places into their account. But Abraham did not work for God's covenant promises, any more than sinners under God's condemnation may work for their acquittal. In every case, God produces the work and freely offers us the fruit of His labors; we simply receive justification by faith.

CSB	KJV	NIV	NASB	ESV
Justified / declared righteous, acquitted	Justified	Justified	Justified	Justified

Comparing English translations of *edikaiothe* in Rom. 4:2

CSB	KJV	NIV	NASB	ESV
Declares ... righteous	Justifieth	Justifies	Justifies	Justifies

Comparing English translations of *dikaiounta* in Rom. 4:5

Rom. 5:1 - "Therefore, since we have been declared righteous (*dikaiothentes*) by faith, we have peace with God through our Lord Jesus Christ."

In this single verse, Paul offers several important truths about justification. First, it is certain, "since we have been declared righteous ..." Second, the means of justification is faith; the Father acquits us based on our faith in His Son, who took upon Himself our guilt, bore our punishment, and clothed us in His righteousness. Third, the result of justification is peace with God. Because of ancient manuscript variances, the phrase "we have peace" could be translated, "let us continue enjoying peace." Once enemies of God and firmly in the crosshairs of His wrath (Rom. 5:10; 8:7), we now have peace with God — lasting, unbreakable peace.

The Christian's peace stands in stark contrast to the unbeliever's condemnation, which is in essence the Father's declaration of war against those who reject His Son (see John 3:18). However, when the enemies of God hear the gospel, come under the conviction of the Holy Spirit, and trust in Jesus, their condemnation melts away as the Father withdraws His battle cry and hoists the flag of perpetual armistice. As Paul writes, "Therefore, there is now no condemnation for those in Christ Jesus ..." (Rom. 8:1).

The glory belongs to God, for He is the one who secures the peace. Faith merely is the outstretched hand that receives the olive branch.

CSB	KJV	NIV	NASB	ESV
Since we have been declared righteous	Being justified	Since we have been justified	Having been justified	Since we have been justified

Comparing English translations of *dikaiothentes* in Rom. 5:1

2 Cor. 5:21 - "He made the one who did not know sin to be sin for us, so that in him we might become the righteousness (*dikaiosune*) of God."

The Father and Son work together for our justification. In verse 19, Paul writes that "in Christ, God was reconciling the world to himself." This message of reconciliation has been given to His followers as "ambassadors for Christ, since God is making his appeal through us" (v. 20). The essence of the message is that God the Father made His innocent Son the object of His wrath, for our sake, by placing the sins of all humanity on Him at the cross. There is no suggestion that Jesus *became* a sinner like us, for Scripture is clear — and Jesus makes plain

— that He is sinless (John 8:46; Heb. 4:15; 1 John 3:5). Rather, it is because of Christ's complete holiness that He may stand in our place and receive the wrath of the Father for our sins.

As a result, the Father declares righteous the person who believes in Jesus for everlasting life. "It is the great exchange: the sinner's sin for His righteousness," writes Dwight Hunt. "There is no greater news that can be spread, which is why Paul was so passionate in sharing this news with others."[15] The innocent Lamb of God is punished voluntarily as if guilty, and the guilty are graciously acquitted. As the apostle Peter writes, "He himself bore our sins in his body on the tree, so that, having died to sins, we might live for righteousness. **By his wounds you have been healed**" (1 Peter 2:24).

In saying "we might become the righteousness of God," Paul seems to be referring to the doctrine of imputation, in which, as a result of Christ's finished work on the cross, we receive a right standing before God while Christ takes on our sins. It's also possible that Paul is describing God's righteous character, which we receive via the indwelling Holy Spirit, enabling us to live holy lives. In either case, justification is the work of God, accomplished through the sacrificial and substitutionary death of Jesus at Calvary.

This should compel us to live as ambassadors for Christ, carrying the message of reconciliation to a lost world in desperate need of peace with God.

CSB	KJV	NIV	NASB	ESV
Righteousness	Righteousness	Righteousness	Righteousness	Righteousness

Comparing English translations of *dikaiosune* in 2 Cor. 5:21

Gal. 2:15-16 - "We are Jews by birth and not 'Gentile sinners,' and yet because we know that a person is not justified by the works of the law but by faith in Christ Jesus, even we ourselves have believed in Christ Jesus. This was so that we might be justified (*dikaioutai*) by faith in Christ and not by the works of the law, because by the works of the law no human being will be justified."

While Paul's audience consists mostly of Gentile readers, Judaizers are hard at work to convince non-Jewish Christians that in order to be right with God, they must conform to the Mosaic Law. The word "Judaizer" comes from a Greek verb *ioudaixein*, meaning "to follow Jewish customs." In Gal. 2:14, Paul recalls a confrontation with Peter, who was compelling Gentile Christians to live like Jews. In Paul's attempt to blunt the advances of the Judaizers, he makes it clear that a person is justified by faith alone. Works of the law, particularly circumcision, cannot secure an acquittal before God's holy bench, or make someone righteous.

Paul's words cut deeply into this first-century false gospel, while dissolving the argument that Jewish ethnicity accounts for anything with respect to eternal life. Not only are Gentiles justified by faith, apart from the works of the law, but Jews are in the same boat. Their appeal to the Mosaic Law as a means by which God acquits them of their sins and brings them into His kingdom is all heat and no light. Salvation is *of* the Jews, meaning that Christ is the seed of Abraham. And certainly, there *are* some advantages to being a Jew, which Paul readily acknowledges (Rom. 9:4-5). But a right standing with God knows no ethnicity. It is God's gift, bestowed on all who trust in His Son for forgiveness of sins and everlasting life.

Paul's reference to "Gentile sinners" apparently is a derogatory phrase common in rabbinical Judaism. The false teachers may have used it to shame Gentile Christians into adding works of the law to their faith in Jesus. Paul puts the slanderous phrase back on his Jewish brothers and sisters to make it plain that everyone is in need of God's grace. Later, he remarks, "There is no Jew or Greek, slave or free, male and female; since you are all one in Christ Jesus. And if you belong to Christ, then you are Abraham's seed, heirs according to the promise" (Gal. 3:28-29).

CSB	KJV	NIV	NASB	ESV
Justified	Justified	Justified	Justified	Justified / counted righteous

Comparing English translations of *dikaioutai* in Gal. 2:16

ROB PHILLIPS

But what about James?

Paul writes in Rom. 3:28, "For we conclude that a person is justified by faith apart from the works of the law." James, on the other
hand, in his general epistle, pens these words, "You see that a person is
justified by works and not by faith alone" (James 2:24).

Viewed in isolation, it appears these two statements are at odds.
But when taken in their proper contexts, these passages reveal that
Paul and James are on the same theological page.

For starters, we should not assume Paul and James use "works" in
the same way. Paul connects works with the Jewish law and its practices, such as circumcision. More importantly, he does so with respect
to an individual *prior to*, or apart from, becoming a Christian. James,
on the other hand, does not address Jewish covenantal ceremonies or
responsibilities. Instead, he describes the outworking of faith *after* one
becomes a Christian.

In other words, Paul and James are in complete agreement. We are
justified — that is, declared in right standing before God — based
solely on our faith in Christ, whose finished work on the cross paid
our sin debt.

As we've seen, Paul is explicit about this in other passages:

- Rom. 4:5 – "But to the one who does not work, but
  believes on him who declares the ungodly to be righteous,
  his faith is credited for righteousness."
- Eph. 2:8-9 – "For you are saved by grace through faith,
  and this is not from yourselves; it is God's gift — not from
  works, so that no one can boast."
- And Titus 3:5 – "[H]e saved us — not by works of
  righteousness that we had done, but according to His
  mercy — through the washing of regeneration and renewal
  by the Holy Spirit."

James has no argument with Paul's teaching on salvation by grace
through faith. He simply builds on that doctrinal truth, exhorting
believers to live in such a way that makes their faith evident to all.

When we trust in Christ for salvation, He not only justifies us by faith. He sends the Holy Spirit, who seals us, sets us apart, places us into the body of Christ, gives us spiritual gifts, and begins the lifelong process of conforming us to the image of Jesus. This creates a new attitude in us, as well as new desires and a new outlook.

Therefore, being made new creations in Christ (2 Cor. 5:17), we find it natural to live moral lives, be generous, and share our faith, because the Spirit now inhabits the temple of our bodies and guides our behavior.

To the outside observer, there is something different about us. Through our attitudes, words, and actions, the Holy Spirit testifies to the saving power of Jesus. That is the justification of which James writes — not justification before God in salvation, but justification before people in our witness.

That's why James writes in the same context, "Show me your faith without works, and I will show you faith by my works" (2:18b). And: "For just as the body without the spirit is dead, so also faith without works is dead" (2:26).

While we must never attempt to judge another person's eternal standing with God, we may witness the evidence of the Spirit's power in believers through their Christlike concern for others, their moral lives, and their selfless works in the name of Jesus.

SUMMARY

The noun *dikaiosis*, or justification, describes the act of God declaring sinners righteous on the basis of the finished work of Christ. Believing sinners are acquitted — freed of all guilt — as their sins are transferred to the account of Christ and exchanged for Christ's righteousness.

Justification is grounded in Christ's death, burial, and resurrection. The apostle Paul puts it succinctly: "He was delivered up for our trespasses and raised for our justification" (Rom. 4:25). Paul further writes, "So then, as through one trespass [Adam's] there is condemnation for everyone, so also through one righteous act [Christ's] there is justification leading to life for everyone. For just as through one man's disobedience the many were made sinners, so also through the one man's obedience the many will be made righteous" (Rom. 5:18-19).

"Christ's one act of righteousness (i.e., his death and resurrection, considered as one event) leads to our justification as an antidote to the one trespass of Adam that brought humankind into the bondage of sin and death," according to the *Expository Dictionary of Bible Words.*[16]

Justification is received by faith, apart from human effort (Rom. 5:1; Gal. 3:24). It is a one-time, instantaneous, non-repeatable act of God, placing us in right standing before His holy bench and ensuring that we are never subject to double jeopardy. To add works to justification, such as returning to old covenant practices that served as types and shadows of greater things to come, is to trample on the Son of God and regard as profane the blood of the new covenant (Heb. 10:29).

Justification is not to be confused with sanctification, which is the work of God setting believers apart and engaging us in a lifelong process by which we become more Christlike (1 Thess. 5:23). Justification and sanctification may be distinguished but not separated; both are divine elements of God's redemption.

Consider these summary statements about justification:

- The Greek verb *dikaioo* is a legal term meaning "acquit" or "declare righteous." It is the opposite of "condemn." In justification, God issues a legal declaration about us. This is why theologians refer to justification as *forensic*, which means "having to do with legal proceedings."
- Every person needs to be justified before God because every person is a sinner. Our sins place us under God's wrath. Further, no one possesses the righteousness necessary to enter the presence of God, whose eyes are too pure to look on evil (Hab. 1:13).
- God the Father is the author of justification. He is the member of the Triune Godhead who declares the believing sinner righteous. He does so, based on the person and work of Jesus Christ, who, acting on behalf of helpless sinners, satisfies the claims of God's law on them.
- Faith is the means by which we receive the offer of right-standing with God. Paul refers us to the case of Abraham,

who "believed God, and it was credited to him for righteousness" (Rom. 4:3ff; Gal. 3:6).

- Two inseparable elements come into play in justification: forgiveness and imputation. In forgiveness, God acquits us, or declares that our sins are forgiven based on the finished work of Christ. At the same time, our sins are imputed, or transferred, to the account of Christ, in exchange for His righteousness.

- The results of justification are evident in the life of believers. For example, justification brings peace with God; it results in the righteousness of God; it yields new attitudes and outlooks that show we are right with God and that His Spirit is working in us; and it produces works appropriate to the nature of the new creature that has come into being.

- Contrary to some arguments, Paul and James are in complete agreement about justification. We are declared in right standing *before God* based solely on our faith in Christ, whose finished work on the cross paid our sin debt. As a result, the indwelling Holy Spirit produces changes in us that justify us *before people* in our holy lifestyles.

THINK
Questions for personal or group study

(1) What is *forensic justification*? In what ways is it helpful for us to envision a courtroom setting when seeking to understand the New Testament concept of justification?

(2) How do the following passages address the reality that we cannot justify ourselves?

- Isa. 64:6
- Matt. 7:21-23
- Matt. 22:1-14
- Luke 18:9-14
- Rom. 3:10-31

(3) How is justification different from pardon? Why is it important for us to understand the distinction?

(4) How can God the Father declare sinners righteous (when He knows full well we are wicked) without negating His holiness? Consider the ways in which the following phrases contribute to the answer:

- Jesus is born "under the law" (Gal. 4:4).
- Christ "redeemed us from the curse of the law by becoming a curse for us" (Gal. 3:13).
- The Father "has sent his Son as the world's Savior" (1 John 4:14).
- Jesus is "obedient to the point of death — even to death on a cross" (Phil. 2:8).
- Through Christ's obedience "the many will be made righteous" (Rom. 5:19).
- "He made the one who did not know sin to be sin for us, so that in Him we might become the righteousness of God" (2 Cor. 5:21).

(5) If justification is the removal of the penalty for *all* believers' sins — past, present, and future — why do Christians need to confess our sins to God on a regular basis?

(6) What is the meaning of *imputation*? What is exchanged between the believing sinner and Jesus in imputation that enables God the Father to declare the sinner righteous?

(7) Read Rom. 3:28 and James 2:24. Paul says we are justified by faith, while James writes that we are justified by works. How might you reconcile these seemingly contradictory statements?

Chapter Seven

YOU ARE INDWELT

P salm 51 is a gut-wrenching prayer of confession and a desperate plea for restoration. King David has lived for some time with the reality of his past deeds. First, he lingers in the palace while his troops are off to war. Next, he sees a beautiful woman bathing; she is Bathsheba, the wife of Uriah. He sends messengers for her, sleeps with her, and impregnates her.

Seeking to cover his sins, he calls Uriah home from the front, urging him to enjoy intimacy with Bathsheba. But Uriah, knowing that service in battle is considered service to the Lord, and remembering that David has required his men to refrain from sexual contact while on active duty (1 Sam. 21:5), he returns to his fellow soldiers without sleeping with his wife.

At last, David desperately orders Joab to put Uriah in the thick of the fiercest fighting, and then to withdraw so that Uriah is killed in battle. After a time of mourning, Bathsheba becomes David's wife.

Living in an Eastern honor/shame culture, rather than a modern Western guilt/innocence culture, David may not have given his misdeeds too much thought.[1] But, "the Lord considered what David had done to be evil" (2 Sam. 11:27b).

So, Yahweh sends Nathan the prophet to the king. Nathan shares a parable of two men in a certain city, one rich and the other poor. When a traveler comes to visit the rich man, the rich man takes the poor man's only possession — one small ewe lamb — and slaughters it to feed his guest. Infuriated at this report, David orders that justice be served, and that no pity be shown to the wealthy plunderer. Nathan replies to David, "You are the man!" (2 Sam. 12:7).

David immediately acknowledges his guilt, and Nathan assures David that Yahweh has taken away his sin and spared his life, even though the Law of Moses requires the death penalty for adulterers. There *are* consequences, however. The child of David and Bathsheba dies, and disaster comes upon the house of the king.

And so, we come to Psalm 51, David's lament over his sin and his cry for God's graciousness. "Completely wash away my guilt and cleanse me from my sin," he prays. "For I am conscious of my rebellion, and my sin is always before me. Against you — you alone — I have sinned and done this evil in your sight. So you are right when you pass sentence; you are blameless when you judge" (Ps. 51:2-4).

In the midst of David's prayer of confession, repentance, and a plea for a clean heart, he makes a request that believers today might find odd: "Do not banish me from your presence or *take your Holy Spirit from me*" (v. 11, emphasis added). Is David afraid his sins are so odious to God that he has lost his salvation? And if King David, a man after God's own heart (1 Sam. 13:14; Acts 13:22), can forfeit his relationship with Yahweh, what hope is there for any of us today?

These questions go to the heart of what it means to be indwelt by the Holy Spirit. And they prompt us to examine the different ways the Spirit worked in Old Testament times in contrast with the Day of Pentecost and beyond.

More to the point, as we read through the Old Testament, we see that the Spirit rushes upon selected leaders for the purpose of empowering them for service. Typically, the Spirit visits national leaders like Moses and Joshua, kings like Saul and David, judges like Samson, and prophets like Elijah and Joel. Meanwhile, the permanent dwelling of the Holy Spirit in the Old Testament is in *places* rather than in persons: the pillar of cloud and fire, the tabernacle, and the temple.

But on the Day of Pentecost, the Holy Spirit fulfills Old Testament prophecies and takes up residence in the human spirits of persons professing faith in Jesus, who ratifies the new covenant in His blood.

While Bible commentators differ in their views about the work of the Spirit in Old Testament times vs. New Testament times, it is biblically faithful for followers of Jesus to say, "I am indwelt."

WHAT DOES IT MEAN TO BE INDWELT?

Indwelling is an act of God in which the Holy Spirit takes up permanent residence in the body of a follower of Jesus Christ. Specifically, indwelling occurs in the human spirit, the innermost part of us that God created as His dwelling place. While regeneration and indwelling are related, and perhaps simultaneous, they may be distinguished. As we saw in Chapter Five, regeneration is the work of the Holy Spirit that brings a sinner from spiritual death to spiritual life. Indwelling is the continuous presence of the Spirit in the believer's body. Put another way, regeneration introduces new life, while indwelling assures its permanence.

A simple illustration may help. Suppose there is an abandoned house on a remote stretch of land. It was built and furnished years ago but never lived in. An explorer locates the structure, overgrown with vegetation and shielded from within by heavy curtains. Taking his lantern, the explorer opens the door and enters, illuminating a treasure trove of breathtaking architecture and ornate furnishings buried beneath cobwebs and dust. Determined to stay, the explorer sets the lantern on a stand, throws open the curtains, and begins to sweep away years of neglect, ultimately revealing a priceless mansion. As we come to discover, the explorer also happens to be the builder and owner, who has come to reclaim his masterpiece.

While this is by no means a perfect analogy, we may liken the entrance of the owner, and the introduction of light, to regeneration. Meanwhile, the permanent residency of the owner symbolizes the Spirit's indwelling. Later in this chapter, we examine the benefits of the Spirit's non-stop presence in our lives. Believers are, in many respects, works in progress. But we are never alone.

Perhaps the best way to understand the indwelling of the Spirit is in terms of Christians replacing the temple as God's dwelling place. In

ROB PHILLIPS

the Old Testament, God reveals Himself in a variety of ways to human beings. He speaks many times in an audible voice (e.g., Josh. 1:1; 1 Sam. 3:11; Isa. 7:3). He appears in a burning bush (Ex. 3:2ff). He rides in a chariot of fire and sits enthroned above the living creatures (Ezek. 1:4-28). He comes in a Christophany as the Angel of the Lord (e.g., Gen. 16:7-12; Judges 2:1-4; 2 Sam. 24:16; Zech. 1:12). Other examples could be cited, but we should remember that God most desires to walk with us "in the garden at the time of the evening breeze" (Gen. 3:8), an intimacy that Adam's sin ruptured.

In His covenant relationship with Abraham and his descendants, Yahweh establishes a more permanent presence. He appears as a pillar of cloud and fire in the wilderness, protecting His people from pharaoh's army, providing cover from the scorching sun by day, and offering light and warmth by night. When Moses consecrates the tabernacle, the Shekinah glory enters the Most Holy Place and dwells there until it's time for the Israelites to break camp and move on. When Solomon dedicates the temple in Jerusalem, the glory again overshadows the structure and resides above the wings of the cherubim in the Holy of Holies. Sadly, it is not to last.

After generations of spiritual adultery, God's people are on the cusp of divine judgment. The prophet Ezekiel sees the glory of God departing the temple (Ezekiel 8-11), to which the glory does not return, even when Herod's temple, built centuries later, shines resplendently in the Judean sunshine. That is, until the Spirit-filled Messiah, who has come to tabernacle with sinful and fallen people (John 1:14), rides triumphantly into Jerusalem on Palm Sunday and enters the temple. At last, the glory returns. But the significance of this event is lost on the tone-deaf religious leaders who call, not for Christ's worship, but His crucifixion. Later, the resurrected and glorified Savior ascends into heaven. Then, in A.D. 70, the temple is destroyed. But the Shekinah glory is not to be denied.

On the Day of Pentecost, not long after Jesus returns to the Father's right hand and sits enthroned as the glorified Son, the glory returns powerfully as the Holy Spirit falls on Jesus' disciples and permanently indwells His new temple — the temple of their bodies. The tabernacle and the temple are no longer the earthly dwelling places of the Shekinah glory. God now resides permanently in the human spirits of those who trust in His Son. It is a breathtaking story of God's faithfulness to call out, save, and secure those who are His own.

The final chapter is yet to come when our Savior returns, creates new heavens and a new earth, and restores face-to-face intimacy with His glorified saints — the same intimacy Adam and Eve experienced in the garden before sin sent creation into a tailspin.

For now, we have the Holy Spirit in us — that is, in our bodies, which are temples of the Spirit. Paul makes this clear in at least two passages of Scripture. He reminds the drifting Corinthians of a coming day of accountability before the judgment seat of Christ (1 Cor. 3:10-15) and then asks, "Don't you yourselves know that you are God's temple and that the Spirit of God lives in you? If anyone destroys God's temple, God will destroy him; for God's temple is holy, and that is what you are" (vv. 16-17). A little later, warning about sexual immorality, he writes, "Don't you know that your body is a temple of the Holy Spirit who is in you, whom you have from God? You are not your own, for you were bought at a price. So glorify God with your body" (1 Cor. 6:19-20).

Keep in mind, as we saw earlier, God created us as three-part beings: body, soul, and spirit. Our bodies are the physical parts of us that relate to the material world in which we live. But we are more than a concoction of elements, biological processes, and five senses. We possess souls — our minds, emotions, and wills — that define the *real* us. Last, we have human spirits. These are the innermost parts of us that God, who is spirit, made as His dwelling place. Unbelievers are only two-thirds alive; that is, they are alive in body and soul, but spiritually dead in sin (Eph. 2:1).

In regeneration, the Holy Spirit enters the dead human spirit and brings it to life. And then, through indwelling, the Spirit takes up permanent residence, beginning the lifelong work of conforming believers to the image of Christ (in sanctification).

It may help to remember several key truths about the indwelling Spirit. First, He is a gift of the Father and Son to *all* believers (John 7:37; Acts 11:16-17; Rom. 5:5; 1 Cor. 2:12; 2 Cor. 5:5); to not possess the Spirit indicates an unsaved condition (Rom. 8:9; 1 Cor. 2:14; Jude 19). Second, the Spirit continues to dwell in us, even when we sin

(1 Cor. 6:19), although sin grieves Him (Eph. 4:30). Third, as Charles Ryrie points out, "The security of the believer and the permanent indwelling of the Spirit are inseparable doctrines."[2] The permanence of the Spirit's presence fulfills Jesus' promise to send "another Counselor to be with you forever" (John 14:16).

Finally, the Spirit's intimate presence motivates us to holiness, "the only kind of character appropriate in the Spirit's temple," according to John Frame. "And when we recognize the promptings of the Spirit, the kind of life he urges upon us, we seek to live in that way, to encourage the growth of his fruits in our lives."[3]

WHAT DOES THE INDWELLING SPIRIT DO?

Once the Holy Spirit inhabits the bodies of new believers, He makes Himself at home and begins producing life-changing results. Specifically, the Spirit:

- Confirms our adoption as children of God (see Chapter Ten). "For all those led by God's Spirit are God's sons. You did not receive a spirit of slavery to fall back into fear. Instead, you received the Spirit of adoption, by whom we cry out, '*Abba*, Father!' The Spirit himself testifies together with our spirit that we are God's children, and if children, also heirs — heirs of God and coheirs with Christ — if indeed we suffer with him so that we may also be glorified with him" (Rom. 8:14-17).
- Places us into the body of Christ as members of the universal church. This is what's known as baptism in the Holy Spirit (see Chapter Eight). "For we were all baptized by one Spirit into one body — whether Jews or Greeks, whether slaves or free — and we were all given one Spirit to drink" (1 Cor. 12:13).
- Seals us, or stamps God's mark of ownership on us, as a guarantee of our salvation (see Chapter Eleven). "In him you also were sealed with the promised Holy Spirit when you heard the word of truth, the gospel of your salvation, and when you believed. The Holy Spirit is the

down payment of our inheritance, until the redemption of the possession, to the praise of his glory" (Eph. 1:13-14).

- Convicts us of our need to confess sins as they grieve Him. "And don't grieve God's Holy Spirit. You were sealed by him for the day of redemption" (Eph. 4:30). "If we confess our sins, he is faithful and righteous to forgive us our sins and to cleanse us from all unrighteousness" (1 John 1:9).
- Gives us spiritual gifts to use in service to Him. "A manifestation of the Spirit is given to each person for the common good ... One and the same Spirit is active in all these, distributing to each person as he wills" (1 Cor. 12:7, 11).
- Helps us understand the Bible, which He authored. "Now we have not received the spirit of the world, but the Spirit who comes from God, so that we may understand what has been freely given to us by God" (1 Cor. 2:12).
- Empowers our prayer life. "In the same way the Spirit also helps us in our weakness, because we do not know what to pray for as we should, but the Spirit himself intercedes for us with unspoken groanings. And he who searches our hearts knows the mind of the Spirit, because he intercedes for the saints according to the will of God" (Rom. 8:26-27).
- Enables us to overcome temptation. "I say then, walk by the Spirit and you will certainly not carry out the desire of the flesh" (Gal. 5:16).
- Produces evidence of His presence in our lives. "But the fruit of the Spirit is love, joy, peace, patience, kindness, goodness, faithfulness, gentleness, and self-control. The law is not against such things" (Gal. 5:22-23).

While the Holy Spirit is the personal presence of the Triune God in our lives, He does not force His will upon us. We continue to sin, which grieves Him and prompts Him to convict us of our need for regular confession and repentance. He urges us to read the Bible, pray, and witness. He comforts us in times of doubt, fear, and disappointment. And He reminds us of our irrevocable citizenship in God's kingdom, even when we sometimes act like vagrants. He works constantly to conform us to the image of Christ — that is, to make us more like Jesus. This is the work of sanctification, which we address in Chapter Nine.

KEY PASSAGES ON INDWELLING

Let's survey several Bible verses that address the indwelling of the Holy Spirit.

John 7:37-39 - "On the last and most important day of the festival [Feast of Tabernacles], Jesus stood up and cried out, 'If anyone is thirsty, let him come to me and drink. The one who believes in me, as the Scripture has said, will have streams of living water flow from deep within him.' He said this about the Spirit. Those who believed in Jesus were going to receive the Spirit, for the Spirit had not yet been given because Jesus had not yet been glorified."

The Feast of Tabernacles, or *Sukkot*, is the most festive of the seven feasts God gives Israel. It is mentioned more often in Scripture than any of the others. All Jewish males are required to come to Jerusalem for the seven-day festival. Throughout the week, families live in temporary shelters to remind them of God's provision during their forty years of wilderness wandering. This happy feast, also called Ingathering because it is observed after the fall crops are harvested, commemorates God's past provision in the desert and His present goodness.

On the final day of the feast, the temple water-pouring ceremony, *Hoshana-Rabbah*, takes on great significance. Jewish tradition holds that it is on this day that God decides whether there will be rain for the next year's crops. It is during this ceremony that Jesus stands up and shouts, "If anyone is thirsty, let him come to me and drink." The Jewish leaders are infuriated; some want to seize Him, but no one lays a hand on Him. A debate ensues among the people, many of whom do not realize, or refuse to believe, He is the Son of David, born in Bethlehem, the Messiah (John 7:40-44). The chief priests and the Pharisees rebuke the temple officers, who have the authority to arrest Jesus for disturbing the ceremony, but the officers reply, "No man ever spoke like this!" (v. 46).

The Gospel writer informs us that Jesus' words prefigure the coming of the Holy Spirit. We also learn several important truths: (1) Belief in Jesus is a prerequisite for receiving the indwelling Spirit; (2) the Spirit is like streams of living water — refreshing, invigorating, and satisfying us continuously; and (3) the Spirit's coming follows the return of the resurrected and glorified Jesus to the Father's right hand.

Jesus' invitation to "come and drink" harks back to Old Testament prophetic passages such as Isa. 55:1: "Come, everyone who is thirsty, come to the water; and you without silver, come, buy, and eat! Come, buy wine and milk without silver and without cost!" Chapter 55 of Isaiah is an invitation to God's people to experience His forgiveness. The reference to water, wine, and milk represent spiritual, as well as physical, nourishment, offered freely by God's grace to those who come to Him.

John 14:16-17 - "And I will ask the Father, and he will give you another Counselor to be with you forever. He is the Spirit of truth. The world is unable to receive him because it doesn't see him or know him. But you do know him, because he remains with you and will be in you (*estai en umin*)."

Jesus promises His disciples that God's presence remains perpetually with them. After His departure, He will send another "Counselor," rendered "Advocate" or "Comforter" in other translations. The "Spirit of truth" is *with* them now and will be *in* them.

"I will not leave you as orphans; I am coming to you," He assures them in verse 18, echoing the parting words of Moses to Israel: "Be strong and courageous; don't be terrified or afraid of them. For the Lord your God is the one who will go with you; he will not leave you or abandon you" (Deut. 31:6). Likely, Jesus has in mind His resurrection and the coming of the Spirit at Pentecost. Later, the writer of Hebrews recalls the message of Moses, offering assurance that the Lord is true to His word: "**I will never leave you or abandon you**" (Heb. 13:5).

The *CSB Study Bible* notes, "The Spirit replaces Jesus' physical presence by permanently indwelling his followers. Divine presence for

Jesus's followers includes the Spirit (14:15-17), Jesus (vv. 18-21), and the Father (vv. 22-24)."[4]

We should note that some early manuscripts of verse 17 say that the Spirit "is" already in the apostles, although most English translations prefer "will be" in them. Bruce Metzger writes, "A majority of the Committee interpreted the sense of the passage as requiring the future *estai* ..."[5]

CSB	KJV	NIV	NASB	ESV
Will be in you/ Is in you	Shall be in you	Will be in you/ Is in you	Will be in you	Will be in you / Is in you

Comparing English translations of *estai en umin* in John 14:17

Rom. 8:9 - "You, however, are not in the flesh, but in the Spirit, if indeed the Spirit of God lives in you (*oikei en umin*). If anyone does not have the Spirit of Christ, he does not belong to him."

We should consider two key truths in this verse. First, Paul reinforces what he writes elsewhere: The indwelling Holy Spirit is the undeniable mark of every true believer. If we have the Holy Spirit taking up residence in our bodies, we are children of God; if not, we are still dead in our sins. Second, Paul notes the intimacy and equality that exist among the persons of the Godhead. To have the Holy Spirit is to have the "Spirit of God" (the Father is implied) as well as the "Spirit of Christ."

Additionally, Paul reminds us that if the Spirit of God lives in us, we are "in the Spirit" as opposed to being "in the flesh." This is a positional statement. No doubt, believers often give in to the desires of the flesh and fall prey to behaviors that grieve the heart of God, necessitating divine discipline. Paul acknowledges his own struggles between the flesh and the law of God — a raging internal battle that prompts him to cry, "What a wretched man I am! Who will rescue me from this body of death?" (Rom. 7:24).

He then answers his own question: "Thanks be to God through Jesus Christ our Lord! So then, with my mind I myself am serving the law of God, but with my flesh, the law of sin" (Rom. 7:24-25). He follows this immediately with a declaration that his position "in Christ

Jesus" ensures his future glory: "Therefore, there is now no condemnation for those in Christ Jesus, because the law of the Spirit of life in Christ Jesus has set you free from the law of sin and death" (Rom. 8:1-2).

Being "in Christ Jesus" is a reflection of the eternal intimacy that exists among the persons of the Godhead. Throughout Scripture, we see the Father, Son, and Holy Spirit in perfect harmony and singleness of mind, working together in creation, providence, and redemption. For example, Jesus tells the Jews who surround Him and demand to know if He is the Messiah, "I and the Father are one" (John 10:30). When they pick up rocks to stone Him for blasphemy, Jesus responds, "If I am not doing my Father's works, don't believe me. But if I am doing them and you don't believe me, believe the works. This way you will know and understand that *the Father is in me and I in the Father*" (vv. 37-38, emphasis added).

Later, when Philip asks Jesus to "show us the Father," Jesus replies, "The one who has seen me has seen the Father. How can you say, 'Show us the Father'? Don't you believe that *I am in the Father and the Father is in me*?" (John 14:8-10, emphasis added). Jesus then offers further assurance, "On that day [likely a reference to Pentecost] you will know that *I am in my Father, you are in me, and I am in you*" (v. 20, emphasis added).

The presence of the Holy Spirit in the heart of believers enables us to "share in the divine nature" (2 Peter 1:4). This does not mean we become little gods, but that we enjoy unbreakable fellowship with the Triune God and participate in His moral excellence.

Equally important, being "in the Spirit" means the Spirit produces fruit in our lives consistent with the character of God: love, joy, peace, patience, kindness, goodness, faithfulness, gentleness, and self-control (Gal. 5:22-23). This work of the Spirit in us stands in stark contrast to the works of the flesh, which reveal the true nature of unbelievers. Among these works are sexual immorality, moral impurity, promiscuity, idolatry, sorcery, hatreds, strife, jealousy, outbursts of anger, selfish ambitions, dissensions, factions, envy, drunkenness, carousing, and so on. Paul makes it clear that those who habitually engage in these behaviors will not inherit the kingdom of God (Gal. 5:19-21).

CSB	KJV	NIV	NASB	ESV
Lives in you	Dwell in you	Lives in you	Dwells in you	Dwells in you

Comparing English translations of *oikei en umin* in Rom. 8:9

1 Cor. 3:16-17 - "Don't you yourselves know that you are God's temple and that the Spirit of God lives in you (*oikei en umin*)? If anyone destroys God's temple, God will destroy him; for God's temple is holy, and that is what you are."

This passage may have both personal and corporate applications. No doubt, God's dwelling place under the new covenant is in the bodies of Jesus' followers, as Paul makes explicit in 1 Cor. 6:19, where he writes, "Don't you know that your body is a temple of the Holy Spirit who is in you ...?" Just as faithful Israelites under the old covenant would be careful not to defile the temple in Jerusalem, believers under the new covenant are to consider our bodies as God's residence, and to keep His dwelling place pure.

At the same time, Paul is writing to the church at Corinth, a city notorious for its idolatry and sensual pleasures. Many believers have come out of this lifestyle, as Paul acknowledges. "And some of you used to be like this," he writes (1 Cor. 6:11). Now, he urges them to be mindful of the ultimate identity of their corporate body. Together, believers are a temple that God has built, and in whom the Spirit resides.

Peter makes a similar statement as he implores his readers to rid themselves of "all malice, all deceit, hypocrisy, envy, and all slander" (1 Peter 2:1). He goes on to refer to followers of Jesus as "living stones, a spiritual house ... being built to be a holy priesthood to offer spiritual sacrifices acceptable to God through Jesus Christ" (v. 5).

It's a sobering reminder that our individual conduct may cast shadows on the reputation of the body of Christ, His church.

CSB	KJV	NIV	NASB	ESV
Lives in you	Dwelleth in you	Dwells in your midst	Dwells in you	Dwells in you

Comparing English translations of *oikei en umin* in 1 Cor. 3:16

1 Cor. 6:19-20 - "Don't you know that your body is a temple of the Holy Spirit who is in you, whom you have from God? You are not your own, for you were bought at a price. So glorify God with your body."

Paul notes that sexual immorality is unique in that it is sin against a person's own body (v. 18). It defiles the temple of the Holy Spirit, who resides permanently in the innermost sanctum of a believer's body. Just as sexual misconduct dishonors the sanctity of God's intention for men and women, who are to engage only in sexual relations within the confines of monogamous, lifelong, heterosexual marriage, it also sullies the wedding covenant we have entered into with Christ, our Bridegroom. He has courted us, and we have accepted His marriage proposal. And now, during our engagement period, as we await His glorious coming, we are to remain "a pure virgin to Christ" (2 Cor. 11:2).

As the *CSB Study Bible* observes, "The point is that the believer's body is a sacred vessel, bought at a price by the Son of God. Believers thus have no business doing anything with the Lord's body that does not glorify him."[6] Paul's reference to us as being "bought at a price" directs us back to the cross, where the one who did not know sin became sin for us, so that in Him we might become the righteousness of God (2 Cor. 5:21).

The Lord redeemed us; that is, He purchased us out of the slave market of sin, adopted us as children, and made us joint heirs with Jesus. This came at the incalculable cost of His Son's blood, as Peter reminds us, "For you know that you were redeemed from your empty way of life inherited from your fathers, not with perishable things like silver or gold, but with the precious blood of Christ, like that of an unblemished and spotless lamb" (1 Peter 1:18-19).

In a message on 1 Cor. 6:19-20, Charles Spurgeon said, "That the blood of Christ was shed to buy our souls from death and hell is a wonder of compassion which fills angels with amazement, and it ought to overwhelm us with adoring love whenever we think of it, glance our eye over the recording pages, or even utter the word 'redemption.'"[7]

Col. 1:27 - "God wanted to make known among the Gentiles the glorious wealth of this mystery, which is Christ in you, the hope of glory."

Jesus has promised not to leave His disciples as orphans. "I am coming to you," He assures them in John 14:18. He has asked the Father, who has granted that another Counselor, the Spirit of truth, be sent to them. In a very real sense, just as the entire fullness of God's nature dwells *bodily* in Jesus (Col. 2:9), the completeness of deity rests *mysteriously* in the Holy Spirit, so that the Father's promise never to leave us, and the Son's promise to come to us, are both fulfilled in the indwelling Holy Spirit.

Paul writes that this is good news for Gentiles as well as Jews. The same Holy Spirit who fills Jewish believers on the Day of Pentecost (Acts 2) is poured out on Cornelius and his household, who are Gentiles (Acts 10), and finally comes upon the disciples of John the Baptist (Acts 19). This is the permanent presence of the Triune God in the hearts of all believers. This Spirit, who distinguishes the true body of Christ (Rom. 8:9), is for all who receive Jesus by faith. Paul writes to the Galatians, "There is no Jew or Greek, slave or free, male and female; since you are all one in Christ Jesus. And if you belong to Christ, then you are Abraham's seed, heirs according to the promise" (Gal. 3:28-29).

Paul often repeats the theme of "Christ in you" throughout his epistles (see Rom. 8:10; 2 Cor. 13:5; Gal. 4:19; Eph. 3:17). But in Col. 1:27, he makes it known that part of his mission as apostle to the Gentiles is to reveal that the indwelling Christ is "the hope of glory." Followers of Jesus are to live in the light of eternity. The Lamb of God is returning one day as the Lion of the tribe of Judah — a glorious, personal, physical return during which He resurrects and perfects our bodies and sets all things right.

As Paul writes in Rom. 8:18, "For I consider that the sufferings of this present time are not worth comparing with the glory that is going to be revealed to us." And he adds in 2 Cor. 4:17, "For our momentary light affliction is producing for us an absolutely incomparable eternal weight of glory."

1 John 4:15 - "Whoever confesses that Jesus is the Son of God — God remains in him (*ho theos menei en auto*) and he in God."

The apostle John uses "remain" or "remains" six times in verses 12-16. In God's self-revelation in creation, conscience, Christ, and the canon of Scripture, He does many wonderful works *for* us. But after we place our faith in Jesus, He does something truly unique *in* us, taking up permanent residence in our spirits by means of the Holy Spirit. God "remains in us" and we "remain in him" (vv. 12-13). All of this flows from His limitless love for us, which we are to enjoy, return, and share with one another.

John has just finished imploring his readers to "test the spirits to see if they are from God" (v. 1). False prophets — likely Docetists, who affirm the deity of Christ but deny His humanity — have infiltrated the first-century church. John calls them spirits of the antichrist, for by denying the humanity of Jesus, they negate His suffering and death on the cross, His burial, and His bodily resurrection, without which there is no gospel. His rebuke of the false prophets is sharp, and his words of exhortation to followers of Jesus are strong.

Then, without skipping a beat, he emphasizes love as essential for knowing God (vv. 7-16). John ends the chapter with these words: "If anyone says, 'I love God,' and yet hates his brother or sister, he is a liar. For the person who does not love his brother or sister whom he has seen cannot love God whom he has not seen. And we have this command from him: The one who loves God must also love his brother and sister" (vv. 20-21).

Warren Wiersbe writes, "'God is love,' then, is not simply a profound biblical statement. It is the basis for a believer's relationship with God and with his fellowman. Because God is love, *we* can love. His love is not past history; it is present reality. 'Love one another' begins as *a commandment* (1 John 4:7), then it becomes *a privilege* (1 John 4:11). But it is more than a commandment or a privilege. It is also the thrilling *consequence* and evidence of our abiding in Christ (1 John 4:12). Loving one another is not something we simply *ought* to do; it is something we *want* to do."[8]

CSB	KJV	NIV	NASB	ESV
God remains in him	God dwelleth in him	God lives in them	God abides in him	God abides in him

Comparing English translations of *ho theos menei en auto* in 1 John 4:15

WERE OLD TESTAMENT SAINTS INDWELT?

Was the coming of the Holy Spirit on the Day of Pentecost a watershed event in which the Spirit, for the first time, permanently indwelt believers? Or did Old Testament saints experience the indwelling as well?

The Old Testament clearly says that some people had the Spirit (e.g., Num. 27:18), but it isn't clear that this was the experience for every participant under the old covenant. In contrast, the New Testament teaches that the Spirit indwells *all* believers. In fact, His presence in the spirit of every believer is the distinguishing mark of the true church (Rom. 8:9-11).

There are many and varied positions on the question of whether believers under the old covenant were indwelt. James Hamilton identifies six views, ranging from "complete continuity," which posits that old-covenant believers were both regenerated and indwelt by the Holy Spirit, to "complete discontinuity," which holds that the Spirit had nothing at all to do with the faithfulness of those under the old covenant.[9]

It may help our understanding to distinguish between regeneration and indwelling. They are related, but not identical, works of God. As we learned in Chapter Five, regeneration is the work of the Holy Spirit, bringing a sinner from spiritual death into spiritual life. It is a one-time, non-repeatable act. In comparison, indwelling is the ongoing presence of the Spirit in the hearts of believers in Jesus Christ. Indwelling is a permanent and continuous action by the Spirit in the believer's human spirit. Regeneration brings new life to sinners, while indwelling sustains that life forever and ensures that God completes the work of redemption He has begun in us (Phil. 1:6).

John's Gospel is helpful in addressing the issue of the Spirit's indwelling in Old Testament vs. New Testament saints. Certain statements in this Gospel suggest that believers would not be indwelt by the Spirit until Jesus was glorified. Consider:

John 7:38-39 - "'The one who believes in me, as the Scripture has said, will have streams of living water flow from deep within him.' He said this about the Spirit. Those who believed in Jesus were going to receive the Spirit, for the Spirit had not yet been given because Jesus had not yet been glorified."

John 14:16-17 - "And I will ask the Father, and he will give you another Counselor to be with you forever. He is the Spirit of truth. The world is unable to receive him because it doesn't see him or know him. But you do know him, because he remains with you and will be in you."

John 16:7 - "Nevertheless, I am telling you the truth. It is for your benefit that I go away, because if I don't go away the Counselor will not come to you. If I go, I will send him to you."

Commenting on Jesus' statement in John 14:17 — "he remains with you and will be in you" — James Hamilton writes, "Here Jesus encapsulates the Bible's teaching on God's dwelling in relation to believers in the old and new covenants. In the old covenant God faithfully remained *with* His people, accompanying them in a pillar of fire and cloud, then dwelling among them in the tabernacle and temple. Under the new covenant, the only temple is the believing community itself, and God dwells not only among the community corporately (Matt. 18:20; 1 Cor. 3:16; 2 Cor. 6:16), but also *in* each member individually (John 14:17; Rom. 8:9-11; 1 Cor. 6:19)."[10]

Further, it appears that John's Gospel teaches that the continual indwelling of the Holy Spirit begins only after Jesus completes the work the Father gave Him to do (John 17:4). In other words, once Jesus ascends into heaven and sits down at the Father's right hand, the indwelling ministry of the Spirit begins.

It seems best to conclude that old covenant believers experience the Holy Spirit in some way. Perhaps even they are regenerated. But they are not indwelt. That is, the Spirit's permanent residence in the hearts of believers is a distinguishing feature of the new covenant. Keep in mind that Jesus tells Nicodemus a person must be born again, or born from above, in order to see the kingdom of God, let alone enter it (John 3:3, 5-7). Jesus speaks of regeneration to a Jewish religious leader under the old covenant, and the necessity of new birth doesn't change under the new covenant.

So, if Old Testament saints could be "born again" but not indwelt, what is the Spirit's ministry to them? The focus seems to be on God's presence with the nation of Israel, not with individual covenant members permanently possessing the Spirit. Even so, the Spirit is at work, empowering individual leaders for service but not permanently indwelling them. "In the Old Testament, it was primarily the mediators of God's covenant — political leaders and prophets — who experienced the Spirit on an individual basis.... in every instance the Spirit's presence *distinguishes* a person from the rest of the nation and thereby qualifies him for his function as an advocate for God's kingdom."[11]

Some leaders, like Joshua, are said to have the Lord's Spirit in them (Num. 27:18). However, it does not seem the Spirit's presence is necessarily permanent, but rather for empowerment for service. For example, consider the confession of Moses that he cannot bear the burden of the nation alone (Num. 11:14). Yahweh tells Moses to select seventy elders. Then, He promises to "take some of the Spirit who is on you and put the Spirit on them" (vv. 16-17).

Or consider King Saul. The Spirit of the Lord comes powerfully on Saul, and he prophesies (1 Sam. 10:6, 10). But later, the Spirit departs from Saul when Samuel anoints David as king. Now, the Spirit comes powerfully on David (1 Sam. 16:13-14). In fact, the Spirit not only flees Saul, but God sends an evil spirit to torment him — a maddening frame of mind that Israel's future king, David, soothes with music (1 Sam. 16:23; 18:10). It's important to note that even though the Spirit leaves Saul, the king does not lose his salvation. That's made clear when Samuel, in a rare post-mortem appearance, assures Saul that after death, Saul and his sons will be with Samuel in *Sheol* (1 Sam. 28:19).

The Spirit also rushes upon prophets to empower them to deliver messages. A curious example of this is Balaam, son of Beor. The Spirit comes on Balaam (Num. 24:2), enabling him only to bless Israel, although Balak, king of Moab, has hired Balaam to curse Yahweh's people. It appears this false prophet-for-hire is never regenerated, for he dies making war on the people of God (Num. 31:8), and the New

Testament writer, Jude, condemns him, along with first-century false teachers, as people who "create divisions and are worldly, not having the Spirit" (Jude 19).

Meanwhile, the prophet Joel speaks of an experience that is not occurring in his day. The Lord declares through the prophet, "After this I will pour out my Spirit on all humanity; then your sons and your daughters will prophesy, your old men will have dreams, and your young men will see visions" (Joel 2:28). It seems likely he is pointing to the fulfillment of Moses' wish that Yahweh would put His Spirit on all people (Num. 11:29) — a wish Peter declares fulfilled on the Day of Pentecost as the Spirit permanently indwells followers of Jesus (Acts 2:14ff.).

Last, when we look at David's cry to the Lord in Psalm 51:11 — "Do not banish me from your presence or take your Holy Spirit from me" — he is not addressing the issue of indwelling but of empowerment for service as Israel's God-anointed leader. As the Spirit comes powerfully on David at the time of his anointing (1 Sam. 16:13), David also knows the Spirit may be withdrawn, as He was from Saul. As a man after God's own heart, David makes no excuses for his sin. He cries out to God in humility and repentance, imploring the Spirit to enable him to continue his call to service.

Other examples could be cited, but the point is that the Spirit temporarily empowers certain Old Testament leaders for service without permanently indwelling them. He comes for a time on His servants but makes no guarantees of remaining with the unfaithful. The indwelling is reserved for new covenant believers who, receiving the Holy Spirit, are sealed, sanctified, and given spiritual gifts that remain throughout their earthly lives.

ARE INDWELLING AND FILLING THE SAME THING?

Let's address one final question about indwelling: Are the Holy Spirit's ministries of indwelling and filling the same thing? Like regeneration and indwelling, there is a relationship between indwelling and filling, although they are not synonymous terms. Persons must be indwelt by the Spirit in order to be filled. In other words, they must be born-again (regenerated) followers of Jesus and possess the indwelling

Spirit. At the same time, being indwelt by the Spirit is no guarantee of filling.[12] Unlike regeneration and indwelling, the filling with the Holy Spirit is temporary, conditional, and repeatable. Further, it is a command for all believers.

The apostle Paul writes to the Ephesians, "And don't get drunk with wine, which leads to reckless living, but be filled by the Spirit: speaking to one another in psalms, hymns, and spiritual songs, singing and making music with your heart to the Lord, giving thanks always for everything to God the Father in the name of our Lord Jesus Christ, submitting to one another in the fear of Christ" (Eph. 5:18-21).

Paul's commands are plural, meaning they refer not only to individuals, but to the entire community of faith. Just as getting drunk requires a decision to drink to excess, and results in rash behavior, being filled with the Spirit requires us to "understand what the Lord's will is" (v. 17), leading to obedient acts of worship, praise, fellowship, and service.

While we are commanded to be filled with the Spirit, we are never explicitly told how, nor are we ever commanded in Scripture to ask for the filling of the Spirit. The verb *plerousthe* ("filled") in Eph. 5:18 is in the passive voice, meaning that the Spirit acts on us. Still, we play a part as we obey and yield to the Lord. Paul's message may be translated, "Be you continuously filled," bringing together a command and a call to lifelong vigilance.

Put simply, it does no good to pray for the Spirit's filling when the heart is in rebellion. But filling comes naturally — or perhaps we should say, supernaturally — as we walk in obedience to God's will as revealed in Scripture and respond to the inner call of the indwelling Spirit.

Robert Gromacki writes, "Although a believer may consciously yield himself to the Holy Spirit for the first time in a crisis experience, that act of submission must be repeated daily. It is possible to be filled with the Spirit on Sunday and not be filled on Monday. Each Christian must ask himself or herself, 'Am I at this moment spiritually clean and submissive to the leadership of the Spirit?'"[13]

The Bible speaks of filling in many different ways. In each case, the context makes it clear that the writer refers to a temporary condition. For example, a wedding banquet hall is filled with guests (Matt.

22:10). A sponge is filled with sour wine (Matt. 27:48). And boats are filled with fish (Luke 5:7). In addition, people are filled with awe (Luke 5:26), rage (Luke 6:11), jealousy (Acts 13:45), and confusion (Acts 19:29).

The same verb forms are used to describe people filled with the Spirit. Note the difference between the filling of banquet halls, sponges, and boats by *external* sources or circumstances, and the filling of the Holy Spirit, which is generated *internally*:

- Zechariah is told that his future son, John the Baptist, will be "filled with the Holy Spirit while still in his mother's womb" (Luke 1:15). Later, as the unborn child leaps for joy while his mother receives word of the coming Messiah, Elizabeth is "filled with the Holy Spirit" (Luke 1:41).
- Zechariah is "filled with the Holy Spirit" and prophesies on the day of John the Baptist's circumcision (Luke 1:67-79).
- Believing Jews on the Day of Pentecost are all "filled with the Holy Spirit" and begin speaking in different languages (Acts. 2:4).
- Standing before Caiaphas and the other members of the high-priestly family, Peter is "filled with the Holy Spirit" and speaks boldly about the name of Jesus (Acts 4:8-12).
- After Peter and John are released from the Sanhedrin, they gather with fellow believers and pray for boldness to witness. When they finish praying, the place where they assemble is shaken, and they are all "filled with the Holy Spirit" and begin to speak the Word of God boldly (Acts 4:31).
- Ananias lays hands on Saul and tells him the Lord Jesus has sent him so that Saul may regain his sight and be "filled with the Holy Spirit" (Acts 9:17).
- Paul, "filled with the Holy Spirit," tells the sorcerer Elymas that God is going to strike him with blindness, which immediately takes place, leading to the conversion of Sergius Paulus, a proconsul who has heard the gospel proclaimed (Acts 13:8-12).

In none of these cases does the person filled with the Spirit stop and pray for the filling, or fast for a period of time, or engage in rituals. The Holy Spirit simply fills the open heart — even the heart of an unborn child — and produces His fruit: joy, praise, a prophetic word, a bold witness, a miraculous work.

It should be noted that in the examples of Zechariah and Elizabeth in Luke 1, the Holy Spirit fills devout Jews long before the Day of Pentecost. Further, John the Baptist is filled with the Spirit while still in his mother's womb. These instances of filling may be likened to the work of the Spirit in the Old Testament illustrations cited earlier as the Spirit temporarily empowers God's chosen vessels for service.

While the New Testament does not give Christians step-by-step instructions for being filled with the Spirit, it does offer three commands involving the Spirit that seem related to His work of filling. At their core are an understanding of God's Word and an obedient response. Consider what we are to do and not do:

1. **Walk by the Spirit.** Paul tells the Galatians, "I say then, walk by the Spirit and you will certainly not carry out the desire of the flesh" (Gal. 5:16). This imperative is in the present tense. We are to "keep on walking" by, or in, the Spirit. This enables us to avoid giving in to the lusts of the flesh. Believers can't walk both paths at the same time, any more than a spring can pour out both sweet and bitter water, or a fig tree can produce olives (see James 3:9-12).

2. **Don't grieve the Spirit.** To the Ephesians, Paul writes, "And don't grieve God's Holy Spirit. You were sealed by him for the day of redemption" (Eph. 4:30). The Greek verb translated "grieve" is *lypeo* and means "to feel sorrow or pain." Evidently, we cause the third person of the Trinity anguish when we sin deliberately. In the previous verses, Paul warns against lying, anger, stealing, and foul language, reminding us that these sins often are premeditated and are always defiant acts of the will, which cause the Holy Spirit very real and personal grief. In 1 Cor. 10:13, Paul reminds us that when we are tempted to sin, our faithful God always provides "a way out."

3. **Don't quench the Spirit.** In one of the shortest verses in the Bible, Paul simply tells us, "Don't stifle the Spirit" (1 Thess. 5:19). Various forms of the verb *sbennymi*, which literally means "to quench," are found throughout the New Testament. For example, the foolish virgins ask their wise counterparts for oil because their lamps are *going out* (Matt. 25:8, emphasis added). Jesus describes hell as a place where "the fire is not *quenched*" (Mark 9:48, emphasis added). And Paul assures us that the shield of faith can *extinguish* all the flaming arrows of the evil one (Eph. 6:16, emphasis added). So, perhaps Paul, in saying, "Don't stifle the Spirit," is urging us to do nothing that dampens the purifying and empowering work of the Holy Spirit in our lives.

Indwelling and filling are not the same, but they are related ministries of the Holy Spirit that apply only to believers. To be indwelt is to have the Spirit dwelling permanently in our hearts. To be filled is to be under the unbridled control of the Spirit, which produces the fruit of the Spirit: love, joy, peace, patience, kindness, goodness, faithfulness, gentleness, and self-control (Gal. 5:22-23).

SUMMARY

Followers of Jesus may take comfort in knowing that the Holy Spirit indwells us. That is, the third person of the Triune Godhead has taken up permanent residence in our human spirits, from which He engages in the lifelong ministry of conforming us to the image of Jesus Christ. While regeneration is the work of the Holy Spirit that brings a sinner from spiritual death to spiritual life, indwelling is the continuous presence of the Spirit in the believer's life.

Without the Spirit's continuous abiding in our hearts, we could have no assurance of salvation, no soothing balm in times we are hurting and seemingly alone, no unbroken protection against the Devil's false claims of ownership, no spiritual growth, and no means by which both the Father and Jesus keep their promise to abide in us forever.

It may be rightly said that the Spirit's residence in our hearts is purchased, not rented. We are bought with a price — the redemptive work of Christ (1 Cor. 6:20; 7:23) — and we belong to the One who has promised that the Spirit abides with us forever (John 14:16).

Consider these summary statements about indwelling:

- Indwelling is an act of God in which the Holy Spirit takes up permanent residence in the bodies of believers in Jesus Christ. Specifically, indwelling occurs in the human spirit, the innermost part of us that God created as His dwelling place.
- Perhaps the best way to understand the indwelling of the Spirit is in terms of Christians replacing the temple in Jerusalem as God's dwelling place. On the Day of Pentecost, not long after Jesus returns to the Father's right hand, the glory of Yahweh returns powerfully as the Holy Spirit falls on Jesus' disciples and permanently indwells His new temple — the temple of their bodies.
- The Holy Spirit is a gift of the Father and Son to *all* believers, not just to some; to not possess the Spirit indicates an unsaved condition. Further, the Spirit continues to indwell us, even when we sin, although our sin grieves Him. The security of the believer and the permanent indwelling of the Spirit are inseparable doctrines. And the Spirit's intimate presence motivates followers of Jesus to holy living.
- The Spirit produces many life-changing results in us. He confirms our adoption as children of God; places us into the body of Christ as members of the universal church; seals us; convicts us of our need to confess sins; grants us spiritual gifts for service; helps us understand the Bible, which He authored; empowers our prayer life; enables us to overcome temptation; and produces evidence of His presence in our lives.
- Regeneration brings new life to sinners, while indwelling sustains that life forever and ensures that God completes the work of redemption He has begun in us.

- There is a relationship between indwelling and filling with the Spirit, but they are not the same thing. Indwelling occurs continuously and is permanent. Filling, however, is temporary, conditional, and repeatable. Further, it is a command for all believers.

THINK
Questions for personal or group study

(1) Numerous Old and New Testament passages refer to the "Spirit of God" (e.g., Gen. 1:2; Ex. 31:3; Matt. 3:16; 1 Cor. 2:11; 2 Cor. 3:3; 1 Peter 4:14). Look up these passages and consider: How is the Holy Spirit a person distinct from the Father and the Son, yet of the same divine nature?

(2) How are regeneration, indwelling, and filling related works of the Holy Spirit? In what ways may they be distinguished? Check the boxes below that correspond to the manner in which each of these works of the Spirit is applied to a believer's life.

MINISTRY	ONE-TIME	CONTINUOUS	PERMANENT	REPEATABLE
Regeneration				
Indwelling				
Filling				

(3) Why is it important to understand the *permanence* of the Holy Spirit's presence in believers' spirits? If the indwelling of the Spirit is temporary, what impact does that have on the other salvific works of the Spirit: the inward call, regeneration, filling, sealing, sanctification, the endowment of spiritual gifts, and so on?

(4) If the Holy Spirit truly resides permanently in the temples of our bodies, why do we continue to sin as children of God? Why aren't we immediately made perfect the moment He enters our hearts? Do you think it's possible, with much prayer and effort, to become sinless as a follower of Jesus in our earthly lives? Why or why not?

(5) Why is the Day of Pentecost a watershed event in the ministry

of the Holy Spirit? What happened on that day that differentiates followers of Jesus from Old Testament saints?

(6) The Bible commands us to be filled with the Holy Spirit, yet it doesn't tell us *how*. Even so, there are three New Testament commands involving the Spirit that seem related to the Spirit's filling. Look up the following passages and identify the commands:

- Gal. 5:16
- Eph. 4:30
- 1 Thess. 5:19

(7) The indwelling Spirit produces many life-changing results in us. What are these divine benefits, according to the following passages of Scripture:

- Rom. 8:14-17
- Rom. 8:26-27
- 1 Cor. 2:12
- 1 Cor. 12:7, 11
- 1 Cor. 12:13
- Gal. 5:16
- Gal. 5:22-23
- Eph. 1:13-14

Chapter Eight

YOU ARE BAPTIZED IN THE SPIRIT

The men of Pentecost Island in the South-Pacific archipelago known as Vanuatu engage in a daring rite of passage. They climb a rickety ninety-eight-foot-tall tower, tie vines to their ankles, and dive toward the ground at speeds reaching forty-five miles per hour. When their dives go according to plan, they get close enough to touch the ground with their shoulders or heads. But a slight miscalculation may result in cracked skulls, busted bones, or even death. Boys as young as seven years of age may participate, but from shorter towers. When youngsters engage in their first dives, their mothers hold items representing their childhood, and then throw the items away, signifying passage into manhood.[1]

"Land diving" is one of many rites of initiation practiced around the world. Like cow-jumping by men of the Hamar tribe in Ethiopia, which confirms their worthiness to marry, or teeth-sharpening by young women of the Mentawai Islands, which beautifies them so their souls remain satisfied, such rites demonstrate a person's quest for worthiness.

Similarly, many of the world's major religions feature important ceremonies that confirm believers' sincerity or earn divine favors for them. Examples include the Hindu practice of *sati*, in which a recently widowed woman immolates herself on her husband's funeral pyre, thus becoming a deity (a practice now banned by the Indian government); the Muslim *hajj*, or pilgrimage to Mecca, one of the five pillars of Islam; and the Mormon rite of baptism for the dead, which qualifies certain deceased persons to enter the celestial kingdom.

Christianity has a rite of passage as well — a work that confirms divine acceptance and ensures a place in the community of believers. It is baptism in the Holy Spirit. What makes this initiation so unique is that God Himself conducts it — unseen, silently, supernaturally — as a work of grace. Believing sinners are instantaneously declared righteous before God in justification (Chapter Six), indwelt by the Holy Spirit (Chapter Seven), and placed positionally into the body of Christ in Spirit baptism.

This is not an earned benefit. Believers make no pilgrimages, perform no ceremonies, and run no risk of bodily harm to prove themselves worthy. They simply believe on the Lord Jesus Christ, and His Spirit brings them into unbreakable fellowship with all other followers of Jesus via the miracle of Spirit baptism. Although there is much misunderstanding about this divine work, and much disagreement among Evangelical Christians as to its meaning and visible proof, it is biblically faithful for the follower of Jesus to say, "I am baptized in the Holy Spirit."

WHAT DOES IT MEAN TO BE BAPTIZED IN THE SPIRIT?

The baptism in the Holy Spirit is the means by which God places new believers into the body of Christ. Just as water baptism is the immersion of professing Christians into water — symbolizing the death, burial, and resurrection of Christ, and signifying new believers' identification with Christ in the death of their old lives and resurrection into new life — Spirit baptism is the placing of new believers, positionally, into the universal church.

When we talk about baptism *in* the Spirit, we should note that the Greek work *en* may be rendered "in," "by," "of," or "with." Many modern English versions use footnotes to indicate the nuances in translation. The meaning, however, is the same: As the Holy Spirit regenerates and indwells our human spirits, bringing us new life and ensuring our everlasting fellowship with God, the Spirit also immerses us into the invisible church. New believers share the common bond of the indwelling Spirit with every other person around the world who has been born of the Spirit (see Rom. 8:9). All followers of Jesus are given "one Spirit to drink" (1 Cor. 12:13), regardless of our denominational affiliation, language, nationality, ethnicity, or culture. We truly are the recipients of "one baptism" (Eph. 4:5).

Charles Stanley defines baptism in the Holy Spirit simply as, "The initial coming of the Holy Spirit into the hearts of believers."[2] He notes that Jesus does not speak about the baptism in the Holy Spirit until He prepares to ascend into heaven. In John 14:16-17, just before His arrest, Jesus promises to send the Spirit: "And I will ask the Father, and he will give you another Counselor to be with you forever. He is the Spirit of truth. The world is unable to receive him because it doesn't see him or know him. But you do know him, because he remains with you and will be in you."

Then, after His resurrection, Jesus meets again with His disciples. Luke records, "While he [Jesus] was with them, he commanded them not to leave Jerusalem, but to wait for the Father's promise, 'Which,' he said, 'you have heard me speak about; for John baptized with water, but you will be baptized with the Holy Spirit in a few days'" (Acts 1:4-5). Jesus equates baptism in the Holy Spirit with the "Father's promise" and links it back to His conversation with His disciples in John 14, where He assured them He will ask the Father, who will send the Spirit. Stanley writes, "Jesus was describing the baptism of the Spirit. He didn't use the exact phrase. But His comments in Acts 1:5 link these two discussions. He was not talking about two different events — the coming of the Holy Spirit (John 14) and the baptism of the Spirit (Acts 1:5). They are identical."[3]

Seven passages in the New Testament speak of someone being baptized in the Holy Spirit. We explore these in more detail shortly, but it should be noted that in the first four references (Matt. 3:11; Mark 1:8; Luke 3:16; John 1:33), John the Baptist is speaking of Jesus and declaring that He *will* baptize people in the Spirit. The next two passages (Acts 1:5; 11:16) refer directly to the Day of Pentecost, when Spirit baptism takes place. And the seventh verse (1 Cor. 12:13) comes from the pen of Paul, who reminds believers that we *were* all baptized by one Spirit into one body. So, something dramatic happens at Pentecost, just as Jesus predicts and Peter affirms (Acts 11:16). Yet, the work of the Spirit at Pentecost continues, as He keeps on baptizing new believers into the church.

Even so, when the Day of Pentecost comes, Luke does not use the phrase "baptized" to describe the miraculous work of the Spirit. He writes that the disciples "were all *filled* with the Holy Spirit" (Acts 2:4, emphasis added). Later, Peter and John lay hands on new Samaritan believers and they "*received* the Holy Spirit" (Acts 8:17, emphasis added). Then, as Peter preaches to Cornelius and his household, "the Holy Spirit *came down* on all those who heard the message" (Acts 10:44, emphasis added). Finally, as Paul shares the gospel with disciples of John the Baptist in Ephesus, "the Holy Spirit *came* on them" (Acts 19:6, emphasis added).

What's happening here? Are new believers baptized? Filled? Recipients of the Holy Spirit? In a word, yes. They are all of the above. Not that these terms are synonymous, but simultaneous. Since the Day of Pentecost, when the promise of the Father is fulfilled and the Holy Spirit is given as the permanent, indwelling presence of God in the spirit of every believer, various terms are used to describe the Spirit's work. Spirit baptism is that rite of initiation whereby the Spirit places us into the body of Christ (the universal church). New believers also "receive" the indwelling Spirit, who "comes down" (or "falls") on them and takes up residence in their spirits. And the Spirit "fills" new believers, although Paul later commands all Christians to be filled with the Spirit, an indication that filling, unlike indwelling and Spirit baptism, is not permanent (Eph. 5:18).

It should be noted that when believers are filled with the Spirit, amazing things happen, indicating that the filling of the Spirit is empowerment for service. For example, those who are filled speak in human languages they haven't learned (Acts 2:4; 10:46; 19:6). They prophesy (Acts 2:14-36; 4:8-12; 19:6). They speak the Word of God boldly (Acts 4:31). They are appointed as deacons (Acts 6:3-5). They are sent out to confirm the faith of many (Acts 11:24). They are chosen as God's spokespersons (Acts 9:17). They perform miracles

(Acts 13:9-12). They receive visions of heaven (Acts 7:55). And they are joyful (Acts 13:52).

So, just as water baptism is a one-time, non-repeatable act in which new believers publicly profess their identification with Jesus in His death, burial, and resurrection, Spirit baptism is a one-time, non-repeatable act in which He immerses believers into the fellowship of all other followers of Jesus, who are members of the universal church. The Spirit also regenerates, indwells, seals, sanctifies, fills, comforts, convicts, grants spiritual gifts, and does much more over the lifetimes of Christians.

WHEN DOES SPIRIT BAPTISM OCCUR?

Baptism in the Holy Spirit occurs in concert with regeneration and indwelling, perhaps simultaneously but not necessarily so. Recall from previous chapters that regeneration is a work of the Holy Spirit, imparting spiritual life to us when we were dead in trespasses and sins (Eph. 2:1). Indwelling is the Spirit taking up permanent residence in our regenerated human spirits. And baptism in the Spirit is the work whereby we are placed positionally into the body of Christ.

Every follower of Jesus has been born again (regenerated), indwelt, and baptized in the Spirit. John Frame writes that "the baptism of the Spirit includes *all* believers. In fact, the baptism of the Spirit is what makes us one body. Without the baptism, we are not part of the body of Christ. So everyone in the body has been baptized in the Spirit.... In the baptism of the Spirit, the Spirit comes on us with power to serve Jesus as his covenant people. He unites us to all the other people in his body, so that together with them we may do God's work in the world."[4]

ARE THERE MULTIPLE SPIRIT BAPTISMS IN ACTS?

Those who contend that Spirit baptism is a second experience after conversion, evidenced by speaking in tongues, often cite unique events involving the Spirit on the Day of Pentecost and beyond, specifically among the Samaritans (Acts 8), Cornelius and his household (Acts 10), and the Ephesian disciples (Acts 19). Taking these events in the context of the entire Book of Acts, we should see that they are dramatic ways God confirms His new covenant with all people as the gospel spirals outward from Jerusalem. We should not expect these experiences to occur in the life of every believer.

Let's look briefly at each of these "baptisms."

Acts 2. On the Day of Pentecost, the promised Holy Spirit comes to reside in the hearts/spirits of those who have committed their lives to Christ. Dramatic signs take place to confirm that the Lord is ushering in a new work of redemption. First, there is a sound like that of a violent, rushing wind coming from heaven and filling the house of Jesus' disciples (v. 2). The disciples see tongues like flames of fire that separate and fall on each of them (v. 3). They are all filled with the Holy Spirit and begin speaking in different languages as the Spirit enables them (v. 4). This activity attracts a crowd of Jews from "every nation under heaven" (v. 5). Their astonishment at hearing the "magnificent acts of God in our own tongues" (v. 11) causes confusion, giving Peter the opportunity to explain what is taking place, and to call them to repentance and faith in Jesus (vv. 14-41).

It's important to note that these stunning events occur during the Jewish feast of Pentecost. It is one of three Jewish festivals for which God requires every male Jew to be present in Jerusalem. So, the gospel is first proclaimed to Jews, the people through whom God is fulfilling His promise to Abraham and blessing the whole world (Gen. 22:18). These Jews are witnessing the fulfillment of Joel's prophecy that in the last days God will pour out His Spirit on all people (Acts 2:16-17; cf. Joel 2:28-32). The tongues being spoken not only convey the message of God in languages that all the Jews from around the world gathered in Jerusalem can understand, but they also are a sign to unbelieving Israel that judgment is about to fall because of the nation's rejection of its Messiah (1 Cor. 14:21-22; cf. Isa. 28:11-12).

This is the baptism in the Holy Spirit that Jesus foretold would occur "not many days from now" (Acts 1:5). But as the gospel goes out from Jerusalem, so does the confirming work of the Holy Spirit, who ensures that Samaritans, Gentiles, and even disciples of John the Baptist are joined to the bride of Christ, the universal church.

Acts 8. As severe persecution scatters the followers of Jesus, Philip enters a city of Samaria and proclaims "the good news about the kingdom of God and the name of Jesus Christ" (v. 12). He performs many signs, casting out unclean spirits, and healing the paralyzed and lame. Great joy comes to the city. News that Samaria has received the Word of God makes its way back to the apostles in Jerusalem.

They send Peter and John, who pray that the Samaritans might receive the Holy Spirit "because he had not yet come down on any of them. They had only been baptized in the name of the Lord Jesus" (vv. 15-16). When Peter and John lay their hands on the Samaritans, they receive the Holy Spirit (v. 17). While not stated explicitly, it appears the Samaritans exhibit the same signs of Spirit baptism as the Jews on the Day of Pentecost, because a former sorcerer named Simon offers Peter and John money in exchange for the power to lay hands on people and dispense the Holy Spirit (vv. 18-19).

Here, the baptism in the Holy Spirit is depicted as being *received* and *coming down* (v. 15). So, why don't the Samaritans receive the Holy Spirit immediately upon confessing Jesus as Lord? Why is it necessary in this instance for two apostles to lay their hands on new believers in order for them to experience Spirit baptism? Two thoughts may help clarify the significance of this event.

First, the church up to this point is Jewish. All those who received the Spirit on the Day of Pentecost, as far as we know, are Jews from around the world. Philip is plowing new ground as he shares the gospel with Samaritans. Recall that Jesus tells a Samaritan woman "salvation is from the Jews" (John 4:22), and He explains to a Canaanite woman whose daughter is tormented by a demon, "I was sent only to the lost sheep of the house of Israel" (Matt. 15:24). Yet, He also assures the Samaritan woman that an hour is coming when "true worshipers will worship the Father in Spirit and in truth," not on Mount Gerizim, the Samaritans' rival place of worship, nor in Jerusalem (John 4:21, 23). And He acknowledges the great faith of the Canaanite woman by healing her daughter.

So, while Jews are the first recipients of the new covenant, Jesus clearly has in mind an everlasting kingdom that extends far beyond ethnic and geographical borders. Nevertheless, Jewish Christians wrestle with this realization, as we read throughout the Book of Acts.

Second, the Jews universally despise Samaritans as "half breeds" and exclude them from worship in the temple in Jerusalem. The

Samaritans practice a hybrid religion of Judaism and idolatry (2 Kings 17:26-28). They have intermarried with foreigners and embraced their religious practices. They have built their own temple on Mount Gerizim, receiving the five books of Moses but rejecting the writings of the prophets and Jewish traditions. They opposed the rebuilding of the temple in Jerusalem after the Babylonian exile, and they welcomed criminals from Judea into their communities. For all these reasons, Jews reckoned Samaritans to be the dregs of humanity and thus had nothing to do with them.

Charles Stanley comments, "If the Samaritan believers had automatically received the Holy Spirit the day Philip preached to them, what do you think would have happened? There would have been a First Church of the Samaritans and a First Church of Jerusalem. The delay forced the Jews to acknowledge that their God accepted the Samaritans just as He accepted them. The delay united the early church."[5]

So, the indwelling Spirit, once the exclusive guest in the hearts/spirits of Jewish Christians, is now baptizing Samaritans into the body of Christ. Both Jews and Samaritans need to see that they are one body, not two. And the highest leadership in the Jerusalem church needs to understand that Samaritans are not second-class citizens but full members of the church. And it gets even better.

Acts 10. This chapter records the spread of the gospel to the Gentiles. Cornelius, a devout and God-fearing Roman centurion who resides in Caesarea, has a vision. An angel instructs him to send for Peter, who's in Joppa. Meanwhile, Peter has a vision of his own, in which the Lord prepares him to engage Gentiles. Escorted to the home of Cornelius, Peter addresses a gathering of the centurion's relatives and close friends: "Now I truly understand that God doesn't show favoritism, but in every nation the person who fears him and does what is right is acceptable to him" (vv. 34-35). Peter shares the message of Jesus with the Gentiles, concluding with these words, "All the prophets testify about him [Jesus] that through his name everyone who believes in him receives forgiveness of sins" (v. 43).

While Peter is speaking, the Holy Spirit *comes down* on all those who hear the message. The circumcised believers who have come with Peter are amazed because the *gift of the Holy Spirit* has been *poured out* on the Gentiles, for they hear them speak in other tongues and declare the greatness of God (vv. 44-46). Peter then responds, "Can anyone withhold water and prevent these people from being baptized, who have *received* the Holy Spirit just as we have?" (v. 47, emphasis added).

When Peter returns to Jerusalem, the "circumcision party" criticizes him for interacting with uncircumcised men (11:2-3). Peter explains everything that has taken place over the last several days, summarizing, "As I began to speak, the Holy Spirit came down on them, just as on us at the beginning. I remembered the word of the Lord, how he said, 'John baptized with water, but you will be baptized with the Holy Spirit.' If, then, God gave them the same gift that he also gave to us when we believed in the Lord Jesus Christ, how could I possibly hinder God?" (vv. 15-17).

When the Jews hear Peter's testimony, they fall silent. At last they glorify God and say, "So then, God has given repentance resulting in life even to the Gentiles" (v. 18).

While Cornelius is a God-fearing and devout man, it appears he doesn't hear the gospel until Peter delivers it. Certainly, he has not previously trusted in Christ for salvation. So, he becomes one of the first examples of the way in which the gospel is going out to the ends of the earth (Acts 1:8). The baptism in the Holy Spirit, accompanied by speaking in tongues and prophesying, is not to be seen as the norm for believers today. Rather, it is a dramatic confirmation of salvation coming to the Gentiles, and the same Holy Spirit placing Gentiles into the body of Christ along with Jews and Samaritans.

Acts 19. In verses 1-7, we see another example of people who have not heard the gospel of Jesus Christ. The apostle Paul arrives in Ephesus and finds some disciples of John the Baptist. Paul asks them, "Did you receive the Holy Spirit when you believed?" They respond, "No, we haven't even heard that there is a Holy Spirit." Paul asks them, "Into what then were you baptized?" And they reply, "Into John's baptism." Paul says, "John baptized with a baptism of repentance, telling the people that they should believe in the one who would come after him, that is, in Jesus." When they hear the gospel, they are baptized into the name of the Lord Jesus. Paul then lays hands on them. The Holy Spirit *comes on* them, and they begin to speak in other tongues and prophesy.

These twelve disciples of John the Baptist probably heard him preach, or talked to others who heard him, and were baptized in water as a sign that they were repenting of their sins and preparing for the coming Messiah. They had not heard the story of Christ's death, burial, and resurrection. Nor had they any inkling of the "promise of the Father," the Holy Spirit who would indwell them.

As Wayne Grudem explains, "Therefore these 'disciples' in Ephesus did not have a new covenant understanding or new covenant faith, and they certainly did not have a new covenant empowering of the Holy Spirit — they were 'disciples' only in the sense of followers of John the Baptist who were still waiting for the Messiah. When they heard of him they believed in him, and then received the power of the Holy Spirit that was appropriate to the gospel of the risen Lord Jesus Christ."[6]

So, this passage describing the experiences of the Ephesian disciples should not be seen as a normative "second blessing" for believers today. We do not have faith in a coming Messiah, but in the crucified, buried, and resurrected Messiah who has finished the work of redemption. When we receive Him by faith, we are baptized into fellowship with Him by the Holy Spirit, and then are commanded by Jesus to be water baptized as a testimony of our identification with Him.

By now, it should be clear that the events in Acts 2, 8, 10, and 19 are historical accounts of Spirit baptism in the hearts of new believers who are Jews, Samaritans, Gentiles, and old-covenant disciples. As followers of Jesus obediently become His witnesses in Jerusalem, in all Judea and Samaria, and to the end of the earth, the Lord confirms the spread of the gospel with dramatic baptisms in the Holy Spirit. These are not standard experiences for all believers in the first century, or today, for the apostle Paul reminds us that we all are baptized by one Spirit into one body — whether Jews or Greeks, whether slaves or free — and we are all given one Spirit to drink (1 Cor. 12:13).

DID THE DISCIPLES RECEIVE SPIRIT BAPTISM BEFORE PENTECOST?

On the evening of Jesus' resurrection, He appears to the disciples as they gather behind locked doors. "Peace be with you," He tells them before showing them His hands and His side, no doubt bearing the marks of His crucifixion. The disciples rejoice at the confirmation of reports that He has risen from the dead. Then, something curious happens. Jesus breathes on them and says, "Receive the Holy Spirit. If you forgive the sins of any, they are forgiven them; if you retain the sins of any, they are retained" (John 20:22-23). What's happening here? Is this a mini-Pentecost? A prophetic word about what is to happen fifty days later and fulfilled in Acts 2? And how is it that the disciples are given the authority to forgive sins?

Bible commentators offer different views about this unique event. Some contend that this is John's version of what Luke depicts as taking place in Acts 2. Others believe Jesus is offering a symbolic promise of the Spirit's coming in power on the Day of Pentecost. And still others suggest that the disciples receive the Spirit in different ways on both occasions.[7]

A few observations may prove helpful:

- It's important to see this passage in light of the Great Commission. As Jesus is the one sent from the Father, He now sends His messengers, as noted in John 20:21: "As the Father has sent me, I also send you." All three persons of the Godhead are active in this commissioning. As Jesus is sent by God the Father, so He, the Son, sends out His disciples, whom the Holy Spirit equips.
- Whatever occurs behind these closed doors with respect to the Holy Spirit, it is not Spirit baptism, for several weeks later Jesus tells the disciples they *will be* baptized with the Holy Spirit "in a few days" (Acts 1:5).
- It doesn't seem that Jesus is telling a parable, either, or painting a prophetic picture of Pentecost. His words, "Receive the Holy Spirit," are direct. They follow His act of breathing on the disciples, and they precede His instructions with regard to their mission of forgiving or retaining sins — a heavy responsibility for which the Spirit must provide guidance.
- Therefore, it seems best to understand this difficult passage as Jesus giving His disciples the indwelling Holy Spirit in

advance of Pentecost, at which time they would be filled and empowered for service. No doubt, Jesus has much to teach the disciples in the forty days between His resurrection and ascension, and the indwelling Holy Spirit enables them to receive His words and be comforted by them.

But what about Jesus' commissioning of the disciples to forgive or retain sins? Isn't God alone the one who forgives (Mark 2:7)? How can any mere human being absolve the sins of another? Jesus' words here may echo a reference to "the key of the House of David" in Isa. 22:22 (see also Rev. 3:7). The *CSB Study Bible* notes, "Jesus bestowed on his followers authority to announce access or disbarment from God's kingdom based on reception or denial of the gospel message. For those who reject Jesus, his messengers are commissioned to say that they do not have forgiveness of sins."[8]

This may be similar to Jesus' words to Peter in Matt. 16:19, where He tells Peter He will give him "the keys of the kingdom of heaven." Jesus goes on to say to Peter, "whatever you bind on earth will have been bound in heaven, and whatever you loose on earth will have been loosed in heaven." The keys are a symbol of authority. Rabbis used the words "bind" and "loose" to denote decisions about what was or was not permitted. Peter is simply an agent of divine revelation. He may only permit or prohibit what has already been permitted or prohibited in heaven.

OTHER VIEWS OF SPIRIT BAPTISM

There are many views about the proper meaning of baptism in the Holy Spirit.[9] Some Puritans, for example, concluded that baptism in the Spirit constitutes a sealing by the Spirit, which produces assurance of salvation. Certain Holiness teachers, like John Fletcher, proposed a two-stage process of salvation and sanctification, interpreting the second stage as Spirit baptism. Proponents of Keswick theology argue for a genuine reception of the Spirit at conversion but contend that a subsequent "baptism" or "filling" gives believers power over sin. Reformed scholars, such as James Dunn, generally hold that Spirit baptism occurs at conversion; they reject the idea of a two-stage process of salvation.[10]

James Hamilton, in *God's Indwelling Presence*, suggests that Spirit baptism is "the powerful, dramatic, visible, audible manifestation of the Spirit" that "marks divine approval of a significant movement in the church's advance."[11] He explains: "This baptism in the Spirit is not the same as or simultaneous with initial conversion or indwelling. Rather, baptism in the Spirit is God's public mark of approval — first for believers in Jesus who are in Jerusalem (Acts 2), then for the Samaritans (Acts 8), then for the Gentiles (Acts 10), then for the followers of John the Baptist (Acts 19). The evidence from Acts indicates that the whole church was representatively baptized when these groups were baptized on these four occasions."[12]

Put another way, Hamilton argues that Spirit baptism is a unique marker in the transition from the old covenant to the new covenant and, as such, is not the normal experience for followers of Jesus. In referring to Luke's record of the "baptisms" in Acts, Hamilton writes, "These instances of baptism in the Spirit are not recorded to show what happens at conversion. Nor are these 'baptisms' necessary for indwelling, for Luke seems to show people who are 'full of the Spirit' ... whom he has not shown being 'baptized' in the Spirit."[13]

As we can see, interpretations of Spirit baptism cover a wide spectrum, from a work of God in every Christian's spirit, to an available benefit conditioned on seeking or performing sacramental acts, to a historical marker in God's divine plan that no longer is to be expected or experienced. The scope of this book does not allow us to unpack every view of Spirit baptism, but it may prove helpful to briefly survey one of the more popular views today, a view clearly defined and consistently practiced by the Assemblies of God, and generally embraced by many Pentecostals and Charismatics.

THE ASSEMBLIES OF GOD VIEW

Some Evangelical Christians understand the Scriptures to describe the baptism in the Holy Spirit as an experience subsequent to conversion that equips believers for godly living and effective service. The

Assemblies of God, for example, defines baptism in the Holy Spirit this way:

> All believers are entitled to and should ardently expect and earnestly seek the promise of the Father, the baptism in the Holy Spirit and fire, according to the command of our Lord Jesus Christ. This was the normal experience of all in the early Christian church. With it comes the enduement of power for life and service, the bestowment of the gifts and their uses in the work of the ministry (Luke 24:49; Acts 1:4, 8; 1 Corinthians 12:1-31). This experience is distinct from and subsequent to the experience of the new birth (Acts 8:12-17; 10:44-46; 11:14-16; 15:7-9). With the baptism in the Holy Spirit comes such experiences as:
>
> • an overflowing fullness of the Spirit (John 7:37-39; Acts 4:8)
>
> • a deepened reverence for God (Acts 2:43; Hebrews 12:28)
>
> • an intensified consecration to God and dedication to His work (Acts 2:42)
>
> • and a more active love for Christ, for His Word and for the lost (Mark 16:20)
>
> The baptism of believers in the Holy Spirit is witnessed by the initial physical sign of speaking with other tongues as the Spirit of God gives them utterance (Acts 2:4). The speaking in tongues in this instance is the same in essence as the gift of tongues, but is different in purpose and use (1 Corinthians 12:4-10, 28)."[14]

In response, a few observations may prove helpful. First, this issue should be considered a secondary doctrine. That is, it *is* important, but it may be distinguished from primary issues — such as the Trinity, the deity of Christ, justification by faith, and the inspiration and authority of Scripture — in that Christians may disagree on secondary issues without accusing one another of heresy. Nevertheless, disagreement on second-order doctrines leads to significant boundaries between local churches and/or Christian denominations.[15]

Second, nowhere does the New Testament instruct believers to seek baptism in the Spirit. It is a promise of Christ to His followers without qualification (John 14:16-17; Acts 1:4-5).

Third, baptism in the Spirit and baptism in fire are not parallel terms (Matt. 3:11-12). These are separate baptisms: one for followers of Jesus, and the other for unrepentant sinners. Many times, the holiness of God is depicted in Scripture in fiery terms. It is a glowing coal that purifies the lips of His spokesmen (Isa. 6:6-7); a message that burns in the bellies of his prophets (Jer. 20:9); tongues of fire that fall on His church on the Day of Pentecost (Acts 2:3); and fiery torches burning before the throne of God in heaven (Rev. 4:5).

At the same time, fire is used to describe the everlasting destiny of those who reject God's gracious offer of salvation. That John the Baptist proclaims two separate baptisms — one with the Holy Spirit and one with fire — is clear by what follows: "His winnowing shovel is in his hand, and he will clear his threshing floor and gather his wheat into the barn. But the chaff he will burn with fire that never goes out" (Matt. 3:12).

Fourth, it seems best to understand "enduement of power for life and service" as a benefit of indwelling, and particularly filling, not baptism in the Spirit.

Fifth, while tongues are associated with the filling of the Spirit in Acts, Paul makes it clear that this gift is a sign to unbelieving Israel that God is working through a new people under a new covenant (1 Cor. 14:22; Isa. 28:11). He also reminds carnal Corinthians that *all* of them have been baptized in the Holy Spirit, yet many of them have not spoken in tongues (1 Cor. 12:13, 30).

Last, while Evangelicals hold a variety of views on the definition of baptism in the Holy Spirit and its evidence in their lives, we should be gracious to one another and stand united in our affirmation of the core doctrines that truly define what it means to be a follower of Jesus.

Key passages on baptism in the Spirit

Let's survey several Bible verses that address baptism in the Holy Spirit.

Matt. 3:11-12. John the Baptist declares, "I baptize you with water for repentance, but the one who is coming after me is more powerful than I. I am not worthy to remove his sandals. He himself will baptize you with the Holy Spirit and fire (*autos umas baptisei en pneumati agio kai puri*). His winnowing shovel is in his hand, and he will clear his threshing floor and gather his wheat into the barn. But the chaff he will burn with fire that never goes out."

Mark 1:7-8. John the Baptist proclaims, "One who is more powerful than I am is coming after me. I am not worthy to stoop down and untie the strap of his sandals. I baptize you with water, but he will baptize you with the Holy Spirit."

Luke 3:16-17 - "John answered them all, 'I baptize you with water, but one who is more powerful than I am is coming. I am not worthy to untie the strap of his sandals. He will baptize you with the Holy Spirit and fire. His winnowing shovel is in his hand to clear his threshing floor and gather the wheat into his barn, but the chaff he will burn with fire that never goes out.'"

John 1:29-34 - "The next day John saw Jesus coming toward him and said, 'Here is the Lamb of God, who takes away the sin of the world! This is the one I told you about: "After me comes a man who ranks ahead of me, because he existed before me." I didn't know him, but I came baptizing with water so he might be revealed to Israel.' And John testified, 'I saw the Spirit descending from heaven like a dove, and he rested on him. I didn't know him, but he who sent me to baptize with water told me, "The one you see the Spirit descending and resting on — he is the one who baptizes with the Holy Spirit." I have seen and testified that this is the Son of God.'"

These four passages record a consistent message from the lips of John the Baptist. While they don't tell us exactly what this baptism truly is, they declare to us that Jesus is the baptizer; that the baptism is future; that Spirit baptism is distinct from water baptism; and that a baptism of judgment falls on those who reject Jesus.

It appears more natural in the Gospels to understand Jesus as the baptizer and the Spirit as the sphere into which people are baptized. In Acts and 1 Corinthians, the Spirit is the agent of baptism, and the body of Christ is the sphere into which believers are baptized. However, these distinctions are not hard and fast, as Charles Ryrie points out: "Both Christ and the Spirit are Agents, and both the Spirit and the body are spheres. Christ is the ultimate Agent for He sent the Spirit who is, so to speak, the intermediate Agent (Acts 2:33). Clearly the body is one sphere, and the Spirit is another. This is similar to the Spirit's work in sealing — He is both the Agent who seals and the sphere in which we are sealed."[16]

A few thoughts about these passages:

- John seeks to make it clear that he is a forerunner of the promised Messiah, not the Messiah Himself. Thus, he is inferior to the Messiah and should not be the ultimate object of people's devotion. When he declares his unworthiness to remove Jesus' sandals, he expresses deep humility. Removing the master's sandals is a task so menial in first-century Jewish life that Hebrew slave owners may not require it of their servants.

- Spirit baptism is superior to water baptism. John's baptism is an outward expression of repentance, but it cannot change the heart. Baptism in the Holy Spirit, in contrast, is an inward work of God that establishes His presence in our lives and secures final, full, and future Christlikeness.

- Spirit baptism is a distinguishing mark of the new covenant. John reminds his disciples that this baptism is both future and tied to Jesus, the Mediator of the new covenant (Heb. 9:15).

- Those who reject this Mediator should expect a baptism of fire, a reference to divine judgment that falls upon the nation of Israel in the destruction of Jerusalem in A.D. 70, and upon individual unbelievers at the great white throne (Rev. 20:11-15).

- John stresses the divine nature of the one who baptizes in the Spirit. Jesus is "the Lamb of God, who takes away the sin of the world!" In other words, He is the promised

Messiah. Through His sinless life and substitutionary death on the cross, He fulfills the law, completes the sacrificial system, and satisfies the wrath of God. In addition, John makes it clear that Jesus existed before he did, even though John is born before Jesus. This is an acknowledgement of Christ's eternal nature. Finally, John affirms that Jesus is the Son of God, a divine title that separates Jesus from angels and people, who sometimes are called "sons of God" in Scripture.

CSB	KJV	NIV	NASB	ESV
He himself will baptize you with the Holy Spirit and fire	He shall baptize you with the Holy Ghost, and with fire	He will baptize you with (or *in*) the Holy Spirit and fire	He will baptize you with (or *in, by*) the Holy Spirit and fire	He will baptize you with the Holy Spirit and fire

Comparing English translations of *autos umas baptisei en pneumati agio kai puri* in Matt. 3:11

Acts 1:4-5 - "While he [Jesus] was with them, he commanded them not to leave Jerusalem, but to wait for the Father's promise, 'Which,' he said, 'you have heard me speak about; for John baptized with water, but you will be baptized with the Holy Spirit (*en pneumati baptisthesesthe agio*) in a few days.'"

Luke begins his narrative in the Book of Acts with a reminder that Jesus spent time with His apostles between His resurrection and ascension. These forty days were crucial. Christ's bodily appearances provided "many convincing proofs" of His victory over sin and the grave to the men He authorized to speak on His behalf after His departure (v. 3). What's more, Jesus gave them instructions and spoke to them about the kingdom of God (vv. 2-3). Among these directives was the command that the apostles remain in Jerusalem and wait for the Father's promise: the baptism with the Holy Spirit (vv. 4-5).

Jesus ties this command to the ministry of John the Baptist, who baptized with water as a sign of repentance. Now, the apostles are to experience a greater baptism — Spirit baptism — in a few more days. As they remain in Jerusalem for the feast of Pentecost, Christ sends His Spirit in dramatic fashion (Acts 2:1-4). And, this promise of the Father is made available to all who repent and believe. Peter tells the Jews gathered for the feast in Jerusalem, "Repent and be baptized, each of you, in the name of Jesus Christ for the forgiveness of your sins, and you will receive the gift of the Holy Spirit. For the promise is for you and for your children, and for all who are far off, as many as the Lord our God will call" (Acts 2:38-39).

Certainly, the "Father's promise" is the Holy Spirit, who proceeds from the Father and whom Jesus sends. Prior to His passion, Jesus tells His apostles, "And I will ask the Father, and he will give you another Counselor to be with you forever. He is the Spirit of truth" (John 14:16-17a). Later, He tells them, "When the Counselor comes, the one I will send to you from the Father — the Spirit of truth who proceeds from the Father — he will testify about me" (John 15:26). In his Gospel account, Luke records the words of Jesus prior to His ascension: "And look, I am sending you what my Father promised. As for you, stay in the city until you are empowered from on high" (Luke 24:49).

Now, just days before the promise is fulfilled, Jesus commands His apostles to stay in Jerusalem. Why here? This is where Abraham obediently offers his son on Mount Moriah (Gen. 22:1-19). It's where the Lord has chosen to place His name (2 Chron. 6:6). It's where the Shekinah glory fills the temple in Solomon's day (2 Chron. 7:1-3). It's where Jesus enters triumphantly on Palm Sunday, openly declaring Himself the Son of God (Matt. 21:1-10). And it's where Jewish men from around the world gather three times a year for the feasts of Passover/Unleavened Bread, Pentecost, and Tabernacles. It's the spot from which Jesus ascends into heaven, and to which He returns one day. What better place for God's people to witness the coming of the Spirit, who bridges the gap on earth between Christ's ascension and His glorious appearing.

Matthew Henry writes, "There [Jerusalem] Christ was put to shame, and therefore there he will have this honour done him, and this favour is done to Jerusalem to teach us to forgive our enemies and persecutors. The apostles were more exposed to danger at Jerusalem than they would have been in Galilee; but we may cheerfully trust God with our safety when we keep in the way of our duty."[17]

CSB	KJV	NIV	NASB	ESV
Baptized with the Holy Spirit	Baptized with the Holy Ghost	Baptized with (in) the Holy Spirit	Baptized with (in) the Holy Spirit	Baptized with (in) the Holy Spirit

Comparing English translations of *en pneumati baptisthesesthe agio* in Acts 1:5

Acts 11:15-17 - "As I [Peter] began to speak [to the Gentile Cornelius and his household], the Holy Spirit came down on them (*epepesen to pneuma to agion ep autous*), just as on us at the beginning. I remembered the word of the Lord, how he said, 'John baptized with water, but you will be baptized with the Holy Spirit.' If, then, God gave them the same gift that he also gave to us when we believed in the Lord Jesus Christ, how could I possibly hinder God?"

Peter is called to report to the "circumcision party" in Jerusalem about what he has witnessed in the home of Cornelius. He tells them, step by step, what transpired. The Holy Spirit "came down" on the Gentiles "just as on us at the beginning." He remembers Jesus' words about the baptism with the Holy Spirit on the Day of Pentecost. And now he identifies the Spirit's appearance as "the same gift." These are significant statements because they tie together the coming-down of the Spirit, the baptism with the Spirit, and the gift of God, which also is the promise of the Father (Acts 1:4).

It is a dramatic event that changes Peter, convincing Him that "God doesn't show favoritism" (Acts 10:34b). The experience in the home of Cornelius is so similar to what occurs on the Day of Pentecost — although on a much smaller scale — that Peter is forced to embrace Gentile believers as brothers and sisters in Christ. His story convinces the Jews in Jerusalem, as Luke records: "When they heard this they became silent. And they glorified God, saying, 'So then, God has given repentance resulting in life even to the Gentiles.'" (Acts 11:18).

Unfortunately, this does not end the matter completely, "for this same legalistic party later debated with Paul about the salvation of the Gentiles (Acts 14:26-15:2). Even after the Jerusalem Conference, legalistic teachers continued to attack Paul and invade the churches he founded. They wanted to woo the believers into a life of obedience to the Law (Gal. 1:6ff; Phil. 3:1-3, 17-21). It is possible that many of these legalists were genuine believers, but they did not understand their freedom in Jesus Christ (Gal. 5:1ff)."[18]

CSB	KJV	NIV	NASB	ESV
The Holy Spirit came down on them	The Holy Ghost fell on them	The Holy Spirit came on them	The Holy Spirit fell on them	The Holy Spirit fell on them

Comparing English translations of *epepesen to pneuma to agion ep autous* in Acts 11:15

1 Cor. 12:13 - "For we were all baptized by one Spirit into one body (*en heni pneumati emeis pantes eis en soma ebaptisthemen*) — whether Jews or Greeks, whether slaves or free — and we were all given one Spirit to drink."

This is one of the clearest statements in Scripture about Spirit baptism. Paul is writing to the Corinthians, a greatly gifted and notoriously carnal lot. He has just written about the diversity of spiritual gifts, while appealing for unity in the one Spirit who has granted these gifts. "Now there are different gifts, but the same Spirit. There are different ministries, but the same Lord. And there are different activities, but the same God produces each gift in each person. A manifestation of the Spirit is given to each person for the common good ..." (vv. 4-7a). Then, Paul reminds them that, regardless of their gifts — or even their degree of spiritual maturity — all of them are baptized by one Spirit into the body of Christ.

All Corinthian believers were baptized in the Holy Spirit and, as a result, became members of the body of Christ. We shouldn't miss the profound simplicity of verse 13. Baptism in the Holy Spirit must refer to the work of the Spirit — whom both the Father and Son have sent — building upon regeneration and indwelling as He secures new believers' place in the universal church.

We should note that the previous six passages on Spirit baptism tell us that Jesus is the agent; that is, He is the one who baptizes new believers in the Holy Spirit, thus placing them positionally into the body of Christ. But many English translations of 1 Cor. 12:13 read "baptized *by* one Spirit," seemingly indicating that the Holy Spirit, not Jesus, is the agent. As many Pentecostals argue, this baptism is a different baptism — a baptism *by* the Spirit, not *in* the Spirit. If this is correct, it supports the Pentecostal position that all believers receive the Holy Spirit at conversion, but only those who earnestly seek the "second blessing" are granted baptism *in* the Holy Spirit, and as proof they speak in tongues.

Is this the case? Are there two Spirit baptisms? And if not, why does 1 Cor. 12:13 appear to indicate there are? Wayne Grudem brings clarity to this issue: "Although the distinction makes sense from some English translations, it really cannot be supported by an examination of the Greek text, for there the expression is almost identical to the expressions we have seen in the other six verses. Paul says *en heni pneumati ... ebaptisthemen* ('in one Spirit ... we were baptized') .... The reason [some] translations have chosen the word 'by' has apparently been a desire to avoid an appearance of two locations for the baptism in the same sentence. The sentence already says that this baptism was 'into one body,' and perhaps the translators thought it seemed awkward to say, '*in* one Spirit we were all baptized *into* one body.' But this should not be seen as a great difficulty, for Paul says, referring to the Israelites, 'all were baptized *into* Moses *in* the cloud and *in* the sea' (1 Cor. 10:2) — a very closely parallel expression ..."[19]

As we see in the chart below, many modern English translations that use "by one Spirit" also acknowledge "with" or "in" as alternative renderings.

CSB	KJV	NIV	NASB	ESV
We were all baptized by (*with, in*) one Spirit into one body	By one Spirit are we all baptized into one body	We were all baptized by (*with, in*) one Spirit so as to form one body	By (*in*) one Spirit we were all baptized into one body	In one Spirit we were all baptized into one body

Comparing English translations of *en heni pneumati emeis pantes eis en soma ebaptisthemen* in 1 Cor. 12:13

SUMMARY

The Holy Spirit engages in a multi-faceted ministry in the hearts of Jesus' followers. He brings conviction to them in their lost state by illuminating the truth of God's Word and convincing them of their desperate need for Christ (John 16:7-11). He makes them spiritually alive via regeneration, takes up permanent residence in their spirits through indwelling, and places them into the body of Christ through Spirit baptism. There's more, which we explore in future chapters.

Baptism in the Holy Spirit is key to our security and spiritual growth. The Spirit's unbroken fellowship with us ensures our eternal destiny as adopted children of the King and citizens in the kingdom of heaven. Further, once He baptizes us, the Spirit begins the lifelong work of making us more like Jesus (sanctification).

This requires our obedience. We may produce much fruit — or face divine discipline for spiritual rebellion. But we may rest assured that the Spirit faithfully carries us toward the goal and across the finish line, where the work that God began in us comes to fruition in glorification — the full conformation of believers to the image of Christ.

Consider these summary statements about baptism in the Holy Spirit:

- Baptism in the Holy Spirit is not an earned benefit. Believers make no pilgrimages and perform no ceremonies. They simply believe on the Lord Jesus Christ, and His Spirit brings them into unbreakable fellowship with all other followers of Jesus via the divine work of Spirit baptism.
- The baptism in the Holy Spirit is the means by which God places new believers into the body of Christ. Just as water baptism is the immersion of professing Christians into water, Spirit baptism is the placing of new believers into the universal church.
- Baptism in the Holy Spirit occurs in concert with regeneration and indwelling. Every follower of Jesus has been born again (regenerated), indwelt, and baptized in the Spirit.
- Those who contend that Spirit baptism is a second experience after conversion, evidenced by speaking in tongues, often cite unique events involving the Spirit on the Day of Pentecost and beyond (Acts 2, 8, 10, 19). However, taking these events in the context of the entire Book of Acts, we should see that they are dramatic ways

God confirms His new covenant with all people as the gospel spirals outward from Jerusalem.

- Based on Jesus' words to His disciples, "Receive the Holy Spirit" (John 20:22-23), it appears they were indwelt by the Spirit in advance of Pentecost, at which time they would be filled and empowered for service. Every other believer at that time received the Spirit on the Day of Pentecost.
- There are many different views about the proper meaning of baptism in the Holy Spirit, including the Assemblies of God position that it is an experience subsequent to conversion that equips believers for godly living and effective service. While Evangelicals may disagree, it's important that we recognize this as a secondary issue that should not divide us as followers of Jesus committed to fulfilling the Great Commission.
- The apostle Paul's statement in 1 Cor. 12:13 is one of the clearest in Scripture about Spirit baptism. He reminds the Corinthians that, regardless of their gifts — or even the degree of their maturity — *all* of them are baptized by one Spirit into the body of Christ.

THINK
Questions for personal or group study

(1) What would you say are the outward signs that a person has been baptized in the Holy Spirit?

(2) Why do you think John the Baptist and Jesus both speak about baptism in the Holy Spirit as an impending work of God, yet Luke never uses the term "baptism" to describe what happens on the Day of Pentecost?

(3) Consider the seven New Testament references to baptism in the Holy Spirit and answer these questions:

PASSAGE	WHO IS SPEAKING?	WHO IS THE BAPTIZER?	WHEN DOES IT OCCUR?	WHO GETS IT?	HOW DO WE KNOW?
Matt. 3:11					
Mark 1:8					
Luke 3:16					
John 1:33					
Acts 1:5					
Acts 11:16					
1 Cor. 12:13					

(4) What are the similarities and differences between baptism in the Holy Spirit and the filling of the Spirit?

(5) What happens in the following verses when believers are filled with the Spirit:

- Acts 2:4; 10:46; 19:6
- Acts 2:14-36; 4:8-12
- Acts 4:31
- Acts 6:3-5
- Acts 7:55
- Acts 9:17

- Acts 11:24
- Acts 13:9-12
- Acts 13:52

(6) How would you respond to someone who says baptism in the Holy Spirit is a second experience that follows conversion, a blessing that must be sought and, when received, results in speaking in tongues?

(7) Many Evangelical Christians consider Spirit baptism to be a "secondary issue." That is, while it *is* an important issue that separates us into local congregations and even into Christian denominations, it should not cause us to accuse those who disagree with us of heresy. Do you agree with this assessment? Why or why not? As a broader question, do you think denominations are a good thing or a bad thing for the body of Christ?

Chapter Nine

YOU ARE SANCTIFIED

When services ended around noon on December 31, 1961, at Highland Crest Baptist Church in Green Bay, Wisconsin, my dad gave me the car keys while he and Mom visited with guests and locked the church doors. A quarter-mile to the east, 39,029 fans streamed into the new City Stadium (now Lambeau Field) for the 1 p.m. kickoff of the NFL championship game between the Packers and New York Giants. The temperature was twenty degrees, and while the players were deciding whether to wear sneakers or cleats on the frozen field, I pulled my collar up tight to my ears and opened the car door, faithful to the task of starting the engine and coaxing out enough heat to make the ride home tolerable.

As my dad, mom, brother, and sister finally made their way across the snowy parking lot and jostled into their seats, we noticed a box tucked away on the floor beneath the console. Inside was a plastic-wrapped Duke football with the autographed names of the Packers players and coaching staff. We later learned who left this prize on the very day the Packers trounced the Giants 37-0 for their first NFL title under Vince Lombardi: Packers defensive back Hank Greminger, a future Packer Hall of Famer, an active member of our church, and a friend of the family.

My father took the Duke out of the plastic bag and let my brother and me behold this treasure for a fleeting moment. Then, he put it back, never again to be touched by human hands. Dad kept the football on a high shelf in his closet. Week after week we begged him to let us play with the ball. We promised never to let Duke touch the ground, or soak up a drop of rain, or ricochet off the side of the house. And we swore to return the ball to its plastic prison after a few brief moments in the yard. Always, the answer was the same: no. This ball was a valuable gift, not an object of play. It was meant for the trophy case, not the frozen tundra. In a fashion, this Duke football was made and autographed for a higher purpose.

Dad never yielded to our requests to treat the gift of Hank Greminger like a common pigskin. When Dad passed away, my brother took possession of the valuable relic, keeping it in a glass case in his home. It has yet to feel the grip of a kid's hands, or experience the scuff of deep fescue after an errant pass. This Duke was not meant for the playing field. You might say it was *sanctified*.

In a similar manner, followers of Jesus should recognize that we are set apart for God. We belong to Him. He has marked us as His own. From the moment we trust in Him for everlasting life, He begins a lifelong process of making us the way He intended us to be. Sanctification is both a position — a one-time act of God marking us as His own — and a process, which is not a steady progression toward perfection, but a bumpy ride through a sinful and fallen world until, in glorification one day, we are fully conformed to the image of Christ.

While there are different views about this pilgrim's journey, it is biblically faithful for the follower of Jesus to say, "I am sanctified."

WHAT DOES IT MEAN TO BE SANCTIFIED?

Sanctification is the work of God making followers of Jesus more like Him. In sanctification, the Holy Spirit produces holiness, which means bearing an actual likeness of God in our thoughts, words, and deeds. While sanctification is a unique process that requires our cooperation with God, we should not think it possible to become little gods; rather, our role is to be imitators of Christ.

As Millard Erickson puts it, "Sanctification is a process by which one's moral condition is brought into conformity with one's legal status before God. It is a continuation of what was begun in regeneration, when a newness of life was conferred upon and instilled within the believer. In particular, sanctification is the Holy Spirit's applying to the life of the believer the work done by Jesus Christ."[1]

Sanctification involves all three persons of the Godhead. In a reference to the Father, Paul prays, "Now may the God of peace himself sanctify you completely" (1 Thess. 5:23). He further reminds the Philippians, "For it is God who is working in you both to will and to work according to his good purpose," indicating that the Father implants a desire for holiness in His children and then enables us to achieve it (Phil. 2:13). And the writer of Hebrews illustrates the Father's role in sanctification as one of chastening His own children (Heb. 12:5-11).

The role of the Son in sanctification is, first, that He earned sanctification for us. That's why Paul writes that Jesus "became wisdom from God for us — our righteousness, sanctification, and redemption" (1 Cor. 1:30). Further, Jesus is our example for living the sanctified life. The writer of Hebrews urges us to look to Jesus, "the source and perfecter of our faith" (Heb. 12:2). And Peter writes that "Christ also suffered for you, leaving you an example, that you should follow in his steps" (1 Peter 2:21). Finally, John tells us that if we claim to remain in Christ, we should "walk just as he walked" (1 John 2:6).

But it seems that the Holy Spirit is the primary agent of sanctification, working within us to produce greater degrees of holiness. Paul and Peter speak of the sanctification of, or by, the Spirit (2 Thess. 2:13; 1 Peter 1:2). What's more, the Spirit produces in us the "fruit of the Spirit" (Gal. 5:22-23), those godly traits that reveal Christlikeness. We grow in sanctification as we "walk by the Spirit" and are "led by the Spirit" (Gal. 5:16-18); that is, we become increasingly responsive to the promptings of the indwelling Spirit.

POSITIONAL AND PRACTICAL

Sanctification may be understood in two ways, both of which relate to holiness. First, there is *positional sanctification*, the state of being separate, set apart from the common and dedicated to a higher purpose.[2] The Hebrew word *qados* literally means "separate" and is used to designate particular places (like the Holy of Holies), objects (such as Aaron's garments and the Sabbath Day), and persons (especially priests and Levites). For example, God commands the Israelites to consecrate, or set apart, every firstborn male (Ex. 13:2).

Positional sanctification finds its place in the New Testament as a work of God occurring at the beginning of conversion. John Frame, who prefers the term *definitive sanctification*, calls this "a once-for-all event, simultaneous with effectual calling and regeneration, that transfers us from the sphere of sin to the sphere of God's holiness, from the kingdom of Satan to the kingdom of God. It is at this point that each of us joins the people of God."[3]

The apostle Peter refers to his readers as "a chosen race, a royal priesthood, a holy nation, a people for his possession, so that you may proclaim the praises of the one who called you out of darkness into his marvelous light. Once you were not a people, but now you are God's people; you had not received mercy, but now you have received mercy" (1 Peter 2:9-10).

Robert Morey describes this initial step of sanctification: "There is a radical break with the total dominion and tyranny of sin, so that the believer now struggles with remaining sin instead of reigning sin.... sin is dethroned, the believer dies to sin, the old self is crucified and there is a new principle of holiness implanted in the heart of the believer which will not allow sin to ultimately and permanently regain dominion over the believer."[4]

Second, there is *practical sanctification*, the lifelong process by which the Spirit makes us more like Jesus.[5] This requires our ongoing submission to Christ and our obedience to the voice of the indwelling Spirit. It is the daily taking up of our cross and following Jesus (Luke 9:23), which means being "willing to die in order to follow Jesus. This is called 'dying to self.' It's a call to absolute surrender."[6]

Practical sanctification means not only that believers are set apart, belonging to Christ, but that our conduct naturally aligns with the revealed Word of God and the indwelling Spirit of God.

Over the course of our Christian walk, we are conformed to Christ's character in two ways. First, the Lord implants and nurtures

Christ's righteousness within us (Phil. 2:13). Second, as regenerate believers, we obey the Scriptures under the power and guidance of the Spirit so that we "grow in grace and knowledge of our Lord and Savior Jesus Christ" (2 Peter 3:18).

Sanctification, then, is more than a past event. It's an ongoing process. "It begins in regeneration, and we can think of sanctification as the outworking of the new life given in regeneration. In that ongoing process, God works in us (1 Thess. 5:23; Heb. 13:20-21), but he also calls us to work out our salvation (Phil. 2:12-13).... divine sovereignty and human responsibility are not opposed. The former works through the latter (as well as sometimes working above and beyond it). The latter always depends on the former. But our role in sanctification is never passive. Our work is to fight, to run the race, to pursue holiness."[7]

WHEN DOES SANCTIFICATION OCCUR?

Sanctification begins the moment people place their trust in Jesus. The blood of Jesus cleanses us from sin (redemption). The Father declares us righteous in heaven (justification). The Holy Spirit indwells us and places us positionally into the body of Christ (Spirit baptism). The Spirit seals us with God's mark of ownership and sets us apart as belonging to Him (positional sanctification). All of these divine saving acts occur simultaneously, or nearly so. But sanctification is unique in that it continues throughout our lifetimes. It is both an event and a process — an ongoing work that God completes in our future resurrection and glorification.

This is not to say that the other saving works of God have no lasting effects. Quite the contrary. In regeneration, for example, the Spirit brings everlasting life to our dead human spirits — a life that by its very definition never ends. In justification, we are declared in right standing before God, with the ongoing assurance that we do not face the prospect of double jeopardy. In indwelling, the Holy Spirit takes up permanent residence in the temples of our bodies. All of these are completed acts with continuing results, whereas sanctification is a work in progress that God begins at conversion and completes in glorification.

When Paul writes to the Corinthians, "But you were washed, you were sanctified, you were justified in the name of the Lord Jesus Christ and by the Spirit of our God," he assures them that their positional sanctification is an accomplished fact (1 Cor. 6:11). And in his farewell address to the Ephesian elders, Paul commits them to God and to the word of His grace, "which is able to build you up and to give you an inheritance among all who are sanctified" — again offering assurance that those who trust in Christ are set apart and marked as His own (Acts 20:32).

Like justification, sanctification is received by faith and has everlasting benefits. Yet there are important distinctions between the two. For example:

- Justification is instantaneous and complete, while sanctification begins at the same time as justification but requires a lifetime to complete.
- Justification is a full acquittal of the guilt of sin, based on the imputation of our sins to the account of Christ and the imputation of His righteousness to us. A person either is justified or not, whereas a Christian may be more or less sanctified (although never unsanctified).
- Justification is a legal declaration of righteousness in heaven, while sanctification is the actual transformation of the acquitted person's character.
- Justification is an objective work that affects our standing with God, while sanctification is a subjective work that affects our inner person.[8]

As we begin our walk with Jesus, we learn that sanctification is a lifelong journey. It commands our submission to Christ as King and our obedience to the indwelling Holy Spirit. The degree to which we become like Christ matches the degree to which we allow His Spirit to take control of our thoughts, words, and deeds.

Throughout His earthly life, Jesus was completely submissive to the will of the Father and dependent on the Spirit. As such, He overcame fierce temptation from the evil one, the flattery of people, and the pull of worldly charms. As the writer of Hebrews notes, "Although he was the Son, he learned obedience from what he suffered" (Heb. 5:8).

Of course, we're not God incarnate, so we should not expect sinless perfection. We may be overcome by sin at different periods of time, yet the overall characteristic of our lives is a pursuit of holiness. "Sin can never again ultimately and permanently enslave the believer, even though it can and does temporarily regain its old dominion through the devices of Satan and corruption of the heart. Grace will soon reassert itself and dethrone sin."[9]

WHAT IS OUR PART IN SANCTIFICATION?

Wayne Grudem writes, "The role that we play in sanctification is both a *passive* one in which we depend on God to sanctify us, and an *active* one in which we strive to obey God and take steps that will increase our sanctification."[10] We may demonstrate this with Scripture. Numerous passages urge us to trust God for our sanctification.

For example, Paul tells his Roman readers to "offer yourselves to God, and all the parts of yourselves to God as weapons for righteousness," and "present your bodies as a living sacrifice, holy and pleasing to God" (Rom. 6:13; 12:1b). At the same time, he writes, "But if by the Spirit you put to death the deeds of the body, you will live" (Rom. 8:13).

Other New Testament passages exhort us to "pursue ... holiness" (Heb. 12:14), "keep away from sexual immorality" (1 Thess. 4:3), "cleanse ourselves from every impurity of the flesh and spirit" (2 Cor. 7:1), and "make every effort to supplement your faith with goodness, goodness with knowledge, knowledge with self-control, self-control with endurance, endurance with godliness, godliness with brotherly affection, and brotherly affection with love" (2 Peter 1:5-7). The point seems clear: We have a role to play in becoming more like Jesus.

Peter tells us that, in our hearts, we are to "regard [sanctify; set apart] Christ the Lord as holy, ready at any time to give a defense to anyone who asks you for a reason for the hope that is in you" (1 Peter 3:15). In other words, while the Spirit does the work of making us more like Jesus, it's our responsibility to relinquish control of our lives and allow the Spirit to take the helm. Only then does He right the ship and sail it toward the harbor of heaven.

Paul further exhorts his readers to "work out your own salvation with fear and trembling" (Phil. 2:12). Then, he reminds them, "For it is God who is working in you both to will and to work according to his good purpose" (v. 13). As followers of Jesus, we are not working *for* our salvation; rather, we are working *out* our salvation as we remove the barriers in our lives that prevent the Lord from making us more like Him.

The believer's role in sanctification is practical: "Do everything without grumbling and arguing, so that you may be blameless and pure, children of God who are faultless in a crooked and perverted generation, among whom you shine like stars in the world, by holding firm to the word of life" (vv. 14-16a). But sanctification also is supernatural. That is, only the indwelling Spirit truly can make us more like Jesus. We can neither manufacture sanctification nor multiply it.

As we submit to the Spirit, we find that sanctification is a progressive work, completed over a lifetime and — if we evaluate ourselves honestly — fraught with fits and starts as our fleshly desires wrestle with the wooing of the Spirit. Even the most mature Christians sometimes say horrible things, act rashly, or allow ourselves to get caught in an addictive pattern of sin.

But God has made provision for that. First, there is the indwelling Holy Spirit who convicts us of our sins — initially, in whispers of exhortation, and then in escalating decibels if we ignore His warnings. Second, there is church discipline, in which fellow believers come to us humbly, and in full recognition of their own frailties, to bring us back to Christ (Matt. 18:15-20; Gal. 6:1; 2 Thess. 3:14-15; 1 Tim. 5:19-22). This occurs one-on-one first, then with others, and finally before the entire church if necessary. Finally, there is divine discipline, in which the Lord may inflict rebellious believers with some infirmity, or even take them home, because they resisted the Spirit, rejected church discipline, and now find themselves in danger of working against the kingdom (see 1 Cor. 11:17-34, particularly vv. 29-30).

Sanctification is wholly the work of God, but it is not passive on the believer's part. The New Testament writers urge us to labor for spiritual maturity. Paul instructs us to practice virtues and avoid evil (Rom. 12:9, 16-17). We are to put to death the deeds of the body (Rom. 8:13) and present our bodies as living sacrifices (Rom. 12:1-2). So, while sanctification is God's work, it is very much our business as well, involving the removal of sin and the addition of holiness.

Despite the fears we may have about losing our salvation, the Spirit ensures that we persevere. Paul writes that the preaching of the cross is foolishness to those who are perishing, but "it is the power of God to us who are being saved" (1 Cor. 1:18). He uses a present participle here to convey the idea of ongoing activity. Further, Paul tells us, "I am sure of this, that he who started a good work in you will carry it on to completion until the day of Christ Jesus" (Phil. 1:6). Not to put too fine a point on it, the Lord promises to fully conform us to the image of Christ — even if He has to take us out early to do so.

IS SINLESS PERFECTION POSSIBLE THIS SIDE OF HEAVEN?

If the goal of God is to fully conform believers to the image of Christ, is it possible to attain sinless perfection within our lifetimes? The issue of *complete sanctification* has generated much disagreement throughout church history.

Generally speaking, those who answer the question in the affirmative are considered *perfectionists* and are Arminian in their doctrine, stressing human freedom and responsibility. This includes denominations such as Church of the Nazarene and some Pentecostal groups. Those who argue against perfectionism tend to be Reformed, or Calvinistic, in their doctrine, emphasizing the sovereignty of God over the free will of His creatures. This is a broad generalization, however, which only serves as a point of reference.

Basically, perfectionists contend that it is possible for believers to arrive at a sinless state prior to physical death. And, they argue, some do. This does not mean a person *cannot* sin any longer; rather, it means he or she *does not* sin. Further, as John Wesley points out in *A Plain Account of Christian Perfection*, the believer who has achieved the sinless state still needs the grace of God and the indwelling Holy Spirit to overcome temptation and to grow even further in his or her walk with the Lord.[11]

While perfectionists say it's possible for a person who has attained complete sanctification not to sin, this, of course, is true of all believers. We are no longer slaves to sin, and God always provides an avenue of escape from temptation (1 Cor. 10:13). But the difference, perfectionists point out, is that some Christians truly reach a state of complete abstinence from evil.

Several passages of Scripture are used to support this view, including:

- Matt. 5:48 - "Be perfect, therefore, as your heavenly Father is perfect."
- Eph. 4:13 - "... until we all reach unity in the faith and in the knowledge of God's Son, growing into maturity with a stature measured by Christ's fullness."
- 1 Thess. 5:23 - "Now may the God of peace himself sanctify you completely. And may your whole spirit, soul, and body be kept sound and blameless at the coming of our Lord Jesus Christ."
- Heb. 13:20-21 - "Now may the God of peace, who brought up from the dead our Lord Jesus — the great Shepherd of the sheep — through the blood of the everlasting covenant, equip you with everything good to do his will, working in us what is pleasing in his sight, through Jesus Christ, to whom be glory forever and ever. Amen."
- 1 John 3:6 - "Everyone who remains in him does not sin ..."

These verses seem to imply that total sanctification is achievable for all believers on this side of heaven.

Going even further, it seems, are Eastern Orthodox leaders who speak of *deification* or *theosis*. This does not mean the pantheistic absorption of Christians into the person of God. Rather, it indicates that believers may acquire "supernatural attributes" and exercise divine energies.[12] "The goal of salvation is that the personal life which is realized in God should also be realized on the level of human existence."[13]

Such a view goes beyond the Evangelical understanding of a believer's union with Christ. To partake in the divine nature does not mean sharing in unique attributes of God, such as eternality, omniscience, or omnipresence. Rather, it means that Christians may exhibit high levels of divine attributes such as mercy, love, and forgiveness. As Christ lives through us, we are vessels of these so-called communicable attributes, yet we never own them in the eternal, unblemished way God does.

In any case, non-perfectionists argue that total sanctification is achieved only in glorification, when followers of Jesus are physically resurrected, given new bodies, and enabled to experience the completion of God's work of salvation as they are freed from the power and presence of sin. While non-perfectionists agree that every believer should strive to be like Jesus, they insist that the effects of the Fall are so great that perfection is unrealistic while we still live in a sinful and fallen world.

In fact, the apostles Paul and John seem to state that sin is an inescapable reality we must endure while we remain on this side of heaven. Consider:

- Rom. 7:18-24 - "For I know that nothing good lives in me, that is, in my flesh. For the desire to do what is good is with me, but there is no ability to do it. For I do not do the good that I want to do, but I practice the evil that I do not want to do. Now if I do what I do not want, I am no longer the one that does it, but it is the sin that lives in me. So I discover this law: When I want to do what is good, evil is present with me. For in my inner self I delight in God's law, but I see a different law in the parts of my body, waging war against the law of my mind and taking me prisoner to the law of sin in the parts of my body. What a wretched man I am! Who will rescue me from this body of death?"
- 1 John 1:8-10 - "If we say, 'We have no sin,' we are deceiving ourselves, and the truth is not in us. If we confess our sins, he is faithful and righteous to forgive us our sins and to cleanse us from all unrighteousness. If we say, 'We have not sinned,' we make him a liar, and his word is not in us."

Other passages in both the Old and New Testaments make clear that sinless perfection is a noble but unattainable goal in this lifetime. In Solomon's prayer at the dedication of the temple, he says, "for there is no one who does not sin" (1 Kings 8:46). Proverbs 20:9 asks rhetorically, "Who can say, 'I have kept my heart pure; I am cleansed from my sin'?" And Jesus' model prayer indicates that prayer for bread and forgiveness go hand in hand every day (Matt. 6:11-12).

So, what do we make of this doctrinal divide? A few observations. First, sin is more subtle and pervasive than we care to admit. Jesus made it clear that our thoughts and attitudes, not just our words and deeds, are sinful if they do not align with His perfect standards (Matt. 5:21-28). It seems unrealistic to think that any person, no matter how godly, can mature to a point where a careless thought is never produced and a hasty word is never spoken. Certainly, however, it's biblically faithful to say that as Christians mature, they take on a heightened sensitivity to sin and develop disciplines to overcome the fiery darts of Satan's temptations.

Second, it may prove helpful to examine the word translated "perfect" in Matt. 5:48. The Greek *teleioi* does not mean perfect in the sense of flawless. Rather, it means "complete." So, we may become mature believers without totally avoiding sin. We may possess the fullness of Christ (Eph. 4:13) and exhibit the fruit of the Spirit (Gal. 5:22-23) without becoming sinless. In addition, John's statement that "everyone who remains in him does not sin" (1 John 3:6) does not teach that some of us attain sinless perfection. As Wayne Grudem notes, "the present-tense Greek verbs are better translated as indicating continual or habitual activity: 'No one who lives in him keeps on sinning ...'"[14]

Last, we should note the absence of sinless characters in the Bible. While the standard for which we strive is complete freedom from sin, the reality is that even the godliest of men and women sometimes fall into grievous sin. When Isaiah comes into the presence of God, he cries out, "Woe is me for I am ruined because I am a man of unclean lips and live among a people of unclean lips" (Isa. 6:5). Daniel includes himself as a guilty party in Israel's sins (Dan. 9:1-19). Paul confronts Peter for his hypocrisy with respect to his treatment of Jews and

Gentiles (Gal. 2:11-14). And an angel rebukes John for bowing to him in worship (Rev. 22:8-9).

One of the great dangers of perfectionism is legalism, enslaving adopted sons and daughters of God by "teaching as doctrines human commands" (Matt. 15:9). While there is never an excuse for believers to sin, our eyes should be fixed on Jesus, the author and finisher of our faith (Heb. 12:2 KJV), rather than on our attempts to gain earthly glorification.

KEY PASSAGES ON SANCTIFICATION

Let's survey several Bible verses that address sanctification.

John 17:17-19 - "Sanctify (*hagiason*) them by the truth; your word is truth. As you sent me into the world, I also have sent them into the world. I sanctify (*hagiazo*) myself for them, so that they also may be sanctified (*hagiasmenoi*) by the truth."

These words of Jesus are part of His high-priestly prayer to the Father in which Jesus intercedes for Himself, His disciples, and all believers. Take note especially of verses 6-19 as Jesus prays for His disciples. They already are sanctified in a sense. That is, they are given to Jesus by the Father (v. 6); they have believed the Father sent Jesus (v. 8); they still belong to the Father (v. 9); they are guarded and kept — none is lost except "the son of destruction" (v. 12); and they are not of the world, just as Jesus is not of the world (vv. 14, 16). These are qualities of persons belonging to God and set apart for His service. And yet, Jesus prays, "Sanctify them by the truth." What does this mean?

Matthew Henry paraphrases Jesus' prayer: "Confirm the work of sanctification in them, strengthen their faith, inflame their good affections, rivet their good resolutions. Carry on that good work in them, and continue it; let the light shine more and more. Complete it, crown it with the perfection of holiness; sanctify them throughout and to the end." He continues, "The great thing to be asked of God for gospel ministers is that they may be sanctified, effectually separated from the world, entirely devoted to God, and experimentally acquainted with the influence of that word upon their own hearts which they preach to others. Let them have the *Urim* and *Thummim, light* and *integrity*."[15]

The truth that sanctifies followers of Jesus requires the Word of God (John 17:17), the Son of God (John 14:6), and the Spirit of God (1 John 5:6). We need all three to experience true sanctification. With the mind, we learn God's truth through His revealed word, the Bible. With the heart, we love God's truth, His Son. And with the will, we yield to the Spirit, living out God's truth every day.[16] As James White notes, "Sanctification and revelation are inextricably intertwined, for without God's revelatory word to our life the process of sanctification cannot begin."[17]

One last thought: Note that Jesus prays, "I sanctify myself for them ..." (John 17:19). The basis of our sanctification is none other than the eternal Son of God, "the Lamb slain from the foundation of the world" (Rev. 13:8b KJV).

CSB	KJV	NIV	NASB	ESV
Sanctify	Sanctify	Sanctify	Sanctify	Sanctify / set apart

Comparing English translations of *hagiason* in John 17:17

CSB	KJV	NIV	NASB	ESV
Sanctify	Sanctify	Sanctify	Sanctify	Consecrate / sanctify / set apart
Sanctified	Sanctified	Truly sanctified	Sanctified	Sanctified / set apart

Comparing English translations of *hagiazo* (sanctify) *and hagiasmenoi* (sanctified) in John 17:19

Rom. 6:19b, 22 - "For just as you offered the parts of yourselves as slaves to impurity, and to greater and greater lawlessness, so now offer them as slaves to righteousness, which results in sanctification (*hagiasmon*).... But now, since you have been set free from sin and have become enslaved to God, you have your fruit, which results in sanctification (*hagiasmon*) — and the outcome is eternal life!"

Paul uses slavery and redemption as metaphors for spiritual death and salvation. Just as the ancient Israelites were slaves whom God rescued from bondage in Egypt, Roman Christians once were duty bound to pagan gods, but now they are set free through faith in Christ. Having been slaves of sin, they are now "enslaved to righteousness" (v. 18). Unlike bondage to sin, which results in death, bondage to Christ produces fruit, resulting in sanctification that leads to eternal life. The Christian life is bond-service to a gracious and loving Master, who always acts in our best interests.

Even so, there is a tension in the life of all believers. Though declared in right standing before God through justification, and promised sinless perfection one day in glorification, we bridge the gap between these two saving acts of God by wrestling against the flesh (the disobedient self) and leaning on the indwelling Spirit to produce Christlikeness. This is neither a smooth continuum nor a steady path to the sublime heights of heaven. Rather, it is a bumpy ride with hairpin turns and stomach-churning drops. The new nature Christ gives us overarches the flesh but does not demolish it until the end of the age, when Christ abolishes evil, sets things right, and reigns triumphantly over a world purged of sin and its stain.

The apostle urges his readers to remain vigilant and faithful to their new Master, who carries them through the peaks and valleys of the sinful and fallen world they struggle to navigate.

Royce Gruenler writes that "there is inevitable tension between the authentic self and the inauthentic self, the new and the old, which requires constant vigilance and prodding. Paul is acting as a goad to the Roman Christians and reminds them of their earlier impurity and 'ever-increasing wickedness' as non-Christians, while he encourages them to offer 'the parts of your body [= their whole persons] to righteousness leading to holiness,' a process that requires their utmost attention."[18]

The *CSB Study Bible* cautions, "Lest the figure be misunderstood as a payment for merits earned, eternal life is a gift of God through Christ. One master (sin) pays an earned wage of death; the other master (God) pays in unearned grace, resulting in eternal life."[19]

CSB	KJV	NIV	NASB	ESV
Sanctification	Holiness	Holiness	Sanctification	Sanctification

Comparing English translations of *hagiasmon* in Rom. 6:19b, 22

1 Cor. 1:2, 18 - "To the church of God at Corinth, to those sanctified (*hagiasmenois*) in Christ Jesus, called as saints, with all those in every place who call on the name of Jesus Christ our Lord — both their Lord and ours.... For the word of the cross is foolishness to those who are perishing, but it is the power of God to us who are being saved (*sozomenois*)."

In these two verses, the apostle Paul shows the correlation between positional sanctification and practical sanctification. In verse 2, he writes to "those sanctified in Christ Jesus, called as saints." God's work of setting apart the followers of Jesus is an accomplished fact, resting in the finished work of Christ and carried out in His call to those He foreknew, predestined, and justified (Rom. 8:29-30). Believers are identified with Christ in His death, burial, and resurrection. Thus, we are sanctified "in Christ" and "called as saints." The Greek word translated "saints" is *hagios,* which means "separate from common condition and use; dedicated ... hallowed."[20]

As Paul writes to "the church of God in Corinth" (1 Cor. 1:2), he uses the Greek word *ekklesia*, which means "a called-out people." The church is a body of individuals set apart for God. So, we see the church at Corinth is made up of individuals who are called and sanctified, joining together as the called-out ones in Christ. As Warren Wiersbe notes, "Each church has two addresses: a geographic address ('at Corinth') and a spiritual address ('in Christ Jesus'). The church is made up of saints, that is, people who have been 'sanctified' or 'set apart' by God. A saint is not a dead person who has been honored by men because of his or her holy life. No, Paul wrote to *living* saints, people who, through faith in Jesus Christ, had been set apart for God's special enjoyment and use. In other words, every true believer is a saint because every true believer has been set apart by God and for God."[21]

In verse 18, Paul contrasts those who are perishing with those who are being saved. This is not a reference to position, but to process. While it's true that believers are securely positioned "in Christ" and unbelievers are under God's wrath, both are in a process that either moves them closer to God or causes them to drift farther away from Him. Paul uses the Greek word *sozomenois*, translated "are being saved," to describe the certainty of God's work of sanctification. The root word *sozo* may be rendered "to save, rescue; to preserve safe and unharmed ... to bring safely to ... to bring within the pale of saving privilege."[22]

Meanwhile, those who are perishing (*apollumenois*) find the message of the cross to be foolishness and thus continue down the descending spiral of ungodliness that may lead them past the point of no return (see Rom. 1:18-32). The root word *apollymi* means "to destroy utterly ... to bring to nought, make void ... to lose, be deprived of ... to be lost, to stray."[23] The word is related to Apollyon, the destroyer of Rev. 9:11.

While those who are sanctified in Christ walk a path of good works God laid out "ahead of time" (Eph. 2:10), a path that leads to rewards at the judgment seat of Christ, those who are perishing reject the "foolishness" of the cross and whistle merrily as they walk the highway to hell.

CSB	KJV	NIV	NASB	ESV
Sanctified	Are sanctified	Sanctified	Have been sanctified	Sanctified

Comparing English translations of *hagiasmenois* in 1 Cor. 1:2

CSB	KJV	NIV	NASB	ESV
Are being saved	Are saved	Are being saved	Are being saved / are saved	Are being saved

Comparing English translations of *sozomenois* in 1 Cor. 1:18

Phil. 1:6 - "I am sure of this, that he who started a good work in you will carry it on to completion (*epitelesei*) until the day of Christ Jesus."

While this verse does not use the word "sanctified," Paul assures his Christian brothers and sisters in Philippi that God finishes what He starts — in this case the work of salvation. The Greek word *epitelesei* means "to bring to an end; to finish, complete, perfect ... to carry out to completion."[24]

Roger Ellsworth notes Paul's gift for "slipping little nuggets of breathtakingly glorious truth into the mundane portions of his letter. This verse is one of those nuggets." It tells us:

Salvation is God's work. The Philippians did not begin the work of salvation in themselves only to have God come along and add a little to it. It was entirely his work. God provided the way of salvation through his Son, Jesus Christ, and he even enabled the Philippians to receive that salvation.

Salvation is a good work. Salvation lifts the sinner from eternal condemnation and ruin and makes that person part of God's family and a partaker of God's eternal glory.

Salvation is a sure work. God does not begin it and then abandon it somewhere along the way. He does not pull his people from the flames of destruction only to allow them to slip back and be consumed. God completes the work of salvation.... all his people will make it home. Not one will be missing! The faithful God will faithfully complete his work![25]

CSB	KJV	NIV	NASB	ESV
Carry it on to completion	Perform it	Carry it on to completion	Perfect it	Bring it to completion

Comparing English translations of *epitelesei* in Phil. 1:6

1 Thess. 5:23 - "Now may the God of peace himself sanctify (*hagiasai*) you completely. And may your whole spirit, soul, and body be kept sound and blameless at the coming of our Lord Jesus Christ."

It's important to keep in mind what we've already explored in this chapter. Paul is not teaching sinless perfection. Rather, he is urging the

Thessalonians to give themselves to God without reservation. In this way, they make themselves ready for the coming of Christ, who conforms them fully to His image in glorification.

This is similar to Jude's message of encouragement: "Now to him who is able to protect you from stumbling and to make you stand in the presence of his glory, without blemish and with great joy" (Jude 24).

Paul reminds us that God is the sanctifier. He separates us from profane things, marks us as His own, and engages in the lifelong process of making us holy, as He is holy — a work completed when we see Jesus as He is and become like Him (1 John 3:2). This final act, which follows resurrection, sometimes is called *perfect sanctification*.

Paul asks the God of peace to keep his readers "sound and blameless," that is, with no legitimate ground for accusation, in view of and until the *parousia* — the appearing of the Lord Jesus Christ.

Tim Shenton writes that "it is not our feeble hold of God that makes us secure, but God's strong hold of us. That is why our hope is not in vain. That is why we need not fear the approaching Day of Judgment. Our certainty is wrapped up in God, who will complete what he has begun. Our sanctification and preservation are guaranteed in him."[26]

CSB	KJV	NIV	NASB	ESV
Sanctify	Sanctify	Sanctify	Sanctify	Sanctify

Comparing English translations of *hagiasai* in 1 Thess. 5:23

2 Thess. 2:13 - "But we ought to thank God always for you, brothers and sisters loved by the Lord, because from the beginning God has chosen you for salvation through sanctification (*hagiasmo*) by the Spirit and through belief in the truth."

Paul's gratitude toward God stretches from eternity past to the present day. As the Lord foreknows, elects, and predestines followers of Jesus before the foundation of the world, He carries out His sovereign plan of salvation in human history through the finished work of Christ, and He applies it to us in sanctification as we receive His Son by faith.

The "sanctification by the Spirit" referenced here is not progressive sanctification by which Christians grow in Christlikeness. Rather, it is the initial work of grace in which the Spirit sets apart new believers as belonging to Christ. Though our practical sanctification may experience ups and downs according to our obedience to the Lord, Paul assures us that, positionally, we are forever secure in Christ.

This is grounded in His eternal plan, as Paul expresses elsewhere:

- "For he chose us in him, before the foundation of the world, to be holy and blameless in love before him. He predestined us to be adopted as sons through Jesus Christ for himself, according to the good pleasure of his will, to the praise of his glorious grace that he lavished on us in the Beloved One" (Eph. 1:4-6).
- "He has saved us and called us with a holy calling, not according to our works, but according to his own purpose and grace, which was given to us in Christ Jesus before time began" (2 Tim. 1:9).

CSB	KJV	NIV	NASB	ESV
Sanctification	Sanctification	Sanctifying work	Sanctification	Sanctification

Comparing English translations of *hagiasmo* in 2 Thess. 2:13

1 Peter 1:1-2 - "Peter, an apostle of Jesus Christ: To those chosen, living as exiles dispersed abroad in Pontus, Galatia, Cappadocia, Asia, and Bithynia, chosen according to the foreknowledge of God the Father, through the sanctifying work (*hagiasmo*) of the Spirit, to be obedient and to be sprinkled with the blood of Jesus Christ."

This marvelous passage illuminates the synergistic roles of the persons within the Triune Godhead. Father, Son, and Holy Spirit work together to secure our deliverance from sin and our ultimate conformity to the image of Christ. God the Father chooses us according to His foreknowledge. God the Spirit sets us apart as holy ones and remains with us to make us more like Jesus. And God the Son sheds His blood to secure our redemption. Foreknowledge is *about* us; sanctification is *in* us; and the blood of Jesus is *for* us.

The sanctifying work of the Spirit is the means by which being chosen becomes a reality. Peter writes that the result of the Spirit's work is obedience and sprinkling with the blood of Jesus. While we are declared in right standing with God once and for all based on the shed blood of Jesus at Calvary, Peter's reference to sprinkling harkens back to the Old Testament work of priests at the tabernacle, which required obedience on the part of those offering sacrifices. It could be that he is using the analogy to spur his readers to daily self-denial. As Roger Raymer notes, "One living in obedience is constantly being cleansed with Christ's blood and is thus 'set apart' from the world (cf. 1 John 1:7, 9)."[27]

CSB	KJV	NIV	NASB	ESV
Sanctifying work	Sanctification	Sanctifying work	Sanctifying work	Sanctification

Comparing English translations of *hagiasmo* in 1 Peter 1:2

1 Peter 3:15 - "... but in your hearts regard (*hagiasate*) Christ the Lord as holy, ready at any time to give a defense to anyone who asks you for a reason for the hope that is in you."

The word translated "regard" is *hagiasate* in the Greek and means "to make separate from others." Believers are called to do more than make Christ a priority in our lives; we are to exalt Him above all other priorities since only He is worthy of worship. Peter is writing to encourage those who experience undeserved suffering. He reminds them that they are blessed and should not live in fear of sharing their faith. As they set apart Christ in their hearts, they are better prepared to offer anyone who asks a reason for the hope they exude.

Peter goes on to say in verse 16 that our defense of the Christian faith should always be carried out "with gentleness and respect, keeping a clear conscience, so that when you are accused, those who disparage your good conduct in Christ will be put to shame."

It's interesting to note that while sanctification is an element of God's work of salvation, believers are called to sanctify Christ in our hearts. As Robert Utley explains, "This is the covenant paradox of biblical faith. God is sovereign, yet humans are also free and must exercise that freedom in God's will. And how are we to sanctify Christ? 1. with our love for one another (vv. 8-9); 2. with our lives (cf. vv. 13-14); 3. with our verbal witness (cf. v. 15)."[28]

CSB	KJV	NIV	NASB	ESV
Regard / sanctify / set apart	Sanctify	Revere	Sanctify / set apart	Honor

Comparing English translations of *hagiasate* in 1 Peter 3:15

Summary

Sanctification is the work of God making us more like Jesus. It begins in the eternal mind of God the Father, who foreknows, chooses, and predestines us. It comes to us as a gift, delivered in person by the Son of God who, through His shed blood on the cross, secures salvation for us. And it is applied to us through the Holy Spirit, who marks us as God's own and then stays with us, ensuring that we are conformed to the image of Christ.

As a potter selects a lump of clay and places it on the wheel, the Spirit takes us as rank new believers and sets us apart for holiness. Then, just as the potter spins the wheel and fashions the clay into a beautiful vessel, the Holy Spirit molds our hearts — pressing, shaping, flinging — until our full being takes final shape just as God planned it. It's a lifelong process filled with spins, pressures, fits and starts, but in the end, it results in lives that reflect the Artist's genius and unmatched skill.

While sanctification is wholly the work of God, believers are called to sanctify the Lord Jesus in our hearts — to set Him apart from all competing gods, and to exalt Him in the throne room of our bodies, which are the temples of the Holy Spirit. In the end, God completes the work He began in us, and we are perfectly sanctified in the final act of salvation: glorification.

Consider these summary statements about sanctification:

- Sanctification may be understood in two ways, both of which relate to holiness. First, there is *positional sanctification*, the state of being separate, set apart from the common and dedicated to a higher purpose. Second, there is *practical sanctification*, the lifelong process by which the Spirit makes us more like Jesus.
- Sanctification begins the moment a person trusts in Jesus for salvation. As the blood of Jesus cleanses us from sin; as the Father declares us righteous in heaven; and as the Spirit indwells us and places us positionally into the body of Christ, we are sealed with God's mark of ownership and set apart as belonging to Him.
- While the Spirit does the work of making us more like Jesus, it's our responsibility to relinquish control of our lives and allow the Spirit to take the helm. Only then does He right the ship and sail it toward the harbor of heaven.
- Sanctification is supernatural. That is, it is a work only the indwelling Spirit can do. We cannot manufacture or multiply it. At the same time, it's a progressive work, completed over a lifetime and fraught with fits and starts as our fleshly desires wrestle with the indwelling Spirit.
- Christian *perfectionists* contend that it is possible for believers to arrive at a sinless state prior to physical death. *Non-perfectionists* counter that total sanctification is achieved only in glorification, when followers of Jesus are physically resurrected, given new bodies, and enabled to experience the completion of God's work of salvation as they are freed from the power and presence of sin.
- The *non-perfectionist* view appears more biblically faithful. First, sin is more subtle and pervasive than we may care to admit. Second, the Greek word translated "perfect" in Matt. 5:48 (*teleioi*) is better rendered "complete," or "mature." Finally, there is a striking absence of sinless characters in the Bible (except, of course, for Jesus). Rather than focus on our efforts to gain earthly glorification, we should fix our eyes on Jesus, the author and finisher of our faith (Heb. 12:2 KJV).

THINK
Questions for personal or group study

(1) While sanctification begins at the moment of conversion, how is it different from regeneration? Justification? Spirit baptism?

(2) What do you think Paul means when he writes that God has predestined believers to be "conformed to the image of his Son" (Rom. 8:29)?

(3) What is the difference between positional sanctification, practical sanctification, and perfect sanctification?

(4) Do you think it's possible for a Christian to attain sinless perfection in this lifetime? If not, how do you respond to the following passages of Scripture:

- Matt. 5:48
- Eph. 4:13
- 1 Thess. 5:23
- Heb. 13:20-21

(5) Peter tells us to "regard [set apart, sanctify] Christ the Lord as holy" in our hearts (1 Peter 3:15). If sanctification is totally the work of God, what do you think Peter has in mind here?

(6) In John 17:19, Jesus prays to the Father, "I sanctify myself for them [disciples]." If Jesus is sinless, why does He have to be sanctified? How should we understand Jesus' words?

(7) Why is our obedience so important in practical sanctification? How do you reconcile God's sovereign work of sanctification with our responsibility to be obedient?

Chapter Ten

YOU ARE ADOPTED

The news sickened Bernarda Gallardo. The 55-year-old Chilean picked up a local newspaper, only to read about a newborn baby discarded in the town's rubbish heap. The little girl survived a short time before succumbing to the elements. In Chile, if a family member does not claim the body of a deceased person, the corpse is classified as human waste. Bernarda could not let this stand.

She pleaded with medical officials, who allowed her to take the child's body and adopt the unnamed girl as her own. Six months later, she held a public funeral for her daughter, whom she named Aurora. Five hundred people attended.

Since Aurora's service, Gallardo has adopted and buried three more children — Manuel, Victor, and Cristobal.[1]

Gallardo's remarkable compassion for the discarded dead in her community illustrates an even greater love: the love of God for the spiritually dead, whom He brings back to life and adopts into His family. Just as Gallardo paid a price to provide her adopted children decent burials, God the Father paid the ultimate price. He sent His Son to die on a Roman cross to bear our sin debt. Three days later, He raised Jesus from the grave so that anyone who trusts in His Son is made spiritually alive, receives everlasting life, and is adopted into the family of God. This means enjoying the same relational benefits that the Son and the Holy Spirit enjoy with God the Father.

While such love is unfathomable, and at times misunderstood, it is biblically faithful for the follower of Jesus to say, "I am adopted."

WHAT DOES IT MEAN TO BE ADOPTED BY GOD?

Adoption is an act of God making us members of His family. The Greek word for adoption stems from two words: *huios*, meaning "son," and *thesis*, meaning "a placing." Thus, the word *huiothesia* conveys the idea of "placement into sonship." This biblical term is meant to include both males and females.

From a first-century legal perspective, adoption meant taking a person from another family and making him or her legally a child in a new family. The son's or daughter's former relationships were severed, and the adoptee became a member of the new family under the father's authority.

The New Testament concept of adoption is more sublime since it brings God and redeemed people into an everlasting relationship. Believers in Jesus are both *born again* and thus reckoned as children, and *adopted* into God's family with the full privileges and responsibilities of adults.

Here's how it works: In regeneration, the Holy Spirit makes us spiritually alive. That is, we are born again or born from above (John 3:3-8). God considers us as newborn babes and addresses us as children. In adoption, the Spirit brings us into such a relationship with God that we are not only His sons and daughters, but joint heirs with Jesus, having the full privileges of adults.

Earl Radmacher writes, "As spiritually adopted children, believers enjoy the benefits of being in God's family, including being heirs of God (Rom. 8:17). Adoption, however, does not discount the need for growing in the Christian life. The spiritual resources available from the 'Spirit of adoption' belong to the son or daughter of God from the moment of the new birth."[2]

Adoption into God's family is part of God's predestined plan for everyone who believes. As the apostle Paul writes, God has "predestined us to be adopted as sons through Jesus Christ for himself, according to the good pleasure of his will" (Eph. 1:5). It may help to see adoption in light of other elements of God's work of salvation:

- In *calling*, God extends to us an offer of adoption as the gospel is proclaimed and the Holy Spirit draws us to Christ.
- In *regeneration*, the Holy Spirit awakens our dead human spirits, which have been cut off from the life-giving presence of God by our disbelief and rebellion.
- In *indwelling*, the Spirit takes up permanent residence in our human spirits, the most holy place in the temples of our bodies.
- In *justification*, the Father declares us righteous based on the imputation of our sins to Christ and the imputation of His righteousness to us.
- In *Spirit baptism*, the Holy Spirit places us into the body of Christ, where we share the common presence of the Spirit with all other followers of Jesus.
- In *sealing*, God places His mark of ownership on us, securing our salvation and distinguishing us from those still in the domain of darkness.
- In *sanctification*, the Spirit sets us apart as holy and then engages in the lifelong process of making us so.
- And in *adoption*, the Father brings us into His family as sons and daughters, ensuring us of the same intimacy the Father, Son, and Holy Spirit have enjoyed as persons of the Trinity throughout all eternity.

All of these elements of salvation work together and provide the follower of Jesus lasting benefits, including: a new life; the forgiveness of sins; a right standing with God; a new family; a new destination; a new journey; and a new hope. Jesus may have had the ultimate fulfillment of all these benefits in mind when He declared, "Look, I am making everything new" (Rev. 21:5b).

The legal aspect of the Greek word *huiothesia* is significant. It indicates that believers have been given all the legal privileges of sons and daughters in God's family. "When God adopts believers as His children, He places the Spirit of His Son into their hearts so that they become, in effect, His natural-born children. As such, they are not merely 'adopted' (in the sense the word now conveys) but genuinely 'begotten' by God. God makes 'sons of God' out of 'sons of men.' The term 'sons of God,' a common King James expression, includes believers of both sexes."[3]

The journey into adoption is a treacherous one. Because every person is a naturally born sinner, the New Testament describes us as "children under wrath" (Eph. 2:3) and "children of disobedience" (Eph. 2:2; 5:6 KJV). We are citizens of Satan's kingdom, a domain of darkness. We are spiritually blinded (2 Cor. 4:4), captives to the will of the evil one (2 Tim. 2:26), and dead in our sins (Eph. 2:1). As such, we are under divine wrath (John 3:36b).

But God doesn't leave us there. He sends His Son, who sets aside His privileged position at the Father's right hand and adds sinless humanity to His deity via the miracle of the virgin birth. He goes to the cross, bears our sins, and then rises from the dead to conquer Satan, sin, and death for us. He is not only the unique Son of God; He is the firstborn Son — that is, the first person to rise from the dead never to die again. And by God's grace, through faith in Jesus, we are purchased out of the slave market of sin, released forever from the clutches of the evil one, and welcomed as adopted children into the family of God.

It's important to understand that while believers are called "sons of God" in the Scriptures (Matt. 5:9; Rom. 8:14, 19; Gal. 3:26), the title "Son of God," when used for Jesus, refers to His deity (Matt. 16:16-17). He is one in essence with God the Father and the Holy Spirit. As the second person of the Trinity, Christ is distinguished from the Father as "the only begotten Son."

That's a key distinction. Believers in Jesus do not become little gods. Although adopted as God's sons and daughters, we are not equals with the eternal, all-powerful, all-knowing, everywhere-present God. We do "share in the divine nature" (2 Peter 1:4), however. That means the Holy Spirit takes up residence in the temples of our bodies, enables us to overcome sin, enlightens us to God's perspective of every-thing, and ensures that we are more than conquerors in Christ. What's more, the Spirit assures us that we are indeed God's children

(Rom. 8:16; Gal. 4:6). We may rightly call God our Father (Rom. 8:15), a privilege even the elite religious leaders of Jesus' day could not claim (John 8:39-47).

Although believers are now and forevermore in the family of God, we won't experience the full benefits of adoption until we are raised from the dead in glorification (Rom. 8:21-23). Only then do we receive our full inheritance, being conformed to the image of Christ and enjoying eternity in a sinless state in new heavens and a new earth purged of sin and its consequences (2 Peter 3:10-13; Revelation 21-22).

WHEN DOES ADOPTION OCCUR?

Like so many other acts of salvation, adoption takes place in a moment of time and provides lasting benefits. It appears we are adopted as God's children *after* we are born again, as God responds to our saving faith. Wayne Grudem writes that "the New Testament never connects adoption with regeneration; indeed, the idea of *adoption* is opposite to the idea of being born into a family! Rather, the New Testament connects adoption with saving faith, and says that in response to our trusting in Christ, God has adopted us into his family."[4]

We see this in at least a couple of New Testament passages. The apostle John writes, "But to all who did receive him, he gave them the right to be [or become] children of God, to those who believe in his name, who were born, not of natural descent, or of the will of the flesh, or of the will of man, but of God" (John 1:12-13). Once the Holy Spirit regenerates us and the Spirit of God indwells us, we share in the divine nature as newborn children of God. Then, we become the adopted children of God. Further, Paul writes that "through faith you are all sons of God in Christ Jesus" (Gal. 3:26).

Someone may point to Gal. 4:6 and argue that God first adopts us as children and then sends His Holy Spirit to regenerate us: "And because you are sons, God sent the Spirit of His Son into our hearts ..." However, just a few verses earlier Paul declares our adoption as "through faith." Therefore, it's best to understand Gal. 4:6, not as the work of the Spirit in regeneration, but a subsequent work of the Spirit bearing testimony in our already-regenerated spirits that we are members of God's family. "This work of the Holy Spirit gives us *assurance* of our adoption, and it is in this sense that Paul says that, after we have become sons, God causes his Holy Spirit within our hearts to cry, 'Abba! Father!' (cf. Rom. 8:15-16)."[5]

Just as earthly adoption becomes final when all legal requirements are met, our adoption as children of God is completed when we are born again by the Spirit of God and declared righteous by the Father through justification. A benefit flowing from justification by faith is a new and permanent relationship with God as our Father, with benefits carrying forward throughout the Christian life and perfected in glorification.

In addition to becoming children of God, we are, spiritually speaking, brothers and sisters of all other believers, including believing Jews of the Old Testament. Paul reminds us that Christians are Abraham's children: "Neither are all of Abraham's children his descendants. On the contrary, **your offspring will be traced through Isaac.** That is, it is not the children by physical descent who are God's children, but the children of the promise are considered to be the offspring" (Rom. 9:7-8).

Paul further explains that our status as God's adopted children was not fully realized under the old covenant. He writes, "Before this faith came, we were confined under the law, imprisoned until the coming faith was revealed. The law, then, was our guardian until Christ, so that we could be justified by faith. But since that faith has come, we are no longer under a guardian, for through faith you are all sons of God in Christ Jesus" (Gal. 3:23-26).

This doesn't mean there is no Old Testament concept of a divine family, for in several passages God calls Himself the Father of the Israelites; He even calls them His children (Ps. 103:13; Isa. 43:6-7; Mal. 1:6; 2:10). Even so, the full benefits of membership in God's family do not arrive until Jesus completes His earthly ministry and the Spirit is poured into our spirits.

WHAT ARE THE BENEFITS OF ADOPTION?

Adoption as children of God provides many benefits including:

An intimate relationship with God. Unlike Allah, the god of Islam, who is neither personal, relational, nor knowable, Yahweh is all three. He could have forgiven our sins based on the finished work of Christ and then left us alone as acquitted sinners; justification could have been the end-all to the matter of the debt we owe our offended God. But, instead, we are invited to pray, "Our Father in heaven" (Matt. 6:9). It's true that God is our judge, master, and Lord. "But the role that is most intimate, and the role that conveys the highest privileges of fellowship with God for eternity, is his role as our heavenly Father."[6]

The presence of the Holy Spirit, who enables us to live according to the Father's will. "For all those who are led by God's Spirit are God's sons," Paul writes. "You did not receive a spirit of slavery to fall back into fear. Instead, you received the Spirit of adoption, by whom we cry out, 'Abba, Father!' The Spirit himself testifies together with our spirit that we are God's children ..." (Rom. 8:14-16).

The discipline of God. While this may not be a pleasant reality, it should comfort us to know that God's love for us is so deep, He corrects us to keep us closer to Him. As the writer of Hebrews puts it, quoting from Prov. 3:11-12, **"My son, do not take the Lord's discipline lightly or lose heart when you are reproved by him, for the Lord disciplines the one he loves and punishes every son he receives"** (Heb. 12:5-6).

Sharing in the sufferings and subsequent glory of Christ. Paul writes that we are God's children and heirs, coheirs with Christ, "if indeed we suffer with him so that we may also be glorified with him" (Rom. 8:17).

Membership in the family of God. The New Testament often refers to Christians as "brothers" and "sisters" in Christ (Matt. 12:50; Rom. 1:13; 8:12; 16:1; 1 Cor. 1:10; 6:8; 7:15; Philemon 1:2; James 1:2; 2:15). The idea of believers being part of a family should encourage us to work cooperatively with like-minded Christians, and to be careful about speaking carelessly against those whose beliefs and practices on secondary and tertiary matters differ from ours.[7]

A perfect model for our lives. Paul writes, "Therefore, be imitators of God, as dearly loved children, and walk in love, as Christ also loved us and gave himself for us, a sacrificial and fragrant offering to God" (Eph. 5:1-2). Peter adds, "As obedient children, do not be conformed to the desires of your former ignorance. But as the one who called you is holy, you also are to be holy in all your conduct; for it is written, Be holy, because I am holy" (1 Peter 1:14-16). A consistent pattern of imitating our Heavenly Father demonstrates that we belong to Him and love Him. As the apostle John puts it, "This is how God's children and the devil's children become obvious. Whoever does not do what is right is not of God, especially the one who does not love his brother or sister" (1 John 3:10).

CAN MY ADOPTION BE REVOKED?

If Moses "permitted" Hebrew men to divorce their wives (Matt. 19:8), and if Israelite parents were instructed to stone rebellious children in severe cases (Deut. 21:18-21), what guarantee do Christians have that God won't cancel our adoption if we cross a certain line? Put another way, how secure are we in the family of God?

The apostle Paul likely wrote about our adoption as children of God in the context of Roman law and culture. In his day, the Roman practice of adoption embraced three realities. First, adopted persons lost all rights to their old family in exchange for the privileges of fully legitimate children in their new family. In a binding legal sense, they got a new father. Second, they became heirs of their new father's estate. "No matter how many other sons there were at the time or how many were born thereafter, he [the adopted son] was co-heir with them. This was not subject to change."[8] Finally, the old life of the adoptees was erased. All debts were cancelled, legally and irrevocably. In short, adoption was permanent and irreversible.

In much the same way, when new believers are adopted into God's family, Satan no longer may claim them. Their sin debt is cancelled. Their citizenship in the kingdom of darkness is revoked. Their spiritual chains and blinders, placed there by the evil one, are stripped away. Their sentence of everlasting death is reversed. The "father of lies" no longer takes them captive to do his will (John 8:44; 2 Tim. 2:26).

Instead, believers are given new lives, new natures, new names, a new home, a new family, a new citizenship, and a new hope (John

10:10; 14:3; 2 Cor. 5:17; Eph. 1:5; Phil. 3:20; 1 Peter 1:3; Rev. 2:7; 3:12). They also are given the Holy Spirit, who seals them until the day of redemption — the topic of our next chapter (Eph. 4:30). The Spirit is their pledge of an inheritance with all the children of God. Further, the Spirit witnesses that adoption has taken place and then guarantees its security throughout this life and the life to come.

It's important to see adoption in light of all God's work of salvation. If He foreknew us, elected us to salvation, and predestined us to be conformed to the image of His Son — all in eternity past — then the finished work of Christ on the cross and the regenerating, indwelling, baptizing, and sealing work of the Spirit ensures that the Lord's purposes carry through unhindered. We may call the Lord *Abba* — dearest daddy — because He is loving, merciful, and faithful to His promises.

This does not mean the Lord looks the other way when Christians commit grievous sin. Quite the contrary. Because He has promised to make His adopted children just like His eternal Son, He chastens us for our own good. This takes appropriate forms: the gentle voice of the Spirit, convicting us of sin; church discipline, in which fellow believers walk us through repentance and restoration, or, if we persist in sin, deliver us to a congregational rebuke; or even illness or physical death at the hands of the Lord Himself (Matt. 18:15-20; Acts 5:1-11; 1 Cor. 11:27-32; Gal. 6:1).

While we may lose rewards in heaven for unfaithfulness (1 Cor. 3:11-15), or even find ourselves ashamed at His coming (1 John 2:28), we do not need to fear losing God's gift of everlasting life. The Father who adopted us ensures our inheritance, and He works in our lives to make sure we stand worthy of it one day.

WHAT DOES IT MEAN TO BE A COHEIR WITH JESUS?

In Rom. 8:17, Paul writes that Christians are "heirs of God and coheirs with Christ." A proper understanding of our inheritance as adopted children of God is grounded in Roman law and culture. According to Francis Lyall, there was no Jewish adoption law for the purpose of perpetuating a family line. When a man died without male offspring, his closest male relative was commanded to sleep with the widow and produce an heir. Roman law, in contrast, allowed a man to designate an heir from outside his family.

Further, in modern law, we do not become heirs until someone dies, even though we may be listed as beneficiaries. But in Roman law, all members of a family held property jointly with the *paterfamilias*. All children of any age — natural or adopted — already were heirs even while their father lived, and they had joint control of property. In other words, "Birth, not death, constituted heirship," according to Lyall.[9]

As heirs, we are promised an inheritance that is "imperishable, undefiled, and unfading, kept in heaven" for us (1 Peter 1:4). This inheritance is salvation in all its fullness — our glorification, our rewards for faithfulness, our place around the throne in heaven, and our promise of everlasting life in intimate fellowship with the Triune God in the new heavens and the new earth. Peter makes this clear: "You are being guarded by God's power through faith for a salvation that is ready to be revealed in the last time.... because you are receiving the goal of your faith, the salvation of your souls" (1 Peter 1:5, 9).

This salvation is:

- Imperishable - perhaps a historical allusion to the Promised Land meaning "secure from invasion."[10]
- Undefiled - not tarnished by the presence or power of sin, which dims even the brightest blessings of God on earth.
- Unfading - incapable of losing its luster or longevity; "exempt from the blight which attaches to earthly bloom."[11]
- Kept in heaven - where Satan may neither steal nor defile it, and where God Himself holds it securely. The word *kept*, or *reserved*, is a military term for a guarded or garrisoned fortress (cf. Phil. 4:7).[12]

Jesus, as the eternal Son of God, is the natural heir of the Father. His inheritance is the entire universe — all that exists. The writer of Hebrews notes, "God has appointed him [Jesus] heir of all things and made the universe through Him" (Heb. 1:2b) Being a coheir with Jesus means that we, as adopted children, share in His inheritance.

"What belongs to Jesus will belong to us. Christ gives us His glory (John 17:22), His riches (2 Cor. 8:9), and all things (Heb. 1:2). We are as welcome in God's family as Jesus is; we are 'accepted in the Beloved' (Eph. 1:6 NKJV). All that belongs to Jesus Christ will belong to us, the co-heirs, as well."[13]

It's too much for our limited minds to take in. The universe — the vast, unfathomable created order — is ours. For all eternity. Even better, the eternal, all-powerful, all-knowing, and everywhere-present Creator of it all is ours, now and forevermore.

ARE ANGELS "SONS OF GOD"?

Although both holy and evil angels are called "sons of God" (Job 1:6), this evidently is a reference to their status as special creations of God. It does not seem to indicate that angels share the same privileges that Old and New Testament saints receive as God's adopted children.

In fact, Heb. 2:14-16 distinguishes between our status as God's children and the status of angels: "Now since the children have flesh and blood in common, Jesus also shared in these, so that through his death he might destroy the one holding the power of death — that is the devil — and free those who were held in slavery all their lives by the fear of death. For it is clear that he does not reach out to help angels, but to help Abraham's offspring."

In other words, Jesus did not come to earth in the likeness of fallen angels, but in the likeness of sinful people. As such, there is no redemption for Satan and demons; only hell awaits them (Matt. 25:41). Holy angels enjoy the presence of God in heaven. As beings of greater power and intelligence than humans, angels also serve the Lord as messengers, defenders of God's people, and soldiers against the forces of Satan in the heavenly realm. Even so, holy angels cannot experience redemption; they simply observe it — and wonder (1 Peter 1:12).

Nowhere in Scripture are angels called members of God's family or said to have the privileges that belong to redeemed people — such as being joint heirs with Jesus. Adoption is a remarkable gift of God to creatures made lower than the angels.

Some may raise the issue of the "sons of God" in Gen. 6:1-4. These "sons of God" desire "the daughters of men" and take them as wives. A number of Bible commentators take this to mean that certain fallen angels had sexual relations with the women of earth, producing a wicked hybrid race of people that God ultimately destroyed with the flood. Others contend that the term "sons of God" refers to the godly line of Seth, which intermarried with the wicked line of Cain.

But it seems best to understand the "sons of God" in this passage as mighty, wicked men who willingly became the first objects of demon possession — an unspeakable breach of God's division in creation between angels and people. These "angels who did not keep their own position but abandoned their proper dwelling" are now "kept in eternal chains in deep darkness [in Tartarus] for the judgment on the great day" (Jude 6; cf. 2 Peter 2:4).[14]

CAN I CLAIM MY INHERITANCE NOW?

If we are sons and daughters of God, coheirs with Jesus, and citizens of the King who owns the cattle on a thousand hills (Ps. 50:10), what's to keep us from claiming our inheritance now? Why wait until Christ returns? Why postpone the riches of the New Jerusalem? Why languish in poverty and sickness when no child of the King should experience such wretched circumstances?

Why not speak words of faith over our checkbooks and doctors' charts and live a life free of the consequences of the Fall? If God spoke the world into existence, and we are His adopted children, granted the full privileges of His family, why can't we call "things into existence that do not exist" (Rom. 4:17b)?

While Christians should find such questions absurd, if not heretical, there is a strain of Christianity that answers, "Why not?" to all of these questions. The Word of Faith movement, better known as the prosperity gospel, essentially promotes a gospel in which faith in Jesus is a means to an end — that end being your health, prosperity, and success.

The argument goes something like this: God has made us in His image, and we most please Him when we imitate our Creator. Jesus took our infirmities (read "poverty" and "sickness") on Himself and abolished them through His suffering in hell. So, we are set free from these consequences of the Fall. We may therefore create new realities by speaking words of faith, just as God spoke the world into existence.

This line of thinking continues: If we have enough faith, we may be healed of all illnesses, cured of poverty, cleansed of psychological ailments, and purged of toxic relationships. After all, if we live in the finest homes, drive the most luxurious cars, marry the most gorgeous mates, run the most successful businesses, parade the most adorable children onto the field to be crowned homecoming kings and queens — all in the name of Jesus — who wouldn't want to accept Him as their Savior?

Such a view of adoption is perverse. If Jesus came, not to be served, but to serve, and to give His life as a ransom for us (Matt. 20:28), shouldn't we imitate Him by denying ourselves, taking up our crosses daily, and following Jesus (Luke 9:23)? Isn't a selfish view of sonship, which Word of Faith leaders promote, in reality a wish for the Father's death so the full inheritance may be claimed now? Isn't this the attitude of the son who, in Jesus' parable, seized his share of his father's wealth and then squandered it in foolish living (Luke 15:11-32)?

Being grateful, humble, and self-denying followers of Jesus does not diminish our adoption as children. We still have the promises of our full inheritance: a universe purged of sin and its consequences, freedom from death, grief, crying, and pain, which John calls the "previous things" (Rev. 21:4). But these promises are for the future. Until then, Christians occupy the same sinful and fallen world as the unregenerate do. We're going to get sick, lose our jobs, struggle to make ends meet, grow old, and die.

Further, we are to expect rejection, persecution, and many trials precisely because we are the adopted children of God. If the world hates us, we should remember that it hated Jesus first (John 15:18-25). As the apostle Paul notes, "It is necessary to go through many hardships to enter the kingdom of God" (Acts 14:22).[15]

KEY PASSAGES ON ADOPTION

Let's survey several Bible verses that address what it means to be adopted by God.

Rom. 8:14-17 - "For all those led by God's Spirit are God's sons. You did not receive a spirit of slavery to fall back into fear. Instead, you received the Spirit of adoption (*huiothesias*), by whom we cry out, '*Abba*, Father!' The Spirit himself testifies together with our spirit that we are God's children, and if children, also heirs — heirs of God and coheirs with Christ — if indeed we suffer with him so that we may also be glorified with him."

Paul packs a number of divine truths about adoption into these four verses. First, the Holy Spirit leads all of God's children, who have been born again and adopted into the family of God. The indwelling Spirit does more than pitch His tent in our spirits and passively reside there until we pass through the portal of death to meet the Lord. He places God's mark of ownership on us through sealing. He plunges us into the universal church through Spirit baptism. He sets us apart and works continually to conform us to the image of Christ in sanctification. He empowers us to serve by granting us spiritual gifts. He helps us understand the book He authored as we read it and meditate on its inspired passages. He whispers comfort, encouragement, and correction into our spiritual ears so that we might hear His voice through the white noise of fleshly appeals.

Second, the Spirit advances us in our faith. We should not despair about the slavery of fear, from which Christ has delivered us. Rather, we should rest in the reality of everlasting life, which the "Spirit of adoption" has secured for us. In that warm glow of unbreakable familial love, we may call God *Abba* — our Papa.

Third, the Spirit testifies with our spirits that we are children of God. Just as the third person of the Godhead testifies to the life and work of the eternal Son of God, the Spirit also assures us that as adopted sons and daughters, we possess a secure destiny. Even more, we are coheirs with Christ. The certainty of Jesus' role as the heir of all things should remind us of His words, "I will not leave you as orphans; I am coming to you.... Because I live, you will live too" (John 14:18-19).

Finally, Paul caps this marvelous passage with a sober reminder that we should expect to suffer with Him before we are glorified with Him. Elsewhere in Scripture, the apostle encourages Christ's disciples to continue in the faith, while reminding them, "It is necessary to go through many hardships to enter the kingdom of God" (Acts 14:22). And he warns a young pastor that "all who want to live a godly life in Christ Jesus will be persecuted" (2 Tim. 3:12). Christian suffering is not merely *for* Christ but *with* Him. We may share in His abandonment, rejection, and pain, and yet it is not ours alone; He remains with us through it all.

Warren Wiersbe writes, "There is no need for the believer to be defeated. He can yield his body to the Spirit and by faith overcome the old nature. The Spirit of life will empower him. The Spirit of death will enable him to overcome the flesh. And the Spirit of adoption will enrich him and lead him into the will of God."[16]

CSB	KJV	NIV	NASB	ESV
Adoption	Adoption	Adoption to sonship	Adoption as sons	Adoption as sons

Comparing English translations of *huiothesias* in Rom. 8:15

Rom. 8:23 - "Not only that, but we ourselves who have the Spirit as the firstfruits — we also groan within ourselves, eagerly waiting for adoption (*huiothesian*), the redemption of our bodies."

This is an unusual reference to adoption in that the apostle Paul likens it to the future resurrection of our bodies. The indwelling Holy Spirit is believers' guarantee of glorified bodies when Christ returns for us. We may groan now because of our fallen nature, but the promised redemption of our bodies will conform us to Jesus' glorified body.

Paul describes three related *groanings* in verses 22-26. First, "the whole creation has been groaning together with labor pains until now" (v. 22). That is, the fallen world in which we live agonizes beneath the weight of the curse and cries out for the day when it is set free from bondage to decay.

Second, Christians, "who have the Spirit as the firstfruits, also groan within ourselves, eagerly waiting for adoption, the redemption of our bodies" (v. 23). Put another way, Paul urges us to live in the light of eternity. The indwelling Holy Spirit is our "firstfruits," the down payment on our future inheritance, which is received when

Christ raises us from the dead and perfects our bodies (1 Cor. 15:35-58; Phil. 3:21).

Third, the Spirit intercedes for us "with unspoken groanings" (v. 26). While we wait eagerly for our future glorification, the Holy Spirit sustains us in our present weakness. Often, we are unable to express our fleshly struggles adequately to our loving Heavenly Father. But both the Son and the Spirit come to our aid. Jesus is our intercessor in heaven (Heb. 7:25), and the Spirit is our intercessor on earth, specifically within our spirits.

As the *CSB Study Bible* notes, "We are limited and ignorant, but the Spirit uses unspoken groanings to communicate our needs. This is not 'speaking in tongues or languages' (Gk *glossolalia*). It is instead wordless. Our heavenly Father knows what is happening in our lives and within the deep recesses of our personalities. The Spirit's requests are always according to the will of God and are always answered."[17]

CSB	KJV	NIV	NASB	ESV
Adoption	The adoption	Adoption to sonship	Adoption as sons	Adoption as sons

Comparing English translations of *huiothesian* in Rom. 8:23

Rom. 9:4 - "They are Israelites, and to them belong the adoption (*he huiothesia*), the glory, the covenants, the giving of the law, the temple service, and the promises."

Paul moves from great joy in Romans 8, proclaiming the believer's triumph in Christ, to deep sorrow in Romans 9. There, like Moses, he expresses a willingness to be cursed in exchange for the Israelites' salvation (cf. Ex. 32:30-35). What a grieving heart. Paul is willing to delay his journey into heaven for the sake of the saved (Phil. 1:22-24) and ready to go to hell for the benefit of the lost (Rom. 9:3).

Paul then returns to a listing of national privileges that he began in Rom. 3:1-2. First, the Israelites are entrusted with the very words of God (3:2). Next, to them belong the adoption, the glory, the covenants, the giving of the law, the temple services, the promises, and the ancestors through whom Messiah has been born (9:4-5).

Our focus here is on the adoption of Israel by God, who refers to

His chosen people as "my firstborn son" (Ex. 4:22). The Lord instructs Moses to tell Pharaoh, "Let my son go so that he may worship me, but you refused to let him go. Look, I am about to kill your firstborn son!" (Ex. 4:23).[18] The Lord claims Israel as His firstborn, a position of privilege within ancient families that is secured through birth order or by appointment. "In short, Pharaoh was informed that he was merely a vassal ruling a second-rate nation and must answer to the Lord."[19]

Paul's reference to adoption in Rom. 9:4 is the only time in his epistles that he applies the term to Israel. But it is significant for us as Christians. In the same way God chooses the nation of Israel and showers blessings on His "firstborn son," He chooses us as adopted children and then promises us a great inheritance. We already have discussed the benefits of Christians being adopted into the family of God. So, let's briefly survey the blessings of Israel as the Lord's adopted people:

The glory. Yahweh gives the Israelites the Shekinah glory — a blazing, physical manifestation of the divine presence — in the tabernacle and temple (Ex. 40:34-38; 1 Kings 8:10-11). The glory Moses beholds on Mount Sinai comes to dwell with the Lord's people (Ex. 24:16-17). We have no indication in Scripture that this glory resides with pagan peoples.

The covenants. First, God makes a covenant with Abraham, and then Moses, and then David. The Gentiles, before the time of Christ, are "foreigners to the covenants of promise" (Eph. 2:12).

The law. The Lord gives the Israelites His law to govern their political, social, and religious life, and to guarantee His blessings if they obey. This does not excuse non-Israelites for their sins, because God's existence and moral code are revealed to all people through creation and conscience (Rom. 1:18-32; 2:12-16).

The temple service. God establishes the ministry to be performed in the tabernacle and temple, where His people may obtain atonement for their sins and bring their offerings of praise.

The promises. These are the great Abrahamic promises, which unfold over time and are fulfilled only in Christ (Acts 26:6-7; Gal. 3:16, 21; Heb. 7:6).

The ancestors. Through the patriarchs — most notably Abraham,

Isaac, and Jacob (Luke 20:37) — comes the greatest promise of all: "Christ, who is God over all, praised forever" (Rom. 9:5).

The purpose of all these blessings is that Jesus Christ, through Israel, might come into the world. "All of these blessings were given freely to Israel and to no other nation."[20]

CSB	KJV	NIV	NASB	ESV
The adoption	The adoption	The adoption to sonship	The adoption as sons	The adoption

Comparing English translations of *he huiothesia* in Rom. 9:4

Gal. 4:4-5 - "When the time came to completion, God sent his Son, born of a woman, born under the law, to redeem those under the law, so that we might receive adoption as sons (*ten huiothesian*)."

The adoption of believing people as children of God is conditioned on the finished work of Christ. Paul reminds us that the Son's appearance on earth comes at exactly the right moment: "When the time came to completion" (v. 4). This is rendered "the fullness of the time" in the KJV and NASB; "the fullness of time" in the ESV; and "the set time" in the NIV. Just as the Father appointed a day for His Son to come to earth as the Lamb of God who takes away the sin of the world (John 1:29), He also governed human history in such a way that the birth of Jesus would coincide with the world's readiness for a redeemer.

In Jesus' day, the Roman world is in such need of a deliverer that it deifies its Caesars. Old religions give way to new ones, and worn-out philosophies are petty and vain. At the same time, modern roads connect the cities of the Roman Empire, making it easier to spread news and transport people. Roman laws protect the rights of its citizens and preserve the special peace known as *Pax Romana*. Latin and Greek are widely known across the empire. If there ever is a time for a savior to appear, it is now.

Even so, throughout His earthly ministry, Jesus avoids being placed on a throne — or tossed over a cliff to His death. Why? Because the time of His revelation as Messiah, and the hour of His crucifixion, have not yet come. At the scene of His first miracle, Jesus tells His mother, "My hour has not yet come" (John 2:4). Later, Jesus tells His unbelieving brothers, who challenge Him to go to the Feast of Tabernacles and make Himself known, "My time has not yet arrived / fully come" (John 7:6, 8). As He teaches in the temple, the religious leaders try to seize Him. "Yet no one laid a hand on him because his hour had not yet come" (John 7:30).

Then, proclaiming Himself "the light of the world" (John 8:12), Jesus finds Himself opposed by the Pharisees. "But no one seized him, because his hour had not yet come" (John 8:20b). When Jesus proclaims His deity with the words, "Truly I tell you, before Abraham was, I am," the Jews pick up stones to throw at Him. "But Jesus was hidden and went out of the temple" (John 8:58-59). And when He declares, "I and the Father are one," the Jews again seek to stone Him for blasphemy. "Then they were trying again to seize him, but he eluded their grasp" (John 10:30, 39).

The apostle John captures the elusiveness of Jesus, but he doesn't miss the point that the Son of Man has a destiny with the cross. After His triumphal entry into Jerusalem, Jesus tells His followers, "The hour has come for the Son of Man to be glorified" (John 12:23). Not long thereafter, John records, "Before the Passover Festival, Jesus knew that his hour had come to depart from this world to the Father" (John 13:1). And the apostle records these words from Jesus in His high priestly prayer: "Father, the hour has come. Glorify your Son so that the Son may glorify you" (John 17:1).

Not only does the Son's appearance on earth come at exactly the right moment, it comes in a most unusual way. Jesus is "born of a woman" (Gal. 4:4), a reference to His miraculous conception in a virgin's womb. This is the way of the Incarnation, God with us. Through the virgin birth, Jesus does not relinquish His deity. Rather, He temporarily sets aside His privileged position at the Father's right hand, humbling Himself to come to His fallen creatures veiled in human flesh.

Jesus' favorite term for Himself is "Son of Man." No doubt, this is a reference to Daniel 7 and His own deity, but it also demonstrates the manner in which the Messiah comes to us in full humanity as the God-Man. The writer of Hebrews captures this well: "Therefore, he had to be like his brothers and sisters in every way, so that he could become a merciful and faithful high priest in matters pertaining to

God, to make atonement for the sins of the people. For since he himself has suffered when he was tempted, he is able to help those who are tempted" (Heb. 2:17-18). The ancient promise that the Redeemer would be the "seed" or "offspring" of woman is fulfilled in Jesus (Isa. 7:14; Matt. 1:18-25).

Finally, Jesus is "born under the law, to redeem those under the law" (Gal. 4:4b-5a). To redeem is to set free by paying a price. Our Redeemer is born under the Mosaic Law. Rather than do away with the law, He fulfills it through His sinless life, which is then offered up for us (Rom. 5:17; 2 Cor. 5:21; Heb. 4:15-16). His death on the cross, in our place, is the just payment for our sins. While it satisfies God's justice, it also extends to us God's grace and mercy. Since we are slaves to sin and held captive by the evil one, we have no hope for freedom (2 Tim. 2:26). But because Jesus took our place on the cross, as the spotless Lamb of God, He has redeemed us from the slave market of sin. We are bought with a price, and thus we are free (1 Cor. 6:20; 7:23). Even better, we now receive the adoption as children of God.

CSB	KJV	NIV	NASB	ESV
Adoption as sons	The adoption of sons	Adoption to sonship	The adoption as sons	Adoption as sons

Comparing English translations of *ten huiothesian* in Gal. 4:5

Eph. 1:5-6 - "He predestined us to be adopted as sons (*eis huiothesian*) through Jesus Christ for himself, according to the good pleasure of his will, to the praise of his glorious grace that he lavished on us in the Beloved One."

While our adoption as children of God takes place in time, it always has been in the mind of God. Just as the Father chose us in Christ before the foundation of the world (v. 4), He also predestined us to be adopted as His sons and daughters. Throughout the New Testament, the Greek word *proorizo* consistently refers to God's predetermined plan to bring salvation history to its climax in the person of Jesus Christ, "the Beloved One" (v. 6). God the Father always is the subject of this verb in the New Testament.[21]

Paul tells the Corinthians, "we speak God's hidden wisdom in a mystery, a wisdom God predestined before the ages for our glory" (1 Cor. 2:7). This predetermined wisdom is the secret, now revealed, that the Lord of glory is the crucified Christ. The early church sees Jesus' sufferings as the predetermined plan of the Father in harmony with the Old Testament Scriptures (Acts 4:28). And Christians receive their calling and adoption based on the Father's loving determination to conform those He foreknew to the image of Christ (Rom. 8:29-30; Eph. 1:11).

Because God's plan of salvation is eternal and intersects with us in time, we may rest assured of our security in Christ. As Robert Utley writes, "A Roman father had the legal right to disinherit or even kill natural children, but not adopted children. This reflects the believer's security in Christ."[22]

This is a breathtaking truth. Just as it pleased God the Father to smite His own (un-adopted) Son on our behalf (Isa. 53:10), He adopts us "according to the good pleasure of his will" (Eph. 1:5). Not that Jesus is a victim in this divine plan of redemption, for the Son of Man makes it clear that He comes into the world to give His life as a ransom for many (Matt. 20:28). He voluntarily lays down His life (John 10:17-18). And, for joy, He endures the cross (Heb. 12:2). There is no sibling rivalry here between the natural heir of all things and His adopted coheirs. The Father and Son are on the same page. What a remarkable story of divine love and sacrifice for the sake of our adoption.

CSB	KJV	NIV	NASB	ESV
To be adopted as sons	Unto the adoption of children	For adoption to sonship	To adoption as sons	For adoption to himself as sons

Comparing English translations of *eis huiothesian* in Eph. 1:5

SUMMARY

Adoption is an act of God making born-again believers members of His family. As in first-century Roman culture, all former relationships of the adopted child are severed, and the adoptee is made a full-fledged member of his or her family under the father's authority, and with the full privileges and responsibilities of an adult. No longer does the evil one hold his servants captive, in spiritual blindness, alienated from God, and destined for outer darkness. Christ has come to our rescue, redeeming us from the slave market of sin and joyfully welcoming us into the Father's family as His coheirs in the everlasting kingdom.

Adoption into God's family is part of the Father's predestined plan for everyone who believes. It is inextricably bound to all other elements of salvation, spanning from eternity past in foreknowledge to eternity future in glorification. As a consequence, we may rest assured of our salvation, for just as a Roman father could not disown an adopted son, God is faithful to His promise to conform us to the image of His eternal Son.

This does not mean a life of ease for the Father's children. Although He has promised us all things, Jesus and the New Testament writers make it clear that we continue to live in a sinful and fallen world, and thus we are subject to accidents, poverty, lawsuits, sickness, aging, and physical death. In addition, faithful Christians should expect persecution. But one day, after Christ returns, He makes all things new, purging the universe of sin and its stain, and delighting us by revealing that the heartaches of this present age are remembered as "previous things" that have "passed away" (Rev. 21:4).

Consider these summary statements about adoption:

- The New Testament concept of adoption is more sublime even than Roman adoption since it brings God and redeemed people into an everlasting relationship. Believers in Jesus are both *born again* and thus reckoned as children, and *adopted* into God's family with the full privileges and responsibilities of adults.
- The journey into adoption is a treacherous one. Because every person is a naturally born sinner, the New Testament describes us as "children under wrath," citizens of Satan's kingdom, spiritually blinded, and dead in our sins. But God doesn't leave us there. He sends His Son to redeem us

out of the slave market of sin and then welcomes us as adopted children into His family.

- It's important to understand that believers in Jesus do not become little gods. Although adopted as God's sons and daughters, we are not — and never will be — equals with the eternal, all-powerful, all-knowing, everywhere-present God.

- Like so many other acts of salvation, adoption takes place in a moment of time and provides lasting benefits. It appears we are adopted as God's children *after* we are born again, as God responds to our saving faith. While regeneration and adoption may be distinguished, they may not be separated.

- Adoption as children of God provides many benefits, including: an intimate relationship with God; the presence of the Holy Spirit; the discipline of God; sharing in the sufferings and subsequent glory of Christ; membership in the family of God; and a perfect role model for our lives.

- When new believers are adopted into God's family, Satan no longer may claim them. They are granted new lives, new natures, new names, a new home, a new family, a new citizenship, and a new hope. They also are given the Holy Spirit, who seals them until the day of redemption.

- As heirs, followers of Jesus are promised an inheritance that is imperishable, undefiled, and unfading, kept in heaven for us. This inheritance is salvation in all its fullness — our glorification, our rewards for faithfulness, our place around the throne in heaven, and our promise of everlasting life in intimate fellowship with the Triune God in the new heavens and new earth.

- The prosperity gospel's view of adoption — that we should claim our inheritance now, primarily in health and wealth — is perverse. Being grateful, humble, and self-denying followers of Jesus does not diminish our adoption as children. We still have the promises of our full inheritance: a universe purged of sin and its consequences, freedom from death, grief, crying, and pain. These promises, however, are for the future. Until then, we occupy the same sinful and fallen world as the unregenerate do.

THINK
Questions for personal or group study

(1) How is adoption different from, but related to, regeneration?

(2) In what ways do advocates of the prosperity gospel promote a false understanding of adoption into God's family?

(3) What does it mean when the Scriptures tell us that Christians are coheirs with Jesus? Specifically:

- What is our inheritance?
- Are we given the same authority as Jesus?
- Does sharing in the "divine nature" (2 Peter 1:4) mean we become little gods?
- If Jesus has all authority in heaven and on earth *now* (Matt. 28:18), do we, as coheirs, have the right to claim our inheritance whenever we choose?
- How secure is our salvation as adopted children of God?

(4) Fill in the blanks as you consider adoption in light of other elements of God's work of salvation (refer to page 199):

- In *calling*, God extends to us an _____ of adoption as the gospel is proclaimed and the Holy Spirit draws us to Christ.
- In *regeneration*, the Holy Spirit _____ our dead human spirits, which have been cut off from the life-giving presence of God by our disbelief and rebellion.
- In *indwelling*, the Spirit takes up permanent _____ in our human spirits, the most holy place in the temples of our bodies.
- In *justification*, the Father declares us _____ based on the imputation of our sins to Christ, and the imputation of His righteousness to us.
- In *Spirit baptism*, the Holy Spirit places us into the

_____ of Christ, where we share the common presence of the Spirit with all other followers of Jesus.

- In *sealing*, God places His mark of _____ on us, securing our salvation and distinguishing us from those still in the domain of darkness.
- In *sanctification*, the Spirit sets us apart as _____ and then engages in the lifelong process of making us so.
- And in *adoption*, the Father brings us into His _____ as sons and daughters, ensuring us of the same intimacy the Father, Son, and Holy Spirit have enjoyed as persons of the Trinity throughout all eternity.

(5) What are some of the benefits we experience now as adopted sons and daughters of God?

(6) Since both holy and evil angels are called "sons of God" in Scripture, does this mean they are coheirs with Jesus, just as Christians are? Consider:

- The status of angels as special creations of God (Job 1:6)
- The difference between our status as God's children and the status of angels (Heb. 2:14-16)
- The destiny of Satan and demons (Matt. 25:41; 2 Peter 2:4; Jude 6; Rev. 20:10)
- The manner in which holy angels observe Christ's redemption of people, but don't experience it themselves (1 Peter 1:12)

(7) Why do you think God allows His adopted children to experience the same hardships and heartaches as unbelievers?

When a recited prayer and a filled-out pew card pass for genuine conversion, our houses of worship become crowded with people who never grow in faith because they never had it to begin with.

Chapter Eleven

YOU ARE SEALED

S eals — as marks of authenticity, possession, and authority — appear many times and in various forms throughout Scripture. Generally, seals are portrayed in two ways. First, a seal is an object — often a small, semiprecious stone with writing cut into its surface. When pressed into wax or clay, it leaves a distinguishing mark. Second, a seal signifies the impression itself.

When Pharaoh exalts Joseph to second-in-command over Egypt, he removes his signet ring and places it in Joseph's hand as validation of the young man's newly bequeathed authority (Gen. 41:42). Jeremiah's purchase of the field in Anathoth from his cousin Hanamel is documented with a signed scroll that is sealed, likely with wax or clay, and stored in an earthen jar as a testimony of Israel's future restoration to the land (Jer. 32:7-15). As Daniel is thrown into the den of lions, Darius the king orders a large stone to be rolled over the opening. Likely, a cord or clay is affixed to the entrance and then sealed with the impressions of the signet rings of Darius and his nobles to prevent tampering (Dan. 6:16-17).[1]

After Jesus' body is placed in the tomb, Pilate authorizes a Jewish "guard of soldiers" to set a seal on the stone to ensure that the Lord's disciples do not steal the corpse and falsely claim Christ's resurrection

(Matt. 27:62-66). The apostle Paul shares with his Roman readers his intention to seal to them "this fruit" — that is, to safely deliver their contributions to the saints in Jerusalem (Rom. 15:28 KJV). An angel places a seal over the abyss into which Satan is thrown for a thousand years (Rev. 20:3). And the Lamb of God is found worthy to take a seven-sealed scroll from the hand of the Father on the throne in heaven (Rev. 5:1-7).

In all, there are about sixty references to seals in the Bible. For Christians, the most personally significant seal is one that human eyes cannot see. It is the secret work of the Holy Spirit, placing God's mark of ownership on us and ensuring that the work of redemption is completed. While there are certain nuances in this doctrine, and some who debate its timing and permanence, it is biblically faithful for the follower of Jesus to say, "I am sealed."

WHAT DOES IT MEAN TO BE SEALED WITH THE HOLY SPIRIT?

When sinners hear the gospel message and respond in belief and repentance, God the Father gives them the gift of the Holy Spirit. This means placing new believers positionally in Christ through baptism in the Holy Spirit; setting them apart as holy through sanctification; and sealing them with the Holy Spirit, or placing His divine mark of ownership on them, thus ensuring His everlasting presence and their eternal security.

In three New Testament passages, the apostle Paul describes the role of the Holy Spirit in sealing Christians. We look more closely at each passage later in this chapter, but for now, we simply list them:

- 2 Cor. 1:22 - "He [God] has also put his seal on us and given us the Spirit in our hearts as a down payment."
- Eph. 1:13-14 - "In him [Christ] you also were sealed with the promised Holy Spirit when you heard the word of truth, the gospel of your salvation, and when you believed. The Holy Spirit is the down payment of our inheritance, until the redemption of the possession, to the praise of his glory."

- Eph. 4:30 - "And don't grieve God's Holy Spirit. You were sealed by him for the day of redemption."

The Greek verb *sphragizo* means "to seal, to set a seal upon, or to mark with a seal." It appears fifteen times in the New Testament. Ancient documents often are sealed with a waxy substance to protect the contents and to authenticate them by imprinting the seal of its author in the soft wax. This verb also is used in the sense of sealing something in order to make it temporarily inaccessible (Rev. 10:4; 20:3).

Figuratively, *sphragizo* certifies the truth of something (John 3:33); the approval of God (John 6:27); or a pledge or guarantee (2 Cor. 1:22). Similarly, New Testament writers use the noun *sphragis* sixteen times to express ownership or to convey authority.

According to Gerald Cowen, classical Greek employs four basic meanings of *sphragizo*, each of which is applied in the New Testament.

First, *sphragizo* means "to close or enclose with a seal" to protect the contents from tampering or theft. We find this usage in the Gospel of Matthew, where Pilate instructs the chief priests and Pharisees to take a guard of soldiers to make Jesus' tomb secure (Matt. 27:65-66). The apostle Paul also uses *sphragizo* this way when he writes that believers are sealed by the Holy Spirit for the day of redemption (Eph. 4:30). With respect to salvation, this is our *security* as coheirs with Jesus.

Second, the Greek word is used to describe the sealing of a document with hot wax, which is then imprinted with a signet ring. This appears to be what the apostle John witnesses in heaven as Jesus takes the seven-sealed scroll from the hand of God the Father (Revelation 5). Paul uses this imagery when he writes that God has placed His seal on us (2 Cor. 1:22). This is our *authentication* as citizens of God's kingdom.

Third, *sphragizo* refers to the certification of an object as genuine or approved. We see this in Revelation 7, when an angel with "the seal of the living God" comes to "seal the servants of our God on their foreheads ... 144,000 sealed from every tribe of the Israelites" (Rev. 7:2-4). Similarly, Paul's three references to believers as sealed with the Spirit communicate the genuineness of our salvation

(2 Cor. 1:22; Eph. 1:13-14; 4:30). This is God's mark of *ownership* on us.

Finally, the Greek term may describe an article that is sealed to show it has been pledged. The Holy Spirit has been given to us as a "down payment" on our everlasting inheritance (2 Cor. 1:22; Eph. 1:13-14). Further, God has sealed us for the "day of redemption," when He completes our salvation in the resurrection and glorification of the saints (Eph. 4:30; cf. Phil. 1:6). This is our *pledge* from God.

Cowen writes, "It is a great comfort and a tremendous assurance to know if individuals are in Christ. God has sealed them, which means God has put His stamp of ownership upon them, authenticated them as genuine children of God, and secured them against any effort Satan may make to break that seal; and God intends for the soul to be intact 'until the day of redemption.' How much more secure could Christians be?"[2]

As is true of regeneration, indwelling, Spirit baptism, and positional sanctification, sealing with the Holy Spirit occurs for every believer and is a one-time, non-repeatable act of God. Bible commentators differ as to whether Old Testament saints are sealed, or if this is a unique work of the Spirit from the Day of Pentecost forward. The Old Testament does not say explicitly that believers under the old covenant are sealed. Some scholars argue that sealing may be inferred, since the Spirit is active in the hearts of believers looking forward to the coming of Messiah.[3]

In any case, *only* believers are sealed. Further, *every* believer is sealed. If this were not true, Paul could not make it the basis for the exhortation not to grieve the Holy Spirit in Eph. 4:30. He would have to be saying that only a group of believers who are sealed should not grieve the Spirit.

WHEN DOES SEALING OCCUR?

There is some question as to when, exactly, followers of Jesus are sealed with the Holy Spirit. Does it take place at regeneration, when the Holy Spirit brings our dead human spirits to life? Does it happen at indwelling, when the Spirit takes up permanent residence in the temples of our bodies? Does it occur when new believers receive the baptism in the Holy Spirit? Or, does sealing happen at a moment of commitment that finds its expression in, say, water baptism?

While Evangelicals may vigorously debate the timing of this special work of the Spirit, it's important to keep in mind several biblical truths. First, *all* believers are sealed with the Holy Spirit. We must avoid the errant doctrine that conditions God's work of sealing us on a public act such as water baptism or a second expression of surrender after conversion.

Second, the timing is less important than the significance of the Spirit's seal. As we've noted in previous chapters, regeneration and indwelling by the Spirit may be distinguished but not separated. That is, whether one believes faith comes before regeneration, or regeneration before faith, the Bible is clear that every true believer is both regenerated and indwelt; therefore, every believer also is sealed. Whether these saving works of God are simultaneous or successive, they are accomplished facts for Christians.

Third, sealing with the Holy Spirit is permanent and irrevocable, a comforting reality we explore in more detail later in this chapter.

One reason for disagreement over the timing of the Spirit's seal is rooted in Eph. 1:13. The KJV reads, "after that ye believed, ye were sealed with that Holy Spirit of promise." Modern translations render it: "When you believed ..." (NIV); "having also believed ..." (NASB); "when you heard ... and believed ..." (ESV); and "when you believed" (CSB). Charles Ryrie points out that one way to understand this verse is that belief occurs *prior* to sealing, while another is to see believing and sealing occurring *simultaneously.* "Exegetically either could be correct," he writes. "But theologically, both believing and sealing must be simultaneous. Otherwise it would be possible to have unsealed believers."[4]

James Dunn puts a finer point on the issue, stressing the importance of context in Greek grammar: "And the context here indicates that we should take the two verbs [believed / sealed] as the two sides of the one event: it was when they believed that God sealed them with the Spirit. As in Gal. 3:2, the step of faith is met by the gift of the Spirit."[5]

No matter how one views the chronology of the interwoven works of the Holy Spirit, we may take comfort in knowing that these divine acts are inseparable. Paul tells us that God has put His seal on us *and* given us the Spirit as a down payment (2 Cor. 1:22). The *and* in this verse links the giving of the Spirit with the sealing of the Spirit, and we know the Spirit is given to us when we believe in Jesus. The Lord Himself tells listeners on the last day of the Feast of Tabernacles that those who believe in Him *will have* streams of living water flowing from deep within them — a promise of the Holy Spirit, who is given after Jesus is glorified (John 7:37-39). Once Pentecost comes, all believers are described as *having* the Spirit (Acts 11:16-17; Rom. 5:5; 1 Cor. 2:12; 2 Cor. 5:5).

WHO DOES THE SEALING?

It's clear that God seals believers, as Paul notes: "He has put his seal on us ..." (2 Cor. 1:22). Less clear is whether the Holy Spirit is the *agent* of sealing — that is, the one who actually seals us. In Eph. 1:13-14, Paul notes that when his Gentile readers heard the word of truth and believed, they were "sealed in him [Christ] with the promised Holy Spirit. He is the down payment of our inheritance ..." Harold Hoehner comments, "God is the One who seals, Christ is the sphere in which the seal is done, and the Holy Spirit is the instrument of the seal."[6]

A few chapters later, however, Paul seems to indicate that the Spirit is the agent, or at least *an* agent, in sealing, for he writes, "You were sealed *by him* [the Holy Spirit] for the day of redemption" (emphasis added). We should note that the phrase "by him" also may be translated "in him."

So, is the Holy Spirit the one who seals us, or is He the seal God uses to mark new believers as belonging to Christ? The issue is similar to the one we encountered with Spirit baptism: Is the Spirit the one who baptizes us, or the one into whom we are baptized?

In both cases, it may be a distinction without a difference. The Holy Spirit is the third person of the Triune Godhead, and He always acts in complete harmony with the Father and Son. He was fully involved in the creation of all things, and He plays a vital role in our salvation, working seamlessly within the Trinity to redeem people.

Jesus tells His disciples that when He departs and returns to the Father, He will ask the Father to send another Comforter like Himself — the Holy Spirit — who will be with us, and in us forever (John 14:16-17).

Whether the Spirit is the agent of sealing, or the instrument, we may rest assured that the third person of the Trinity has been actively involved in making us spiritually alive (regenerating us), residing in our human spirits (indwelling us), placing us positionally into the body of Christ (through Spirit baptism), setting us apart (in sanctification), and placing God's mark of ownership on us (through sealing).

CAN I BECOME UNSEALED?

We must acknowledge that seals, at times, are broken prematurely. Thieves, conniving stewards, and careless couriers may intentionally or unwittingly tamper with objects secured under someone else's authority. With that in mind, isn't it possible that Satan could snatch away the word sown in some people's hearts (Matt. 13:19)? Don't false teachers make merchandise of certain professing believers, thus leading them astray (2 Peter 2:3)? Aren't some prophets so deceived that they think they are saved, only to discover they're not (Matt. 7:21-23)? Don't we see false brothers, false apostles, and false branches of the vine throughout the New Testament (John 15:1-2, 6; 2 Cor. 11:15, 26; Gal. 2:4)? Were these people never saved? Or, have they fallen away from the faith, thus losing their salvation?

People do sometimes turn away from Christ after professing Him as Lord. Some pillars of the faith even wind up publicly repudiating what they have spent their lifetimes affirming, often creating cottage industries for themselves and their fellow apostates through best-selling books, television appearances, and lively debates. It can be difficult to tell whether a professing believer is true, or merely a pretender. This is nothing new. Consider Heb. 6:4-8:

For it is impossible to renew to repentance those who were once enlightened, who tasted the heavenly gift, who shared in the Holy Spirit, who tasted God's good word and the powers of the coming age, and who have fallen away. This is because, to their own harm, they are recrucifying the Son of God and holding him up to contempt. For the ground that drinks the rain that often falls on it and that produces vegetation useful to those for whom it is cultivated receives a blessing from God. But if it produces thorns and thistles, it is worthless and about to be cursed, and at the end will be burned.

This is a thorny passage for which commentators offer various interpretations. Some say those who have "fallen away" are genuine Christians who have forsaken Jesus and reverted to Judaism. Others contend that the writer is describing sanctification rather than justification, especially since he follows up with these words, "in your case we are confident of things that are better and that pertain to salvation" (v. 9). Still others argue that the author is speaking about apostasy as a possibility rather than a reality.

A fourth view holds that the apostates have approached the threshold of everlasting life, only to turn decidedly away. Like the tares in Jesus' parable, they are sown in the same ground, receive the same sunshine and rain, intertwine their roots, and appear from a distance to promise grain at harvest time. But ultimately, they prove themselves fruitless pretenders who are cast into the furnace (Matt. 13:24-30, 36-43). In a similar way, these false professors of the faith are like bad fish caught in the dragnet (Matt. 13:47-50), or like the rocky and thorny soils (Matt. 13:5-7).

Theologian John Frame supports the fourth view and asks us to consider the case of Judas Iscariot. Judas joins the disciples and follows Jesus, a kind of repentance. He is enlightened by Jesus' teaching. He tastes the heavenly gift as he watches Jesus heal and cast out demons. He shares in the ministry of the Holy Spirit, at least as much as King Saul when he prophesied (1 Sam. 10:11). He tastes the good word and the powers of the coming age through his active involvement in Jesus' earthly ministry, even preaching Christ and working miracles in His name. "But he proved to be reprobate, unbelieving. He betrayed Jesus, who said of him that it would have been better if he had not been born. Externally, he seemed to be a believer, and indeed, he had many advantages that believers have, hearing Jesus' words and watching his miracles."[7]

So, professing Christians may share some of the same blessings as genuine believers without being saved. Sadly, they do not persevere. The apostates of Hebrews 6 do not have true faith and thus have never been regenerated, indwelled, Spirit baptized, and sealed. The writer of Hebrews seems to know, however, that his readers possess saving faith and thus endure to the end, for he writes, "Even though we are speaking this way, dearly loved friends, in your case we are confident of things that are better and that pertain to salvation" (v. 9).

This passage is a warning shot across the bow of the church. When a recited prayer and a filled-out pew card pass for genuine conversion, our houses of worship become crowded with people who never grow in faith because they never had it to begin with. Christianity becomes a means to an end, a social club, a self-help society, when Christ should be exalted as the end Himself. It is disturbing to hear the false gospel of easy believism, in which people are taught that making a minimal commitment to Christianity — by coming forward after the service, being baptized, or joining the church — ensures everlasting life, even if the professing believer never bears spiritual fruit and ultimately walks away from the faith.

We cannot read the minds of people, or judge their hearts, so we should be careful neither to welcome nor condemn professing Christians based solely on what we see. But we should faithfully proclaim the whole counsel of God and seek to earnestly fulfill the Great Commission by making disciples rather than counting noses, though this is far messier and much more challenging.

As Frame summarizes, "Perseverance is not guaranteed to everyone who professes faith, only to those who really trust Christ."[8] Genuine salvation is grounded eternally in God's foreknowledge, election, and predestination. Sealing with the Holy Spirit is His guarantee that He will complete the work He determined in eternity past and began in us when we trusted in Him.

This is not fatalism, for it merges divinely with human responsibility. We are commanded to repent (Acts 17:30). We are called to hear and believe the gospel in order to receive everlasting life (John 5:24).

We are encouraged to hold fast to our profession of faith (Heb. 10:23) and to hold on to what is good (1 Thess. 5:21). Our lives are neither the robotic responses to a divine lever-pulling Wizard of Oz, nor a frenzy of human will over which God has little foreknowledge and practically no control. Rather, divine sovereignty and human responsibility are clear biblical truths that merge mysteriously. There is no doubt that God has endowed people with a capacity to make decisions for which He holds us accountable. Salvation is forced on no one, nor withheld from anyone.

What does sealing have to do with security?

Even so, is it possible for a genuine follower of Jesus to commit such grievous sins that he or she becomes "unsealed" and thus loses the gift of everlasting life? Is there a connection between sealing and security?

The primary terms that relate to the certainty of salvation are *assurance* and *security*. Assurance is the subjective side of the issue, dealing with the sense that one is saved. Security is the objective side, relating to the ultimate reality of salvation. Other words and phrases often are used, such as the perseverance of the saints; eternal security; and once saved, always saved. The doctrine of eternal security is much-debated and beyond the scope of this book. Many have written extensively about the issue,[9] but a brief exploration of the doctrine of perseverance of the saints is in order.

Essentially, this doctrine means two things, according to Daniel Wallace: (1) those who are genuinely saved will be saved forever; and (2) those who continue in the faith are genuinely saved. "All who will be saved forever are saved because of Christ's work on the cross and God's power to keep them saved."[10]

Genuine believers continue in faith and good works throughout their lives, but not in their own strength. Each member of the Trinity works to preserve us. To begin, it is the finished work of Christ, not our merits, that secures salvation (Rom. 3:21-26; 4:4-8; 8:1, 29-30; Eph. 2:8-9; Titus 3:5-7).

Next, genuine believers are sealed with the Holy Spirit as a down payment on all the blessings God has promised us, including everlasting life (Eph. 1:13-14; 4:30). The Spirit assures us of salvation and keeps us secure until the end of our earthly lives (John 10:27; Rom. 8:16; 1 John 2:20, 27; Jude 24).

Finally, the Father holds us securely in His grasp, as Jesus assures His disciples: "I give them [Jesus' sheep] eternal life, and they will never perish. No one will snatch them out of my hand. My Father, who has given them to me, is greater than all. No one is able to snatch them out of the Father's hand" (John 10:28-29).

Wallace asks, "But can't a believer, of his own free will, choose to wander out of the Father's and Jesus's protective hands? No. A good shepherd does not allow his sheep to go astray. As our Good Shepherd, Jesus keeps us safe from the thief (Satan) and from ourselves."[11]

Evangelical Christians differ in their views of the relationship between assurance and security. Norman Geisler notes that Evangelicals hold at least four views on the topic of eternal security:

- Strong Calvinists believe in the security of the elect. Nevertheless, they cannot, at present, be sure they are among them. Each person proves his or her election by persevering to the end.
- Moderate Calvinists believe they are eternally secure and can be sure of it. That is, they claim both eternal security and assurance.
- Classical Arminians, who follow Jacobus Arminius (1560-1609), hold that a saved person can lose salvation, but only by the sin of apostasy — a complete denial of Christ. Once someone has apostasized, he or she may never be saved again.
- Wesleyan Arminians, who follow John Wesley (1703-1791), contend that salvation may be lost through any serious intentional sin. However, salvation may be regained through repentance.[12]

Geisler, who holds a moderate Calvinist position, highlights several theological truths on which eternal security is grounded:

- Salvation is of the Lord. Salvation does not derive from our efforts but from our sovereign God. If salvation does not depend on us, but only on God, our security is as eternal as He is (Jonah 2:9; John 1:13; Rom. 9:16).

- God cannot deny Himself. We can no more lose our salvation than God can cease being God (2 Tim. 2:13).
- Election is from eternity. Salvation was not decided or gained in time, and it cannot be dissolved or lost in time (Eph. 1:4; 2 Tim. 1:9; Rev. 13:8).
- God has infallible foreknowledge. Calvinists and Arminians agree on this point. So, it seems unreasonable to assume that God regenerates people who do not persevere. The idea that God starts what He does not finish is contrary to His knowable character (Isa. 46:10; Phil. 1:6).
- Salvation is completed in Christ. From God's perspective, the work of the cross was an accomplished fact from all eternity (Eph. 1:4; Rev. 13:8). Jesus and the New Testament writers declared His work finished (John 17:4; 19:30; Heb. 10:14).
- Salvation is an irrevocable gift. God is bound by His own unconditional covenant to be faithful, even when we are not (Rom. 6:23; 11:29; 2 Tim. 2:13).
- Salvation is an unconditional promise. God's promises are unbreakable (Rom. 6:23; 11:29, Eph. 2:8-9; Heb. 6:17-18).
- Salvation cannot be gained or lost by our works. "He saved us — not by works of righteousness that we had done, but according to his mercy — through the washing of regeneration and renewal by the Holy Spirit" (Titus 3:5). If salvation is not gained by our works, how can it be lost by our works (John 5:24; Rom. 4:4-5; Eph. 2:8-9)?[13]

Much more could be written in support of eternal security, but perhaps it's helpful at this point to consider the doctrine from another perspective. Let's ask ourselves some fairly raw questions in light of all we've learned so far. *If* we may lose our salvation:

- What, exactly, is lost: Regeneration? Justification?

Indwelling? Spirit Baptism? Adoption? Sanctification?
Sealing?

- What impact does losing salvation have on God's eternal decrees regarding foreknowledge, election, and predestination?
- Does God ever call a saved-then-lost person to Himself again?
- Do we die spiritually a second time and thus come under the wrath of God again?
- Are we subjected to double jeopardy? That is, having once been declared righteous before the Father, are we now retried and condemned for the same sins?
- Does the Holy Spirit vacate the temples of our bodies, never to return?
- Do we require a second baptism in the Holy Spirit, if such a thing is even possible?
- Is our sanctification stopped at the departure point, or completely annulled?
- Is the seal of the Holy Spirit stripped away and our eternal destiny voided?
- Having once been adopted sons and daughters of God, do we become spiritual orphans once again?
- Is our promised future glorification revoked?
- How can we ever rest? If only one sin makes us guilty of all (James 2:10), doesn't one sin cause a redeemed person to be lost again?

These are weighty questions. As we have viewed God's work of redemption throughout this book, we've seen that the elements of salvation are inextricably bound to one another. For example, without foreknowledge there is no predestination. Without predestination there is no calling. Without calling there is no justification. And without justification there is no glorification (Rom. 8:29-30).

Salvation in all of its marvelous facets nevertheless is a singular work of God. The seal of the Holy Spirit is God's mark of ownership, authority, security, and pledge. What He closes, no man opens (Rev. 3:7; *cf* Isa. 22:22). Our assurance — that is, our confidence in the security we have in Christ — is based, not on feelings, words, or works; it is based on the eternal and wholly reliable God. He has known us throughout eternity, chosen us in Christ, redeemed us out of the slave market of sin, made us His adopted sons and daughters, written our names in heaven, prepared a place for us, and assured us through His Son that wherever He is, we'll be there, too.

WHAT DOES IT MEAN TO BE "SEALED FOR THE DAY OF REDEMPTION"?

Followers of Jesus are secure in their relationship with Christ. God has known this throughout eternity, as revealed in the doctrines of foreknowledge, election, and predestination. We should know it with firm conviction as well. Jesus tells us that believers in Him already possess everlasting life, which by its very definition cannot be lost (John 5:24). Our names are written in heaven (Luke 10:20). Jesus prepares a place for us and promises to take us there one day (John 14:1-3). The Father adopts us as children and makes us coheirs with Jesus (Rom. 8:14-17). And the Spirit is given to us as a permanent resident in the temples of our bodies (1 Cor. 6:19). He is our advocate in prayer (Rom. 8:26-27), our counselor in life (John 14:16-17), our illuminator in matters of Scripture (1 Cor. 2:6-16), and our source of spiritual gifts (1 Cor. 12:4-11).

All of this provides evidence that something of enduring consequence is taking place in our lives. We are purchased out of Satan's slave market and adopted as children in the never-ending kingdom of heaven. God did it all, and our salvation is as secure as His faithfulness.

One additional assurance is that the Holy Spirit seals us for the day of redemption (Eph. 4:30). What does this mean? It refers to a future day when God's work of salvation in our lives is completed as we receive glorified bodies. Paul describes this in Rom. 8:23 as "the redemption of our bodies."

Other passages of Scripture point to a day when our bodies, as well as our souls and spirits, are made perfect. Paul assures the Philippians that God does not drop the ball when it comes to our salvation: "he who started a good work in you will carry it on to completion until the day of Christ Jesus" (Phil. 1:6). Paul further writes confidently about the redemption of our bodies (1 Cor. 15:35-58; 1 Thess. 4:13-18).

Peter and John assure us that a day is coming when our glorified bodies inhabit a new world purged of sin and its consequences (2 Peter 3:10-13; Revelation 21-22). And we should take comfort in knowing that one day God Himself wipes every tear from our eyes, assuring us that death, grief, crying, and pain — the realities of living in a sinful and fallen world — are gone forever (Rev. 21:4).

Charles Ryrie comments, "Thus the sealing guarantees the complete fulfillment of God's promises to us. And no believer can become unsealed on his way to heaven.... Sealing assures us of the security of God's promises to us, especially our salvation. We can be certain (a) that He possesses us, (b) that we have a secure salvation sealed by and with the Spirit, and (c) that He purposes to keep us to the day of our full redemption."[14]

Peter reminds Christians that we are being "guarded by God's power through faith for a salvation that is ready to be revealed in the last time" (1 Peter 1:5). The word "guarded" (Greek *phroureo*) can mean both "kept from escaping" and "protected from attack." Perhaps both meanings are intended here. Through the sealing of the Spirit, God keeps us securely in His kingdom and shields us from external attacks.

The salvation to which Peter refers is not a single element of it, such as regeneration or justification, but the future fulfillment of all God's promises in redemption. While our salvation is prepared, it is not fully revealed until Christ steps into the clouds of heaven and calls our bodies from the graves (John 5:28-29). The seal of the Holy Spirit serves as God's pledge to fulfill every promise to us.

KEY PASSAGES ON SEALING

Let's survey several Bible verses that address what it means to be sealed by the Holy Spirit.

2 Cor. 1:21-22 - "Now it is God who strengthens us together with you in Christ, and who has anointed us. He has also put his seal on us (*sphragisamenos emas*) and given us the Spirit in our hearts as a down payment."

These two verses beautifully illustrate the seamless work of the Trinity in salvation. God the Father strengthens the redeemed in Christ (the Son), anoints us, puts His seal on us, and gives us the Holy Spirit as a down payment on our inheritance. This deserves a closer look.

First, the Father *strengthens* us. The NIV reads, "Now it is God who makes both us and you stand firm in Christ." The ESV renders the passage, "And it is God who establishes us with you in Christ." The Greek word translated "strengthens," "stand firm," or "establishes" is *bebaioo*. It means to confirm, establish, or render constant and unwavering. Followers of Jesus may rest assured that God the Father has planted us firmly in Christ. As a complement to that, Paul uses the Greek verb *steko* (stand, be constant, persevere) in a number of other passages to exhort Christians to stand firm in the Lord, especially in the context of false teaching (Gal. 5:1; 2 Thess. 2:15). As the Father affirms our security in Christ, we are urged to remain faithful to Him (1 Cor. 16:13; Phil. 1:27; 4:1; 1 Thess. 3:8).

Next, the Father *anoints* us. As Jesus is the Anointed One (*Christos*), the Father also anoints followers of Jesus with the Holy Spirit. The Greek verb *chrio*, which means to anoint, is used five times in the New Testament — four times referring to the anointing of Jesus. In Luke 4:18-21, Jesus reads from Isa. 61:1-2 and applies it to Himself: "The Spirit of the Lord is on me, because he has anointed me ... Today, as you listen, this Scripture has been fulfilled."

In an early Christian prayer in Acts 4:27 and in a message by Peter in Acts 10:38, Jesus is depicted as anointed by God (the Holy Spirit) to His ministry on our behalf. And in Heb. 1:9, the writer quotes from Ps. 45:7 but applies *chrio* to Jesus as God's Son. The final occurrence of *chrio* is in 2 Cor. 1:21-22, where Paul says the Father anoints us. John uses the corresponding noun *chrisma* to refer to an anointing we have from the Holy One, who remains in us and teaches us all things (1 John 2:20, 27).[15]

Third, the Father *places His seal* on us. As we have learned in this chapter, that seal is the Holy Spirit. His permanent presence in our human spirits confirms that the Father secures us as coheirs with Jesus, authenticates us as citizens of His kingdom, rightfully owns us since He has purchased us out of the slave market of sin, and pledges to fulfill every promise to us.

Last, the Father *gives* us the Holy Spirit in our hearts as a down payment. By that, we take comfort in knowing that God finishes the good work He began in us. The Spirit is His guarantee of a never-ending future in the presence of God. The term "down payment" is rendered "guarantee" in the ESV, "earnest" in the KJV, "pledge" in the NASB, and "deposit" in the NIV. It comes from the Greek word *arrabon* and means "pledge or deposit guaranteeing what is to come."[16] William Mounce explains, "Just as a down payment for a house today serves as a guarantee that the rest of the payment will come, so God sends his Holy Spirit into the hearts of believers as a deposit, guaranteeing that someday the full inheritance of salvation will be ours."[17]

Consider two related passages in Paul's writings. In Rom. 8:16, he states, "The Spirit himself testifies together with our spirit that we are God's children, and if children, also heirs — heirs of God and coheirs with Christ — if indeed we suffer with him so that we may also be glorified with him." In other words, the indwelling Holy Spirit confirms our adoption as sons and daughters of God. Further, He reminds us that while we may suffer for the cause of Christ, we remain coheirs of all that is His, received when we are physically resurrected and fully conformed to His image.

The second related passage is 2 Cor. 5:4-5: "Indeed, we groan while we are in this tent, burdened as we are, because we do not want to be unclothed but clothed, so that mortality may be swallowed up by life. Now the one who prepared us for this very purpose is God, who gave us the Spirit as a down payment." The day is coming when we exchange our mortal bodies for glorified bodies released from the grief, pain, and suffering of this present world. Though followers of Jesus are not exempted from the hardships of living in a sinful and fallen world, the Spirit ensures us that better, never-ending days with Jesus are coming.

CSB	KJV	NIV	NASB	ESV
Put his seal on us	Hath also sealed us	Set his seal of ownership on us	Sealed us	Put his seal on us

Comparing English translations of *sphragisamenos emas* in 2 Cor. 1:22

Eph. 1:13-14 - "In him you also were sealed (*en o esphragisthete*) with the promised Holy Spirit when you heard the word of truth, the gospel of your salvation, and when you believed. The Holy Spirit is the down payment (*arrabon*) of our inheritance, until the redemption of the possession, to the praise of his glory."

Paul assures his Gentile readers that they, like Jewish believers, were sealed with the Holy Spirit *when* they heard and believed. As one commentary phrases it, "The Spirit, like a seal, impresses on the soul at regeneration the image of our Father. The 'sealing' by the Holy Spirit is spoken of as *past* once for all. The witnessing to our hearts that we are the children of God, and heirs, is the Spirit's *present* testimony, the 'earnest of the (coming) inheritance.'"[18]

What's more, the Spirit is *promised*. The Holy Spirit neither came into existence at the baptism of Jesus nor on the Day of Pentecost. Rather, He has existed throughout eternity, engaging with the Father and Son in the creation of all things and displaying His power in Old Testament saints. Equally important, a special ministry of the Spirit in the hearts of believers is promised to future generations throughout the era of the Old Covenant.

For example, the Lord speaks to Israel through the prophet Isaiah: "I will pour out My Spirit on your descendants and my blessing on your offspring" (Isa. 44:3); through Ezekiel: "I will give you a new heart and put a new spirit within you; I will remove your heart of stone and give you a heart of flesh. I will place my Spirit within you and cause you to follow my statutes and carefully observe my ordinances" (Eze. 36:26-27); and through Joel: "After this I will pour out my Spirit on all humanity; then your sons and your daughters will prophesy, your old men will have dreams, and your young men will see visions. I will even pour out my Spirit on the male and female slaves in those days" — a prophecy Peter declares fulfilled at Pentecost (Joel 2:28-29; Acts 2:17-18).

When the promised Messiah comes, He pledges to send the Spirit: "When the Counselor comes, the one I will send to you from the Father — the Spirit of truth who proceeds from the Father — he will testify about me" (John 15:26; see also Luke 24:49; John 14:16; 16:13; Acts 1:5-8).

Next, Paul says the Holy Spirit is the "down payment" (*arrabon*) of our inheritance, a term we saw in 2 Cor. 1:22 and 5:5. In classical and later Greek, *arrabon* is a legal and commercial term that means "first installment, deposit, down payment, pledge," and represents a payment that obligated the contracting party to make further payments.

Wayne Grudem writes, "When God gave us the Holy Spirit within, he committed himself to give all the further blessings of eternal life and a great reward in heaven with him.... All who have the Holy Spirit within them, all who are truly born again, have God's unchanging promise and guarantee that the inheritance of eternal life in heaven will certainly be theirs. God's own faithfulness is pledged to bring it about."[19]

As we saw in 2 Cor. 1:21-22, the Trinity is at work here. The Father is the one who seals. Christ is the sphere in which sealing takes place. And the Holy Spirit is the seal. Believers are sealed "until the redemption of the possession," a guarantee of our inheritance in heaven and, ultimately, the new heavens and new earth. "In essence, the 'deposit' of the Holy Spirit is a little bit of heaven in believers' lives with a guarantee of much more yet to come," according to Harold Hoehner.[20]

Warren Wiersbe points out that "redemption" is experienced in three stages: (1) We *have been* redeemed through faith in Jesus (Eph. 1:7); (2) we *are being* redeemed as the Spirit works in our lives to make us more like Christ (Rom. 8:1-4); and (3) we *shall be* redeemed when Christ returns and we become like Him.[21]

A seal is a mark of ownership, authority, authenticity, and promise. It's also a mantle of security, as Paul writes in 2 Tim. 2:19, "Nevertheless, God's solid foundation stands firm, bearing this inscription: **The Lord knows those who are his** ..." Despite the work of evil doers and the venom of evil teachers, the Lord's church stands firmly on the foundation of Christ.

In quoting from the Old Testament, Paul maintains the tension between divine sovereignty and human responsibility. He refers to the rebellion of Korah, who challenged the authority of Moses and Aaron. After prostrating himself before the Lord, Moses tells the rebels, "Tomorrow morning *the Lord will reveal who belongs to him*, who is set apart, and the one he will let come near him. He will let the one he chooses come near him" (Num. 16:5-6, emphasis added). The Lord, indeed, knows those who are His, and His seal upon us — the indwelling Holy Spirit — is designed to assure us that we are known and kept by the one who claimed us for Himself in eternity past.

CSB	KJV	NIV	NASB	ESV
In him you also were sealed	In whom also ... ye were sealed	You were marked in him with a seal	You were sealed in Him [whom]	In him you also ... were sealed

Comparing English translations of *en o esphragisthete* in Eph. 1:13

CSB	KJV	NIV	NASB	ESV
Down payment	Earnest	Deposit	Pledge	Guarantee [until God redeems his possession]

Comparing English translations of *arrabon* in Eph. 1:14

Eph. 4:30 - "And don't grieve God's Holy Spirit. You were sealed (*esphragisthete*) by him for the day of redemption."

Paul warns followers of Jesus not to grieve the Holy Spirit. The Greek verb *lypeo* means "to grieve, feel sorrow or pain." It refers to the emotional or mental state that results from any situation of grief, such as pain or distress. Paul grieves that he has caused the Corinthians to sorrow when he last saw them (2 Cor. 2:2). The rich young ruler grieves when Jesus commands him to sell all that he has (Matt. 19:22). The disciples grieve at the imminent departure of Jesus (John 16:20), and when they learn that one of them is to betray their Master (Matt. 26:22).

But in this passage, Paul provides proof of the personality of the

Holy Spirit, who grieves at the sins of those He indwells and has sealed. What sins grieve the Holy Spirit? All sins, of course. But in the immediate context, sins of the tongue are highlighted. What comes from our mouths reveals what's in our hearts. The thought of being sealed with the Holy Spirit thus should cause us to guard our hearts and bridle our tongues.

At the same time, we should take comfort in times of suffering and persecution. Peter writes that while we may grieve over our circumstances, we should greatly rejoice (1 Peter 1:6). Paul describes Christians as people who may grieve about present difficulties but should rejoice within (2 Cor. 6:10). Even when we experience spiritual failures, we may take comfort in knowing that the permanent seal of the Holy Spirit is not stripped away. As the Father holds us in His hand, and the Son promises never to leave us or forsake us, the Spirit remains with us as our guarantee of a place in heaven, future resurrection, and eternal life with God in the new heavens and earth.

Matthew Henry writes, "There is to be a day of redemption; the body is to be redeemed from the power of the grave at the resurrection-day, and then God's people will be delivered from all the effects of sin, as well as from all sin and misery, which they are not till rescued out of the grave: and then their full and complete happiness commences. All true believers are sealed to that day. God has distinguished them from others, having set his mark upon them; and he gives them the earnest and assurance of a joyful and glorious resurrection; and the Spirit of God is the seal. Wherever that blessed Spirit is as a sanctifier, he is the earnest of all the joys and glories of the redemption-day…"[22]

CSB	KJV	NIV	NASB	ESV
You were sealed	Ye are sealed	You were sealed	You were sealed	You were sealed

Comparing English translations of *esphragisthete* in Eph. 4:30

SUMMARY

When believing sinners entrust their lives to Christ, the Father seals them with the Holy Spirit, placing His divine mark of ownership on them, thus ensuring His everlasting presence and their eternal security. As the Father's imprint on the surrendered heart, the Spirit reminds followers of Jesus that they are secure as coheirs with Christ; authentic citizens of the kingdom of God; in the permanent grasp of the Father; and recipients of God's divine pledge to finish the work He began in them.

Ralph Earle notes that in modern Greek, the noun *arrabona* is used for an engagement ring. This is similar to *arrabon* in ancient Greek, which is translated in Eph. 1:14 as "down payment," "earnest," "deposit," "pledge," or "guarantee." It suggests that when the Holy Spirit draws sinners to Christ, and they respond by committing their lives to Jesus, they have in essence said yes to a marriage proposal. The Bridegroom and the bride are betrothed. The Spirit is then given as a type of engagement ring, assuring new believers of His enduring faithfulness and their final union with the Lord at the Marriage Supper of the Lamb (Rev. 19:7-9).[23]

Consider these summary statements about the seal of the Holy Spirit:

- As is true of regeneration, indwelling, Spirit baptism, and sanctification, sealing with the Holy Spirit occurs for every believer and is a one-time, non-repeatable work of God, with lasting benefits. *Only* believers are sealed. Further, *every* believer is sealed.
- While Evangelicals may debate the timing of this special work of the Spirit, it's important to keep in mind that: (1) all believers are sealed with the Holy Spirit; (2) timing is less important than the significance of the Spirit's seal; and (3) sealing with the Holy Spirit is permanent and irrevocable, a comforting reality for all followers of Jesus.
- Whether the Spirit is the agent — the one doing the sealing — or the seal Himself, we may rest assured that the third person of the Trinity has been actively involved in

making us spiritually alive (regenerating us), residing in our human spirits (indwelling us), placing us positionally into the body of Christ (through Spirit baptism), setting us apart (in sanctification), and placing God's mark of ownership on us (through sealing).

- Unbelievers who falsely profess faith in Jesus may share some of the same blessings as genuine Christians, but they do not persevere. Like the tares in Jesus' parable, they are sown in the same ground, receive the same sunshine and rain, intertwine their roots, and appear from a distance to promise grain at harvest time. But ultimately, they prove themselves fruitless pretenders who are cast into the furnace (Matt. 13:24-30, 36-43).

- Difficult passages like Heb. 6:4-8 are warning shots across the bow of the church. When a recited prayer and a filled-out pew card pass for genuine conversion, our houses of worship become crowded with people who never grow in faith because they never had it to begin with.

- The sealing with the Holy Spirit is the linchpin of eternal security. Essentially, this doctrine means two things: (1) those who are genuinely saved will be saved forever; and (2) those who continue in faith are genuinely saved.

- Genuine believers continue in the faith and good works throughout their lives, but not in their own strength. Each member of the Trinity works to preserve us. Christ secures our salvation through His finished work on the cross. The Spirit acts as our seal, a down payment on all the blessings God has promised us. And the Father holds us securely in His grasp.

- Followers of Jesus are secure in their relationship with Christ. God has known this throughout eternity, as revealed in the doctrines of foreknowledge, election, and predestination. We should know it with firm conviction as well. Jesus tells us that believers in Him already possess everlasting life, which by its very definition cannot be lost.

- Being sealed with the Spirit for the day of redemption (Eph. 4:30) refers to a future day when God's work of salvation in our lives is completed as we receive resurrected and glorified bodies. Paul describes this in Rom. 8:23 as "the redemption of our bodies."

THINK
Questions for personal or group study

(1) Besides the work of sealing new believers, what other divine acts does the Holy Spirit perform with respect to salvation?

(2) What contribution does sealing with the Holy Spirit make to our *assurance* as Christians — that is, the sense that we are secure in Christ?

(3) Where in the order of salvation does sealing with the Holy Spirit belong? Is it before or after faith? Simultaneous with regeneration, justification, or adoption? Is it possible for a new Christian not to be sealed for a period of time — or ever?

(4) In what ways do the three persons of the Trinity work together for our salvation? What distinct roles does each of them play?

(5) Is it possible for a Christian to become "unsealed" due to grievous sins? If so, how does the removal of God's mark of ownership affect the other elements of salvation, such as regeneration, justification, indwelling, Spirit baptism, sanctification, and adoption?

(6) What's the difference between *assurance* and *security* as they relate to our salvation? What do they have in common?

(7) Read Eph. 4:30 and consider these questions:

- What does it mean to "grieve" God's Holy Spirit?
- What are some ways Christians may grieve the Spirit?
- Why does Paul say that we are sealed by the Holy Spirit "for the day of redemption"? What is that day?
- How is Paul's warning against grieving the Holy Spirit balanced by his reference to the day of redemption?

Section Three

BEYOND TIME

We explored God's work of salvation *before time* in Section One, including foreknowledge, election, and predestination. Then, in Section Two, we moved on to God's work of salvation *in time*, featuring eight facets of redemption: calling, regeneration, justification, indwelling, baptism in the Holy Spirit, sanctification, adoption, and sealing. Now, in this final section, we see the apex of our relationship with Christ.

Glorification is the final stage in God's work of salvation. It is the crowning achievement of sanctification, in which Christians are fully conformed to the image of Christ. It is the perfection of the body, as well as the soul and spirit. Even more, it is the restoration of all creation to its pristine perfection.

Put another way, glorification is the means by which God fully reverses the effects of the Fall, purging sin and its stain from our lives and from the created order. It involves the return of Jesus, the future resurrection and judgment of all people, and the creation of new heavens and a new earth.

Glorification is the means by which God fully reverses the effects of the Fall, purging sin and its stain from the created order. It involves the return of Jesus, the future resurrection and judgment of all people, and the creation of new heavens and a new earth.

Chapter Twelve

YOU ARE GLORIFIED

Memphis Belle is one of the most celebrated aircraft of World War II. Named after the girlfriend of chief pilot Robert Morgan, the lumbering B-17F Flying Fortress carried the first U.S. crew to complete twenty-five combat missions over Europe before returning to America, where the airmen were hailed as heroes during a three-month tour to sell war bonds and raise morale.

Based in Bassingborne, England, Belle coursed through flak-filled skies over France and Germany in 1942-43. The ten-man crew battled Nazi fighter planes while delivering their payloads before returning to base through the same threatening skies. The crew's survival through more than two dozen missions was rare indeed. In all, the Army Air Forces lost thirty thousand airmen in battles against Nazi Germany. During the heaviest fighting, U.S. bomber-crew airmen had a one-in-four chance of survival.

The plane's exploits were featured in a 1944 documentary and retold a generation later in a major motion picture.

For a time after the war, however, Memphis Belle sat outdoors, neglected, until an ambitious restoration project began, requiring more than one hundred workers and thousands of hours to scrape paint, bend metal, and fabricate parts. In May of 2018, on the seventy-fifth anniversary of Belle's historic twenty-fifth mission, the totally restored legend was reintroduced to the public at the National Museum of the U.S. Air Force at Wright-Patterson Air Force Base in Ohio.

Today, Belle stands as chiseled and sleek as when she first rolled off the assembly line, a testament to the people who recognized her intrinsic value and labored to restore her glory for generations to come.[1]

In a manner of speaking, followers of Jesus are like Memphis Belle. We are making our way through perilous times as we live in a sinful and fallen world. We age, get sick, break bones, suffer great disappointment, and sometimes are persecuted for our faith. Christ did not offer us an easy path to everlasting life, but in His work of salvation, He promised to bring us home one day and then fully restore us — body, soul, and spirit.

That's what glorification means. It is the final act of God's redemptive work, in which He raises our lifeless bodies from the grave and fully restores us to a state that's better than the original. That's because we have incorruptible bodies that never again suffer the flak of sin or experience death.

While this final work of redemption is yet to come, for followers of Jesus, it is biblically faithful to say, "I am glorified."

WHAT IS GLORIFICATION, AND WHEN DOES IT OCCUR?

Glorification is the final stage in God's work of salvation. It is the crowning achievement of sanctification, in which Christians are fully conformed to the image of Christ. It is the perfection of the body, rejoined with soul and spirit in resurrection, as well as the restoration of the universe to its original state. Put another way, glorification is the means by which God fully reverses the effects of the Fall, purging sin and its stain from the created order. It involves the return of Jesus, the future resurrection and judgment of all people, and the creation of new heavens and a new earth.

For the most part, when Christians talk about glorification, we are referring to our future resurrection, at which time we receive incorruptible bodies similar to the body Christ had when He rose from the dead. In this respect, Wayne Grudem provides an excellent summary statement: "Glorification is the final step in the application of redemption. It will happen when Christ returns and raises from the dead the bodies of all believers for all time who have died, and reunites them with their souls, and changes the bodies of all believers who remain alive, thereby giving all believers at the same time perfect resurrection bodies like his own."[2]

Even so, glorification is more than this. It is multidimensional, involving time and eternity, individuals and the believing community, saints and their Savior, resurrection of people, and the regeneration of earth. To better understand glorification, let's first define "glory" according to Scripture. Then, let's see how glorification works now, then at our death, resurrection, and the coming of new heavens and a new earth.

THE MEANING OF GLORY

To understand the doctrine of glorification, we should first explore the meaning of *glory*, which translates a number of biblical words. One of these words is the Hebrew *kabod*, which refers to an individual's display of splendor, wealth, and pomp.[3] When used to describe God, however, it does not point to a singular attribute, but to the greatness of His whole nature. For example, Ps. 24:7-10 depicts God as the King of glory, attended by His hosts and distinguished by His infinite splendor and beauty:

> Lift up your heads, you gates!
> Rise up, ancient doors!
> Then the King of glory will come in.
> Who is this King of glory?
> The Lord, strong and mighty,
> the Lord, mighty in battle.
> Lift up your heads, you gates!
> Rise up, ancient doors!
> Then the King of glory will come in.
> Who is he, this King of glory?
> The Lord of Armies,
> he is the King of glory.

In the New Testament, the Greek word *doxa* carries the meaning of honor, splendor, brilliance, fame, and glory.[4] God is the "glorious Father" (Eph. 1:17) and the "God of glory" (Acts 7:2). In the Incarnation, Jesus bears "the glory as the one and only Son from the Father" (John 1:14).

While sometimes used to describe the honor of human beings, or even earthly splendor, *glory* often connects the glory of Jesus with that of God the Father, particularly in His resurrection. For example, Jesus prays that the Father would glorify Him as He glorifies the Father (John 17:1-5). Peter declares that God has glorified Jesus by raising Him from the dead (Acts 3:13-15; 1 Peter 1:21). Paul notes of Jesus, "Therefore we were buried with him by baptism into death, in order that, just as Christ was raised from the dead by the glory of the Father, so we too may walk in newness of life" (Rom. 6:4).

Paul also sees Christ's glorification in His ascension; Jesus is "taken up in glory" (1 Tim. 3:16). Further, the apostles preach that Christ is now exalted at the right hand of God (Acts 2:33; 5:31). And, when He returns, His appearance is glorious (Titus 2:13).

William Mounce writes, "Because God is so glorious, it is only natural that his people want to ascribe 'glory' to him. For this reason, there are many doxologies (ascriptions of glory to God) in the NT. Furthermore, every part of our lives should reflect the fact that the glorious God lives in us — even our eating and drinking."[5]

GLORY NOW

It is our Christian duty to glorify God. As we honor the Father, Son, and Holy Spirit for their divine attributes and redemptive work, we replicate God's glory in our thoughts, words, and deeds. It is more than mere reflection. Consider how the moon, which generates no light, reflects the brilliance of the sun. In a similar way, all of God's creation declares His glory, including His eternal power and divine nature (Ps. 19:1; Rom. 1:20). But followers of Jesus have something more: the Shekinah glory residing in our human spirits; thus, we radiate God's eternal light from within. This should lead us to shine in such a way that others see our good works and give glory to our Father in heaven (Matt. 5:16).

As we exalt God in our lives, He begins the glorification process in us. The apostle Peter writes, "His divine power has given us everything required for life and godliness through the knowledge of him who called us by his own glory and goodness. By these he has given us very great and precious promises, so that through them *you may share in the divine nature*, escaping the corruption that is in the world because of evil desire" (2 Peter 1:3-4, emphasis added). Peter does not mean that believers become little gods or that we acquire the unique qualities of deity such as eternality, omnipotence, omniscience, and omnipresence. Rather, he seems to be saying that we participate in God's moral excellence and one day are morally perfected.

The *ESV Study Bible* notes, "'Divine nature' uses terms familiar to Peter's Hellenistic readership to help them understand the idea of transformation into the image of Christ. Peter emphasizes the moral focus of the believer's transformed life. At conversion, Christians are delivered from the **corruption** of this world, which is rooted in **sinful desire**."[6]

The Lord's "divine nature" in us produces an added benefit: the assurance that the sanctifying work of the Holy Spirit continues until glorification comes in its fullness at the return of Christ. As the apostle John writes, "Dear friends, we are God's children now, and what we will be has not yet been revealed. We know that when he appears, we will be like him because we will see him as he is" (1 John 3:2).

GLORY IN DEATH

There is a sense in which the physical death of the saints is a glorious event. As the psalmist pens, "The death of his faithful ones is valuable in the Lord's sight" (Ps. 116:15). The apostle Paul agonizes over the inevitability of his death, not because he fears it, but because being present with the Lord would leave fellow believers without his tutelage. "For me, to live is Christ and to die is gain," he writes to the Philippians. "Now if I live on in the flesh, this means fruitful work for me; and I don't know which one I should choose. I am torn between the two. I long to depart and be with Christ — which is far better — but to remain in the flesh is more necessary for your sake" (Phil. 1:21-24).

In a similar passage, Paul writes, "So we are always confident and know that while we are at home in the body we are away from the Lord. For we walk by faith, not by sight. In fact, we are confident, and we would prefer to be away from the body and at home with the Lord. Therefore, whether we are at home or away, we make it our aim to be pleasing to him" (2 Cor. 5:6-9).

To pass through the portal of death, followers of Jesus leave their earthly bodies behind (but not abandoned, as we see in the next section). Our souls and spirits pass into the presence of God in heaven, where a place is prepared for us (John 14:1-3). There, we glorify God in ways previously unknown since He endows us with moral and spiritual perfection. We worship around the throne in heaven. And we experience the liberation of sin from our thoughts, words, and deeds.

This is what's known as the *intermediate state*, which falls between our physical death and future resurrection. The New Testament teaches that upon death, believers' souls and spirits separate from our lifeless bodies and enter the presence of God in heaven. There we enjoy intimate fellowship with our Lord while awaiting the future resurrection and glorification of our bodies (John 5:28-29; 1 Cor. 15:51-58; 1 Thess. 4:13-18).

We see magnificent glimpses into the throne room of heaven through the visionary eyes of the apostle John in the Book of Revelation: the Triune Godhead; an emerald-colored rainbow surrounding a glorious throne; living creatures; elders; angels; and redeemed people from every tribe, language, people group, and nation. The combined voices of all creatures in heaven, on earth, under the earth, and in the sea proclaim, "Blessing and honor and glory and power be to the one seated on the throne, and to the Lamb, forever and ever!" (Rev. 5:13).

We may be tempted to stop here, as if heaven is the final destination in life's long journey. It *is* breathtaking. But it gets better. Heaven, a place so awe-inspiring that Paul is not allowed to speak the inexpressible words he hears while visiting there (2 Cor. 12:4), nevertheless is a temporary home for those who rest in the Lord until He returns to earth and brings us with Him. More about this shortly.

Meanwhile, it may be helpful to lay out several biblical truths about the intermediate state of glory in heaven for followers of Jesus:

- The Father, Son, and Holy Spirit reside in heaven, yet they have immediate access to earth (Matt. 3:16-17; Mark 16:19; Acts 9:3-6).
- God's will is done completely in heaven — and one day will be done on earth (Matt. 6:9-11).
- Angels surround the throne in heaven (Matt. 18:10), as do majestic heavenly creatures and redeemed people (Revelation 4-5).
- The heavenly throne is the heart of God's authority and majesty (Mark 16:19).
- Heaven is the place from which Satan fell and in which he has no future part (Luke 10:18; Rev. 20:10).
- Heaven is where believers' names are written down, providing assurance of everlasting life (Luke 10:20; Heb. 12:23).
- Christ is preparing a place for believers in heaven and will take us there one day (John 14:3), bringing us back to earth with Him when He returns (Rev. 19:11-16).
- Our citizenship is in heaven (Phil. 3:20).
- Our inheritance is in heaven — imperishable, undefiled, and unfading (1 Peter 1:4).
- Jesus came from heaven (John 3:31; 6:38, 42); ascended there after His finished work on the cross (Luke 24:51; Eph. 4:10; Heb. 4:14); and will descend from heaven one day to resurrect and glorify believers (1 Cor. 15:51-58; 1 Thess. 4:16-17).
- God brings heaven and earth together one day and dwells with us (Rev. 21:3-4).
- Nothing profane enters heaven — or the new heavens and new earth (Rev. 21:27 - 22:5).

Upon physical death, we experience moral and spiritual perfection in heaven while we await resurrection and the glorification of our bodies. Paul writes, "But now he has reconciled you by his physical body through his death, to present you holy, faultless, and blameless before him ..." (Col. 1:22). We are declared righteous when we place our faith in Christ, and we are made fully righteous when we meet Him in death.

Paul further notes, as he urges us to be faithful in this life:

- "He will also strengthen you to the end, so that you will be blameless in the day of our Lord Jesus Christ" (1 Cor. 1:8).
- "For he chose us in him, before the foundation of the world, to be holy and blameless in love before him" (Eph. 1:4).
- "And I pray this: that your love will keep on growing in knowledge and every kind of discernment, so that you may approve the things that are superior and may be pure and blameless in the day of Christ, filled with the fruit of righteousness that comes through Jesus Christ to the glory and praise of God" (Phil. 1:9-11).

Jude adds, "Now to him who is able to protect you from stumbling and to make you stand in the presence of his glory, without blemish and with great joy ..." (Jude 24).

Accompanying our moral and spiritual purity in heaven is a fullness of knowledge. Not that we become omniscient, for that is an exclusive attribute of God. However, our present incomplete understanding is transformed into a more fully orbed comprehension of all things. Paul encourages the Corinthians with these words: "For now we see only a reflection as in a mirror, but then face to face. Now I know in part, but then I will know fully, as I am fully known" (1 Cor. 13:12).

GLORY IN RESURRECTION

The glory we experience now as Christ lives in and through us, and the glory we experience in death as our souls and spirits ascend into heaven, are partial works of glorification. But full glorification for followers of Jesus takes place when He calls our bodies from the grave and gives us incorruptible bodies similar to the body He bore when He rose from the dead. Physical resurrection is the apogee of personal glorification, for in it we shrug off the last vestiges of sin, which have clung to our mortal bodies. In glorification, the effects of the Fall are fully and finally reversed.

At the return of Christ, all who have died in the Lord are resurrected.[7] Their souls and spirits, which are in heaven with Jesus, are reunited with their bodies, resulting in complete personal glorification; the body, soul, and spirit are fully conformed to the image of Christ and thus free of any effects of the Fall. Christians alive on the earth at the return of Christ are instantly transformed as they are given glorified bodies; at the same time, their souls and spirits are perfected as well.

Three New Testament passages in particular describe the transformation to which all Christians may look forward:

(1) Phil. 3:20-21. Paul writes to the Philippians, "but our citizenship is in heaven, and we eagerly wait for a Savior from there, the Lord Jesus Christ. He will transform the body of our humble condition into the likeness of his glorious body, by the power that enables him to subject everything to himself." The Greek word *summorphon* ("likeness") indicates that our bodies become similar in form to that of Christ. The *CSB Study Bible* notes, "Physical bodies will become glorified bodies in the image of Christ. Salvation has three stages: conversion, moral perfection at death, and the transformation of the body through resurrection at the second coming of Christ."[8]

(2) 2 Cor. 5:1-5. To the church in Corinth, Paul pens these words, "For we know that if our earthly tent we live in is destroyed, we have a building from God, an eternal dwelling in the heavens, not made with hands. Indeed, we groan in this tent, desiring to put on our heavenly dwelling, since, when we have taken it off, we will not be found naked. Indeed, we groan while we are in this tent, burdened as we are, because we do not want to be unclothed but clothed, so that mortality may be swallowed up by life. Now the one who prepared us for this very purpose is God, who gave us the Spirit as a down payment."

Paul compares our mortal bodies to living in an earthly tent, and our resurrection bodies to a heavenly palace. Further, he likens glorification to putting on new clothes that never wear out. The word "naked" is a reference to the human soul and spirit apart from bodily existence. While we are very much alive, conscious, and blessed in heaven, Paul emphasizes that it's far better to be resurrected and glorified, since that is the completion of our salvation and the total reversal of sin and its stain on our lives. While we "groan in this tent," God gives us the Holy Spirit as His guarantee of future glorification. The apostle's tent analogy is quite fitting, since Paul made tents while living in Corinth (Acts 18:3), and the Corinthians likely sold tents to sailors or used them for housing visitors attending the Isthmian Games.[9]

(3) 1 Cor. 15:35-49. While Paul devotes the entire fifteenth chapter to resurrection, he draws a comparison between our present bodies and our resurrection bodies in verses 35-49. Let's look a little closer.

Paul begins by raising two questions: "How are the dead raised? What kind of body will they have when they come?" (v. 35). Evidently, many Corinthian believers fail to understand how their material bodies — with their tendency toward death and decay — can possibly live forever.

The apostle's first question deals with the seeming impossibility that mortal men and women have any hope of escaping the finality of death. The Sadducees, a leading sect of first-century Judaism, denied the resurrection. Greek philosophers understood a human being to have a divine soul of pure fire that in this life is imprisoned in a body; at death, the soul escapes from that prison, returns to the divine fire from which it came, and becomes one of the stars. Thus, the very idea of physical resurrection is abhorrent to the Greek mind. For them, the goal is to endure until death, at which time they discard the body with a sigh of "good riddance."[10] These Jewish and pagan influences evidently led many Christians in Corinth to doubt the possibility of a glorious future beyond the inevitability of an earthly demise.

The second question, while allowing for the improbability of future resurrection, addresses the uncertainty of how a corruptible physical body can ever be restored. The Corinthians don't have to wait long for an answer.

Paul assures them that resurrection is not reconstruction. While there is both continuity and identity in resurrection, our future bodies are significant improvements over our present ones. "You fool!" Paul writes. "What you sow does not come to life unless it dies. And as for what you sow — you are not sowing the body that will be, but only a seed, perhaps of wheat or another grain. But God gives it a body as he wants, and to each of the seeds its own body" (vv. 36-38).

This is the first of three analogies from nature that Paul employs to explain how God takes the bodies of the deceased and prepares them for everlasting glory. A seed of wheat is distinct from the roots, stalk, and fruit, yet there is continuity between them all, and the final product comes from the seed. A fully mature stalk of wheat comes from a wheat seed; the seed of a dandelion or an apple has never been shown to produce wheat. In a similar manner, our earthly bodies, like the seed, eventually go into the ground at death. But in the resurrection, God raises them up into fully mature, completely healthy, everlasting bodies that retain our individual identities.

Kenneth Bailey writes, "The seed is a 'body' that first must die. That body dies naked (bare) and *God gives it a new body* different from the one that dies, and yet it is the same in that each seed has 'its own body.' There is both continuity and discontinuity in this parable. God brings about resurrection *and* transformation."[11]

Without stretching the point too far, it's possible that Paul has in mind the words of Jesus predicting His crucifixion: "Truly I tell you, unless a grain of wheat falls to the ground and dies, it remains by itself. But if it dies, it produces much fruit" (John 12:24). Through Christ's death on the cross, He secures salvation for us. And in His resurrection on the third day, He is "the firstfruits of those who have fallen asleep" (1 Cor. 15:20); that is, He is the first to rise from the dead in a glorified body, paving the way for our future resurrection and glorification.

Next, Paul writes, "Not all flesh is the same flesh; there is one flesh for humans, another for animals, another for birds, and another for fish" (v. 39). Paul uses the word "flesh" (Greek *sarks*) several times in this verse to make a point. Human beings share with animals the reality of physical death and corruption, even though our body types are suited for different earthly environments. Yet followers of Jesus do not need to worry about our skin and bones turning to dust in the tomb because God will bring us back to life one day.

In his third example from nature, Paul notes, "There are heavenly bodies and earthly bodies, but the splendor of the heavenly bodies is different from that of the earthly ones. There is a splendor of the sun, another of the moon, and another of the stars; in fact, one star differs from another star in splendor" (vv. 40-41). The word "splendor" in Greek is *doxa*, which means "glory." The splendor of the heavenly bodies has to do with brightness, while the word *doxa*, when applied to people, often carries the idea of honor, reputation, or esteem.

In any case, the sun "dies" in the evening, only to rise brightly the next morning. The stars, moon, and planets "die" at sunrise, but they return at sunset to illuminate the night sky. In a similar way, believers in all levels of honor and reputation die physically, but God most certainly raises them from the dead in glory, just as reliably as He causes the sun, moon, and stars to fulfill their created purposes each day.

With that as a backdrop, Paul differentiates between the mortal body and the immortal one. "So it is with the resurrection of the dead," he writes (v. 42a). Our bodies therefore are:

- Sown in corruption, raised in incorruption (v. 42b). Physical death is the natural result of living in a perishable body. We get sick, are subject to disease, and simply wear out. Even death by natural causes means the fittest body can't live forever. Even those raised from the dead in Scripture — from the son of the widow at Zarephath to Lazarus — died a second time because they did not receive glorified bodies. However, God fashions our future resurrection bodies in such a way that they are immune to sickness, disease, aging, and decay. Put another way, our glorified bodies are guaranteed to last as long as Jesus' resurrected body endures.
- Sown in dishonor, raised in glory (v. 43a). Paul may be thinking ahead to verses 47-49 in depicting our earthly bodies as dishonorable. The first man, Adam, left us a legacy of dishonor. He willfully disobeyed God, made excuses for his sin, and even implicated God in the process. As a result, he passed to us a natural tendency to live independently of God, which manifests itself in sin and shame in every human life. Our earthly rap sheets are exceedingly long and notoriously disgraceful. Standing in sharp contrast, however, are believers' resurrection bodies,

which are raised in glory. They no longer bear the stamp of sin, and thus they radiate the Christlike qualities of holiness, integrity, reliability, and wisdom.

- Sown in weakness, raised in power (v. 43b). The Greek word rendered "weakness" is *astheneia* and means frailty, sickness, or disease. Our present earthly bodies cannot overpower the effects of living in a sinful and fallen world. Ultimately, the curse of sin is victorious even over the most fit human specimens, and we all succumb to death in a thousand awful ways. But our resurrection bodies are raised in power. The Greek *dynamis* means might, strength, or ability. Often in the New Testament, it is connected with miraculous power, particularly with respect to the power of God and the miracles of Jesus. Our glorified bodies are powered by God, who destroys the vestiges of sin plaguing our earthly bodies.

- Sown a natural body, raised a spiritual body. (v. 44a). Paul distinguishes between the bodies we now possess and the bodies we put on in glorification. Today, we have a *soma psychikos*, or a natural body. This means more than just flesh and blood, however. It refers to a living human being that belongs to the natural world. But in resurrection, we receive a *soma pneumatikos*, or a spiritual body. This means that the Holy Spirit preserves and directs our glorified bodies. Commenting on this verse, early church leader John Chrysostom explains that while the Holy Spirit resides in us now, sin causes the Holy Spirit to "fly away." Yet the resurrected body is different: "Then the Spirit will continually remain in the flesh of the righteous and will be in control, with the soul also being present."[12] Kenneth Bailey puts it this way: "In the resurrection the believer will have a Spirit-constituted physical body. The brokenness and decay of the old body will be gone. The new body will be a physical body like the resurrected body of Christ. Such a truly glorious vision and promise calls for an exuberant hymn of victory."[13]

Paul summarizes in verses 47-49 by contrasting the "first man" and the "second man," that is, Adam and Jesus. While God forms Adam from the ground, and he becomes a "man of dust," Jesus is from heaven — eternal and otherworldly. In our present bodies, we resemble Adam in that we "have borne the image of the man of dust." However, in the resurrection, "we will also bear the image of the man of heaven."

Our glorification in resurrection is not a lengthy process. Rather, Paul reveals to us a mystery: "We will not all fall asleep, but we will all be changed, in a moment, in the twinkling of an eye, at the last trumpet" (vv. 51b-52a). Whether we are raised from the dead or transformed as living Christians on earth into glorified believers, the promise of Christ's return should cause us to rejoice, as Paul does: "But thanks be to God, who gives us the victory through our Lord Jesus Christ!" (v. 57).

GLORY IN RESTORATION

The glorified body of Jesus is able to navigate the ravages of a world still under the curse of sin. After His resurrection, Jesus eats our food, travels our roads, speaks with befuddled eyewitnesses of His death and resurrection, passes through closed doors, transports Himself effortlessly from one location to another, and finally launches from the Mount of Olives into heaven. No doubt, our resurrected bodies will have many of the same capabilities. Yet there's still something missing in the redemptive work of God. The world in which we live was not always cursed, nor will it always be. A day is coming when our sovereign Lord makes all things new (Rev. 21:5).

Jesus refers to this as "the renewal of all things, when the Son of Man sits on his glorious throne" (Matt. 19:28). Peter urges us to wait for "new heavens and a new earth, where righteousness dwells" (2 Peter 3:13). And in his vision of the world to come, John says he sees "a new heaven and a new earth; for the first heaven and the first earth had passed away, and the sea was no more" (Rev. 21:1). All of these passages refer to the future glorification of the created order, a world purged of sin and its stain, where the pristine innocence of all creation is restored.

If salvation is God's work of conquering Satan, sin, and death, then it stands to reason that He not only purges our bodies of the effects of the Fall, He also purifies the environment under sin's curse. Because people are part of the creation, Adam's sin reaps devastating consequences for himself, his progeny, and the world in which we live. The Lord spells out the curse in Gen. 3:14-19. The serpent, once a glorious animal, is consigned to shame beneath the feet of mankind. Satan's offspring are at odds with the children of God. Satan himself is to bite the heel of a future Redeemer, who in turn crushes the evil one's head. The pains of childbirth intensify. Conflict arises between husband and wife. The fruit of the earth is harvested with great difficulty as thorns and thistles arise. Work becomes laborious. And death is inevitable, for man is dust, and to dust he returns.

Since that fateful day, sin has ruined everything. Adam and Eve's first child — perhaps thought to be the Redeemer promised in Gen. 3:15 — turns out to be a murderer. Mighty men of old allow themselves to be demon-possessed, setting a precedent for future generations.[14] Humans become so corrupt, except for one family, that God destroys them in a global flood. Then, survivors build a lofty tower at Babel in utter rebellion against God. The Egyptians enslave the Israelites for more than four hundred years while the Lord delays giving His chosen people The Promised Land. Why the long wait? So the sins of the Amorites reach full measure. After their release from captivity, the Israelites whine and rebel, and thus they are made to wander in the wilderness for forty years.

Once settled in the Promised Land, they fail to completely purge it of wickedness. They demand a king, divide themselves into two kingdoms, fall into idolatry and injustice, and are carried off into captivity. The Shekinah glory leaves the temple and never returns until God in human flesh, Jesus of Nazareth, appears and declares Himself Messiah. Rather than received as King, He is betrayed and arrested, falsely tried and convicted, and hung naked on a Roman cross. Even after He rises from the dead and ascends into heaven, the world gets no better as the followers of Jesus are treated with the same disdain shown their Savior.

Along with this legacy of moral evil, let's not forget the parallel historical record of so-called natural evil: Droughts, famines, flash floods, hurricanes, tornadoes, plagues, infestations, earthquakes, electrical storms, tsunamis, volcanoes, diseases, meteorites ... and on it goes.

By the time of the apostle Paul, he laments, "For we know that the whole creation has been groaning together with labor pains until now" (Rom. 8:22). But there's hope surrounding this verse: "For I consider that the sufferings of this present time are not worth comparing with the glory that is going to be revealed in us. For the creation eagerly waits with anticipation for God's sons to be revealed. For the creation was subjected to futility — not willingly, but because of him who subjected it — in the hope that the creation itself will also be set free from the bondage to decay in the glorious freedom of God's children.... Not only that, but we ourselves who have the Spirit as the firstfruits — we also groan within ourselves, eagerly waiting for adoption, the redemption of our bodies" (Rom. 8:18-21, 23).

Just as Christians look forward to receiving glorified bodies, we delight in knowing that the corrupted world in which we live is going to be redeemed one day as well. Peter writes that it is going to happen like this: "But the day of the Lord will come like a thief; on that day the heavens will pass away with a loud noise, the elements will burn and be dissolved, and the earth and the works on it will be disclosed.... Because of that day, the heavens will be dissolved with fire and the elements will melt with heat. But based on his promise, we wait for new heavens and a new earth, where righteousness dwells" (2 Peter 3:10, 12b-13).

The apostle John describes it this way: "Then I saw a new heaven and a new earth; for the first heaven and the first earth had passed away, and the sea was no more. I also saw the holy city, the new Jerusalem, coming down out of heaven from God, prepared like a bride adorned for her husband. Then I heard a loud voice from the throne: Look, God's dwelling is with humanity, and he will live with them. They will be his peoples, and God himself will be with them and will be their God. He will wipe away every tear from their eyes. Death will be no more; grief, crying, and pain will be no more, because the previous things have passed away" (Rev. 21:1-4).

Millard Erickson writes, "Humanity's original dwelling was in the paradisiacal setting in the garden of Eden; their final dwelling will also be in a perfect setting — the New Jerusalem. Part of the glorification of the human will be the provision of a perfect environment in which to dwell. It will be perfect for the glory of God will be present."[15]

After Christ returns, He resurrects and judges all people, and creates new heavens and a new earth, where the Triune God resides forevermore with redeemed people. Our temporary home is heaven. Our eternal home is earth the way God made it and intended it to be — sinless, perfect, and in the presence of His unveiled glory.

ARE THE WICKED GLORIFIED?

We've focused on the future glorification of the adopted children in God's family. But what about those who reject the revelation of God in creation, conscience, Christ, and the canon of Scripture? What kind of resurrected bodies do they get? And where do they spend eternity?

There is no doubt that unbelievers are resurrected one day and spend eternity apart from God in hell. Jesus tells His followers that "a time is coming when all who are in the graves will hear his voice and come out — those who have done good things, to the resurrection of life, but those who have done wicked things, to the resurrection of condemnation" (John 5:28-29). John foresees that second resurrection — the resurrection of condemnation — in Rev. 20:11-15. There, "the dead, the great and the small," stand before a great white throne (v. 12). More about this later.

Meanwhile, there is less in Scripture about the resurrection of the wicked than there is about the glorification of the just. Nevertheless, the Bible gives us enough information to know that those who reject Christ are physically resurrected one day and separated forever from God.

Daniel gives us the clearest Old Testament glimpse of the resurrection of the wicked and their everlasting destiny: "Many who sleep in the dust of the earth will awake, some to eternal life, and some to disgrace and eternal contempt" (Dan. 12:2). Job and Isaiah also offer insights into future resurrection (Job 19:25-27; Isa. 26:19).

In addition to Jesus' words about a day of reckoning for all (John 5:28-29), the New Testament writers confirm final judgment of the wicked in numerous places, a judgment that presupposes resurrection

(Acts 10:42; 17:31; 2 Thess. 1:5-10; Heb. 9:27; 1 Peter 4:5; 2 Peter 3:7).

We've surveyed the resurrection of life, also known as the "first resurrection" (Rev. 20:5-6). Now, let's look at the resurrection of condemnation, which leads to "the second death, the lake of fire" (Rev. 20:14b). John writes that the wicked dead, great and small, stand before a great white throne and are judged according to their works (vv. 11-13).

Prior to this judgment, Satan is thrown into the lake of fire (v. 10). Presumably, demons are cast there at this time as well (Matt. 25:41). Then, Death and Hades are cast into hell (v. 14). This lends credence to the view that the wicked are the last to be resurrected because no one dies physically anymore (Death), and there is no need for an intermediate abode of the dead (Hades). Last, the wicked, whose names are not found written in the book of life, are thrown into the lake of fire and experience the second death (v. 15).

But what kind of resurrected bodies do the wicked receive? Scripture offers no details like the ones Paul lays out for believers in 1 Corinthians 15. Even so, we may offer a few observations about the resurrected bodies of the damned:

- They are physical bodies, reunited with their souls and spirits, which have been suffering conscious torment in Hades between death and resurrection.
- They are fashioned for everlasting separation from God in hell. Jesus tells us that both the souls and bodies of unbelievers are punished in hell, and hell is forever (Matt. 10:28; 25:41). Scripture does not support the false doctrine of annihilationism.[16]
- They cannot be what Paul describes as "spiritual" bodies in 1 Cor. 15:44, for their owners have rejected Christ and thus are void of the indwelling Holy Spirit.
- They encounter the second death — that is, the lake of fire. There, they exist forever but do not experience true life, for they are in outer darkness, cut off from the Source of Life.

Don Stewart comments on the lack of detail concerning the form of unbelievers' resurrected bodies:

> While the Scripture gives much detail with respect to the body of the saved, there is absolutely nothing said with respect to the body of the lost. We know they are raised and judged. Yet Scripture is silent as to what form they will assume upon their resurrection.... The purpose for their resurrection is judgment and punishment. Only the facts are given. This is a consistent pattern of Scripture. In Genesis 5, there is no age given of those in the ungodly line. The ungodly rich man, in Jesus' story in Luke 16, likewise remains nameless. The fact that their form is not explained is to be expected. What is emphasized in Scripture is God and His relationship with His children. Those who have rejected Him are not the main concern. Therefore their names, as well as their form, is not a subject that is given any explanation.[17]

ARE HEAVEN AND HELL EXPERIENCED THE SAME WAY FOR EVERY PERSON?

We've explored the type of resurrected bodies Christians receive in glorification. But do all Christians experience everlasting life the same way? Yes, and no. Yes, in that every believer receives a glorified body and lives forever in the presence of the Triune God on a restored earth. But no, in the sense that resurrection, followed by judgment and reward, are tied together. In a similar manner, unbelievers experience everlasting existence apart from Christ differently, based on what is found in the books that are opened at the great white throne judgment.

Heaven is not the same for every believer, nor do all those who reject Christ experience hell identically. Our final, personal, individual judgment before Christ is His way, as the righteous Judge, of setting things right for all eternity.

Our short stay on earth is a dress rehearsal for life beyond the grave. One day, we all stand before Jesus to give an account of what we did with the gospel, as well as our time, talents, opportunities, and other gifts of grace God has entrusted to us. The result is varying degrees of reward for believers and varying degrees of punishment for unbelievers.

It's clear from Scripture that followers of Jesus stand in a different judgment than those who reject Christ. The apostle Paul tells us that Christians are summoned to the judgment seat of Christ (Rom. 14:10-12; 2 Cor. 5:10). At the same time, the apostle John is given a glimpse of the great white throne, upon which Jesus sits to judge those whose names are not written in the book of life (Rev. 20:11-15).

Let's look a little closer at these days of reckoning.

The judgment seat of Christ

The judgment seat of Christ is the place where Christians, and perhaps believers of all ages, stand before Jesus to receive His evaluation of our lives. The result is everlasting reward, or loss of reward, based on the degree of faithfulness to walk in the path of good works God "prepared ahead of time for us to do" (Eph. 2:10). Paul writes about this judgment in several places:

- Rom. 14:10-12 - "But you, why do you judge your brother or sister? Or you, why do you despise your brother or sister? For we will all stand before the judgment seat of God. For it is written, **As I live, says the Lord, every knee will bow to me, and every tongue will give praise to God.** So then, each of us will give an account of himself to God."
- 1 Cor. 3:11-15: - "For no one can lay any other foundation than what has been laid down. That foundation is Jesus Christ. If anyone builds on the foundation with gold, silver, costly stones, wood, hay, or straw, each one's work will become obvious. For the day will disclose it, because it will be revealed by fire; the fire will test the quality of each one's work. If anyone's work that he has built survives, he will receive a reward. If anyone's work is burned up, he will

experience loss, but he himself will be saved — but only as through fire."

- 2 Cor. 5:10: - "For we must all appear before the judgment seat of Christ, so that each may be repaid for what he has done in the body, whether good or evil."

The Greek word translated "judgment seat" (or "tribunal" in some translations) is *bema*, a bench or platform from which public or judicial pronouncements are made. Pilate sits on the *bema* (Matt. 27:19; John 19:13), as do Herod (Acts 12:21) and Gallio (Acts 18:12-17). Paul does not specify the exact time of this judgment. However, it seems reasonable to conclude that it is tied to our resurrection rather than to our death so that the full impact of our earthly lives — an impact that continues after our departure from earth — may be fully evaluated and rewarded.

This judgment does not determine a believer's eternal destiny, for that is fixed on this side of the grave with his or her decision to trust in Christ.

Rather, the *bema* judgment is where Christ rewards His followers based on how faithfully we managed the time, talents, spiritual gifts, and other good things we were given. Every Christian is a winner because Jesus has secured his or her everlasting life through His finished work on the cross. But not every Christian is rewarded equally.

Jesus urges His followers to lay up treasure in heaven, where it is kept safe (Matt. 6:20). The apostle Paul informs us that our works of faithfulness, which he likens to gold, silver, and precious stones, are refined in the fires of judgment and emerge purified (1 Cor. 3:11-15). And in the Book of Revelation, Jesus reminds us that our faithfulness is rewarded (Rev. 3:23; 22:12).

In fact, the New Testament mentions at least five "crowns," or rewards, believers may send ahead of us to heaven:

- The imperishable crown, for those who persevere in their Christian walk, living a disciplined, Spirit-controlled life (1 Cor. 9:24-27).
- The crown of exultation, or the disciple-maker's crown,

with which the recipient's joy in heaven is multiplied by the fellowship of those he or she has helped lead to faith in Christ (1 Thess. 2:19-20).

- The crown of righteousness, for those who love the appearing of Jesus and live as if He could return at any moment (2 Tim. 4:7-8).
- The crown of glory, for those who faithfully teach God's Word and shepherd the congregation God has called them to oversee (1 Peter 5:1-4).
- And the crown of life, for those who love the Lord enough to faithfully endure the trials of this life without losing faith or denying Christ — especially enduring to the point of death (James 1:12; Rev. 2:10).[18]

What do these "crowns" really mean? Are they literal crowns for us to wear throughout eternity? Perhaps. But as Robert Jeffress points out, they also represent tangible and eternal benefits given to those whom Christ has rewarded at His judgment seat. These benefits include: (1) special privileges, such as a special welcome by God (2 Peter 1:11), special access to the tree of life (Rev. 2:7), and even special treatment by Christ Himself (Luke 12:37); (2) special positions, or additional responsibilities in heaven; and (3) special praise, such as the words of Jesus, "Well done, good and faithful servant!" (Matt. 25:21).[19]

WHY THE *BEMA* JUDGMENT?

In 1 Cor. 4:1-5, Paul describes God's purpose for the *bema* judgment, as well as our proper perspective of it. "A person should think of us in this way: as servants of Christ and managers of the mysteries of God," he writes. "In this regard, it is required that managers be found faithful.... It is the Lord who judges me. So don't judge anything prematurely, before the Lord comes, who will both bring to light what is hidden in darkness and reveal the intentions of the hearts. And then praise will come to each one from God."

This judgment is a full disclosure of our words and deeds, as Christ uncovers even our secret conversations, as well as our thoughts, intentions, and motivations. Like a purging fire, Christ's impartial evaluation of our lives burns away our worthless works and purifies our righteous ones. For the ones who have built well upon the foundation of our faith, we receive a "well done" from Christ and are given greater positions of authority and greater degrees of responsibility in His eternal kingdom (Matt. 25:21, 23).

Those who squander our Christian lives watch as worthless works are consumed in the fires of judgment. Paul reminds such unfaithful workers, "If anyone's work is burned up, he will experience loss, but he himself will be saved — but only as through fire" (1 Cor. 3:15). The apostle John warns his readers to remain faithful to Christ, lest they be ashamed at His coming (1 John 2:28).

"The judgment seat of Christ focuses on the assessment of a Christian's deeds or lifestyle rather than the determination of their eternal destiny," according to Daniel Hays, Scott Duvall, and Marvin Pate. "Having been saved by grace through faith (Eph. 2:8-9), Christians are nevertheless committed to working out their faith through deeds (e.g., Gal. 5:6; Eph. 2:10; Phil. 2:12-13; 1 Thess. 1:3). Believers are accountable for individual actions and are not exempt from doing good. Eschatology and ethics are bound tightly together. The judgment seat of Christ fulfills God's impartial justice, since not all believers live with the same degree of devotion to Christ. Christians are individually accountable for what they do in this mortal body."[20]

THE GREAT WHITE THRONE JUDGMENT

The great white throne, described in Rev. 20:11-15, is unique among the thrones of God in Scripture. It stands alone. It bears no context. It offers no hope, grace, or mercy. It fulfills no covenant promises. It surrounds itself with no rainbows, flaming torches, seas of glass, or heavenly creatures. It is perhaps the most solemn image of God's throne in the Bible, for it depicts the time and place where Christ — the Creator, Redeemer, and Judge — meets face to face with the wicked, who must now give an account of their lives. It might be said that this is the last stop on the road to hell.

Joseph Seiss writes, "We read of no white robes, no spotless linen, no palms, nothing but naked sinners before the naked majesty of enthroned Almightiness, awaiting their eternal doom."[21]

As unbelievers stand before the great white throne — alone, without a defense, and with no escape — John notes that "books were opened. Another book was opened, which is the book of life, and the dead were judged according to their works by what was written in the books" (Rev. 20:12b). What are these books, and how many are there? What is different about the book of life that it should be named, while the others are mentioned as a group without distinction?

It seems clear that God keeps a record of our lives and holds us accountable for how we manage the time, talents, relationships, and other gifts He has entrusted to us. He knows our thoughts, which form the action plans for good and evil deeds (see, for example, Matt. 5:27-28). He hears our words, which reveal the true nature of our hearts and for which we must give an account (Matt. 12:33-37).

In various places, the Bible depicts God's record of our lives as contained in heavenly books. No person escapes the Creator's interest or avoids a day of reckoning with Him. "Myriads of human beings have lived and died of whom the world knows nothing; but the lives they lived, the deeds they wrought, the thoughts and tempers they indulged, still stand written where the memory of them cannot perish. Not a human being has ever breathed earth's atmosphere whose career is not traced at full length in the books of eternity."[22]

The books that record the deeds of unbelievers are opened in order to show them at least two truths: the full extent of their lifelong wickedness, and the failure of their good deeds to earn the favor of God.

THE BOOK OF LIFE

In addition, there is a search for their names in the book of life, where their everlasting bliss in the presence of Christ may have been secured by faith. But no, their names are not to be found. As a result, they are banished to outer darkness, or hell.

What's so special about the book of life? Its pages list no good deeds, no legacy of charitable acts, no meritorious service worthy of everlasting life. So, it seems there is no reason the names of the wicked are excluded. If they could scour the pages, they would see the names of people great and small — leaders, foot soldiers, neighbors, family members. To the mind of the damned, the listing makes no sense.

There is ample room in the book for every person's name, and yet their names are excluded. Why? An entry in this book is not achieved through human effort but through simple surrender. Those written in the book of life have washed their robes in the blood of the Lamb, and He has written their names with His own blood. Those who would not have the Lamb will not have life. They are thrown into the lake of fire. The difference is that the wicked have pleaded their own righteousness, while the righteous have pleaded the blood of the Lamb.

There are no doubt degrees of punishment in hell just as there are varying rewards in heaven. Eternity in hell is not the same for the mass murderer as for the law-abiding citizen, but it is outer darkness nonetheless.

Jesus saves some of His most graphic depictions of the darkness and loneliness of hell for the most religious people of His day. He calls the Jewish leaders a brood of vipers who shut the door of the kingdom of heaven in people's faces. They don't go in and they don't allow those entering to go in. "How can you escape being condemned to hell?" He asks (Matt. 23:14, 33). He tells the story of Lazarus and the rich man in front of the Pharisees to illustrate that wealth and privilege are not the entitlements God owes an outwardly righteous person; rather, heaven awaits those who humbly trust in Him for salvation (Luke 16:19-31).

What a comfort it is for believers to know their names are written in the book of life, and what a shock it must be for countless unbelievers who discover at the great white throne that their names are absent from heaven's roll. On earth their deeds earned a place in many great books — books of valor, conquest, heroics, feats, discoveries, inventions, charities, religious quests, political coups, scientific breakthroughs, medical advances, social progress, military campaigns, community service, and legendary leadership.

Perhaps their names are inscribed on grand buildings, or chiseled into monuments, or painted on the hulls of ocean-going vessels. At the very least, the newspapers noticed their entrance into the world and their departure from it. Somewhere, their names are etched in family trees or scribbled in the opening pages of family Bibles. How can it be that the God who created all people does not ensure that their names are in His book of life?

There must be some mistake. "Lord, Lord, didn't we prophesy in Your name?" some cry out. "Didn't we drive out demons in your name, and do many mighty works in Your name?" The one seated on the throne does not deny they invoked His name on numerous occasions, no doubt producing some earthly good. But He reveals there is no relationship between them when He utters the seven most tragic words in human history: "I never knew you: depart from me" (Matt. 7:23 KJV).

ANYONE NOT FOUND

Rev. 20:15 is as clear as Scripture can be: "And anyone whose name was not found written in the book of life was thrown into the lake of fire."

There is but one way a person's name is entered into the book of life: God writes it there and never blots it out. Just as He chooses believers in Christ from the foundation of the world, He keeps those who belong to Him and never lets them go.

In previous chapters, we explored whether God's election is anchored simply in divine foreknowledge, or in hard determinism, or even in fatalism. No doubt, much about the will of God is beyond our current understanding. Yet it appears that God's sovereignty encompasses His decision to entrust all people with the ability to make choices for which He holds us responsible. No one is denied a place in the book of life, and no one's name is entered there without that person's consent.

As the wicked pass through the gates of hell in Dante's epic poem *Inferno*, they are greeted with these words: "Abandon hope, all you who enter here." They remind the damned that once inside, there is no escape from the fiery torments they have brought upon themselves.

As Charles Swindoll writes, "Though the details of Dante's fictional picture of heaven, hell, and purgatory range from the fantastic to the heretical, he was right about this: the final destination of the wicked features a one-way entrance. All hope vanishes beyond; there will be no escape from the lake of fire.... The facts of eternal punishment are set forth without a hint of hope ... because no hope exists apart from God."[23]

EVERY KNEE WILL BOW

Paul writes to the Philippians that one day, "at the name of Jesus every knee will bow — in heaven and on earth and under the earth — and every tongue will confess that Jesus Christ is Lord, to the glory of God the Father" (Phil. 2:10-11). Believers' knees bow in humble adoration. Unbelievers' knees bow in grudging acknowledgment that while they will have their way and live forever apart from Jesus, He is the ultimate Master with the authority to rule over the human heart.

It is a common expression at funerals that the deceased have gone on to their eternal reward. Meant to comfort mourners that their loved ones are in "a better place," the statement glosses over the deeper truth that indeed all people ultimately are repaid for their lives on earth.

The reward may be our Savior's greeting, "Come, you who are blessed by My Father; inherit the kingdom prepared for you from the foundation of the world" (Matt. 25:34), followed by the bliss of authority and responsibility in the presence of the Lord in the new heavens and new earth. Or, the reward may be the words of the one seated on the throne of His glory: "Depart from me, you who are cursed, into the eternal fire prepared for the devil and his angels!" (Matt. 25:41).

In the end, everyone gets the eternal destiny they choose, based on their acceptance or rejection of Christ. In addition, everyone spends eternity as close to, or as far away from, their Creator as they desire based on how they lived out their acceptance or rejection of the Source of life.

Jesus reminds us in the Book of Revelation that when He returns, He will set things right: "Look, I am coming soon, and my reward is with me to repay each person according to his work" (Rev. 22:12). His words should prompt all people to search their hearts and take stock of their treasure.

WHAT IF THERE'S NO CORPSE?

Every person is physically resurrected one day, summoned before Christ on His throne of glory, and ushered into eternity, either in a glorified body, or in a physical body prepared for everlasting existence in outer darkness.

What about those whose bodies have been cremated, lost at sea, ravaged in warfare, or otherwise ruined beyond recovery? The God who names the stars (Isa. 40:26) is fully capable of tracing every human atom and resurrecting every person ever conceived, and then fashioning that body for everlasting glory with God or everlasting existence apart from Him.

Resurrection must take place for Christ to set things right. The salvation of believers depends on Jesus' finished work at Calvary, purging sin and its consequences from our entire being, and restoring in eternity what was sacrificed in time for His sake. A young woman beheaded for professing faith in Christ must experience the resurrection power of Jesus, whose brutalized body burst forth from the grave in health and wholeness. The child vanquished in his mother's womb, never allowed to draw his first breath, must experience the joys of childhood innocence and the embrace of a loving Father. And the faithful bond-servant of Christ whose physical vigor erodes with the ravages of time must experience the vitality of being a new creation once again.

Equally important, the punishment of the wicked demands resurrection, for their sins are not confined to the soul. Jesus' story of Lazarus and the rich man illustrates the truth that we reap in eternity what we sow in time. In the resurrection of the wicked, the rich man, perhaps, will forever seek the creature comforts he denied Lazarus. The one who trafficked in human lives may find himself forever on the run as a marked man. And the false teacher who, for personal gain, proclaimed "another Jesus," "a different spirit," and "a different gospel" (2 Cor. 11:4), may find his sensual cravings forever unsatisfied, while he seeks to escape the haunting eyes of those who followed him blindly into hell.

While outer darkness may seem unreasonably harsh, everyone who experiences everlasting existence apart from Christ has chosen it. The rich man in Jesus' parable confesses to being in torment, but he shows no willingness to repent of his sin (Luke 16:19-31). The resurrected wicked summoned before the great white throne watch in stunned silence as books are opened, revealing no evidence of a desire for Christ (Rev. 20:11-15). Even those who dare to offer a word in their own defense are proven to be lawbreakers whom Jesus never knew (Matt. 7:21-23).

When judgment falls on the wicked, it does not produce repentance, for that is the goal of God's kindness, restraint, and patience now (Rom. 2:4; 2 Peter 3:9). In body and soul, the resurrected wicked remain, throughout eternity, what they have proven to be on this side of the grave.

Like a black hole, the second death sucks in everything in its path and permits no escape. The gentle touch of the Savior's hand, the still small voice calling the lost to repentance, the joy of an intimate relationship with the God of the universe — these have been rejected and are not welcome in the second death. Worse, there is no second chance. The second death — experienced in an indestructible body devoid of the Spirit — is final and without appeal.

KEY PASSAGES ON GLORIFICATION

Let's survey several Bible verses that address glorification.

Rom. 8:11 - "And if the Spirit of him who raised (*egeirantos*) Jesus from the dead lives in you, then he who raised Christ from the dead will also bring your mortal bodies to life through his Spirit who lives in you."

As we noted in previous chapters, the Holy Spirit's presence in our lives is God's mark of ownership on us, and His guarantee to finish the good work He began in us. The climax of this work is glorification — the transformation of our corruptible bodies into incorruptible bodies similar to Christ's today. This occurs when Jesus retrieves our corpses from the graves at His return. Or, if we are alive on earth, He instantaneously converts our mortal bodies into glorified ones. The Christian's body still dies today because of sin's destructive power, but the indwelling Spirit assures us that, just as He imparts new spiritual life to us now, He delivers new physical life one day.

The Greek verb *egeiro* (to raise) is used several times in the New Testament to depict getting up after awakening from sleep (Matt. 1:24; 8:25; 25:7). More importantly, it describes people who are known to be dead being raised to life, such as Jairus' daughter (Mark 5:22-24, 35-43) and Lazarus (John 12:1, 9, 17). But the core usage of *egeiro* has to do with Jesus being raised from the dead. Except for Phil. 1:17, the letters of the New Testament never use this verb for anything other than the resurrection of Jesus.[24] In fact, Paul employs the term more than thirty times in Romans and 1 Corinthians to make it clear that Jesus is the firstfruits of the resurrection and thus is qualified to raise us from the dead when He returns to earth.

One last observation should not be lost to us. This verse encapsulates the work of the Trinity in our salvation. While Paul is clear that the Holy Spirit indwells believers (see also 1 Cor. 3:16; 6:19; 2 Tim. 1:14), he also reminds us that the Son and the Father dwell in us as well (Rom. 8:10; 2 Cor. 6:16; 13:5; Gal. 2:20; Eph. 3:17; Col. 1:27).

In a similar manner, the Triune Godhead raised Jesus from the dead. Consider:

- God the Father raised Jesus (cf. Acts 2:24; 3:15; 4:10; 5:30; 10:40; 13:30, 33, 34, 37; 17:31; Rom. 6:4, 9; 10:9; 1 Cor. 6:14; 2 Cor. 4:14; Gal. 1:1; Eph. 1:20; Col. 2:12; 1 Thess. 1:10).
- God the Son raised Himself (cf. John 2:19–22; 10:17–18).
- And God the Spirit raised Jesus (cf. Rom. 8:11). This same Trinitarian emphasis can be seen in the previous two verses (Rom. 8:9-10).[25]

CSB	KJV	NIV	NASB	ESV
Raised	Raised up	Raised	Raised	Raised

Comparing English translations of *egeirantos* in Rom. 8:11a

Rom. 8:16-17, 23 - "The Spirit himself testifies together with our spirit that we are God's children, and if children, also heirs — heirs of

God and coheirs with Christ — if indeed we suffer with him so that we may also be glorified with him (*syndoxasthomen*).... Not only that, but we ourselves who have the Spirit as the firstfruits — we also groan within ourselves, eagerly waiting for adoption, the redemption of our bodies (*apolutrosin tou somatos emon*)."

The indwelling Holy Spirit confirms our relationship with the Father. We may rest assured that we are His adopted sons and daughters, elevated to the status of coheirs with the eternal Son of God. We are joined to Jesus now in suffering, but just as certainly we are united with Him in a glorious future. As Jesus is in glory now, so we will be, as Paul captures in another passage: "And most certainly, the mystery of godliness is great: He was manifested in the flesh, vindicated in the Spirit, seen by angels, preached among the nations, believed on in the world, taken up in glory" (1 Tim. 3:16). One day, we also are taken up in glory.

Until the day Christ comes for us, He gives us the Holy Spirit as the "firstfruits," or the down payment on our inheritance. While in our earthly tents, we may groan with hardship, aging, sickness, and encroaching death, but these only serve as reminders of the glories to come. Just as a farmer's firstfruits are the initial harvesting of his ripened crops, the Holy Spirit offers believers a foretaste of the abundant blessings to come, including living in God's presence forever.

Paul uses the term "adoption" in a unique way in this passage. In other places, he makes it clear that believers already are adopted as sons and daughters of God. At the same time, we anticipate the completion of our adoption, when the full effects of redemption are realized in glorification. Paul refers to this as the revelation of God's sons (Rom. 8:19) and the glorious freedom of God's children (Rom. 8:21).

Warren Wiersbe writes, "We are waiting for 'the adoption,' which is the redemption of the body when Christ returns (Phil. 3:20-21). This is the thrilling climax to 'the adoption' that took place at conversion when 'the Spirit of adoption' gave us an adult standing in God's family. When Christ returns, we shall enter into our full inheritance."[26]

CSB	KJV	NIV	NASB	ESV
Glorified with him	Glorified together	Share in his glory	Glorified with Him	Glorified with him

Comparing English translations of *syndoxasthomen* in Rom. 8:17

CSB	KJV	NIV	NASB	ESV
Redemption of our bodies	Redemption of our body	Redemption of our bodies	Redemption of our body	Redemption of our bodies

Comparing English translations of *apolutrosin tou somatos emon* in Rom. 8:23

Rom. 8:29-30 - "For those he foreknew he also predestined to be conformed to the image of his Son, so that he would be the firstborn among many brothers and sisters. And those he predestined, he also called; and those he called, he also justified; and those he justified, he also glorified (*edoxasen*)."

We've already looked in some detail at the "golden chain of redemption" in these two verses. Here, Paul ties together God's work of redemption, which spans time and eternity. Those whom God has always foreknown and predestined, He draws to Himself and declares righteous in time, and ultimately glorifies in future resurrection — the final act of salvation that extends unbroken into eternity future.

The word "glorified," as applied here, means to admit to a state of bliss, or to beautify.[27] Surely, when Christ calls our corpses out of the graves and transforms them into glorious bodies, we experience not only the newness of life in perfection, but the incomprehensible joy that accompanies it. And we experience first-hand what John hears declared from the throne room of heaven: "He will wipe away every tear from their eyes. Death will be no more; grief, crying, and pain will be no more, because the previous things have passed away" (Rev. 21:4).

But perhaps the most noteworthy feature of the golden chain is that Paul depicts the redeemed as "glorified" — in the past tense. No follower of Jesus has yet experienced resurrection and glorification. We, along with our departed brothers and sisters in heaven, await the return of Jesus to make this a reality. And yet, Paul is so certain of our future glorification that he links it to the already accomplished work of foreknowledge, predestination, calling, and justification.

John Witmer notes that, with glorification, "not a single person is lost. God completes His plan without slippage. 'Glorified' is in the past tense because this final step is so certain that in God's eyes it is as good as done. To be glorified is another way of saying that God's children will be 'conformed' to His Son; and that is God's ultimate 'purpose.' No longer will they 'fall short of the glory of God' (Rom. 3:23)."[28]

CSB	KJV	NIV	NASB	ESV
Glorified	Glorified	Glorified	Glorified	Glorified

Comparing English translations of *edoxasen* in Rom. 8:30

1 Cor. 15:51-54 - "Listen, I am telling you a mystery: We will not all fall asleep, but we will all be changed, in a moment, in the twinkling of an eye, at the last trumpet. For the trumpet will sound, and the dead will be raised incorruptible, and we will be changed. For this corruptible body must be clothed with incorruptibility (*aphtharsian*), and this mortal body must be clothed with immortality (*athanasian*). When this corruptible body is clothed with incorruptibility, and this mortal body is clothed with immortality, then the saying that is written will take place: **Death has been swallowed up in victory.**"

The apostle Paul discloses a "mystery" (*mysterion*), a truth that would remain secret apart from divine revelation. Not every believer is to experience physical death, but all Christians may eagerly anticipate the miraculous transformation of our corruptible bodies into incorruptible ones. This occurs at "the last trumpet," or Christ's return for us (see also 1 Thess. 4:13-17).

The change is more than dramatic; it is instantaneous. Paul says it takes place "in a moment," using the Greek word *atomas*, which signifies the smallest possible division of something, in this case time. The phrase "in the twinkling of an eye" further describes the quickness with which our mortal bodies are made like the glorified body of Jesus. The Greek word for "twinkling" (*rhipe*) is used only here in the New Testament. It is used in classical Greek to depict the rush of a storm, the flapping of wings, the buzz of a gnat, and the twinkling of stars. Generally, it describes very rapid movement.[29]

Paul uses the metaphor of putting on clothing to describe the manner in which our bodies are transformed. Our corruptible bodies must be clothed with incorruptibility, and our mortal bodies must be clothed with immortality. This is an apt depiction of glorification because humans naturally possess neither incorruptibility nor immortality. These must come from God, "who alone is immortal and who lives in unapproachable light" (1 Tim. 6:16a). Just as believing sinners are clothed in the righteousness of Christ now, we look forward to the day when He regales us in His incorruptibility and immortality. When this occurs, then Isaiah's prophecy is fulfilled: "Death has been swallowed up in victory" (Isa. 25:8 - "he will destroy death forever").

The seeming victories of Satan in the Garden of Eden and on many subsequent occasions are reversed on the cross and eradicated by the empty tomb. From the vantage point of glorification, Paul could echo a victorious taunt: "**Where, death, is your victory? Where, death, is your sting?** The sting of death is sin, and the power of sin is the law. But thanks be to God, who gives us the victory through our Lord Jesus Christ!" (1 Cor. 15:55-56; cf. Hosea 13:14).

CSB	KJV	NIV	NASB	ESV
Incorruptibility	Incorruption	The imperishable	The imperishable / incorruption	The imperishable

Comparing English translations of *aphtharsian* in 1 Cor. 15:53-54

CSB	KJV	NIV	NASB	ESV
Immortality	Immortality	Immortality	Immortality	Immortality

Comparing English translations of *athanasian* in 1 Cor. 15:53-54

Phil. 3:21 - "He will transform (*metaschematisei*) the body of our humble condition into the likeness of his glorious body, by the power that enables him to subject everything to himself."

Paul encourages his readers to imitate him, and to follow the example of mature believers around them, for enemies of the cross abound. With tears, Paul reminds the Philippian Christians that false teachers are destined for everlasting separation from God. They are preoccupied with Jewish dietary laws, thus making a god of their bellies. They focus inappropriately on the genitals as they glorify circumcision. And they focus on earthly things (vv. 17-19).

But just as the Philippians are proud of their Roman citizenship, Paul urges them to embrace the greater citizenship of heaven. From there, a Savior far superior to Caesar is returning one day (v. 20). When He comes, a miraculous transformation takes place. By the same power He exhibits in resurrection (v. 10) and applies in kingly rule, Jesus transforms our earthly bodies into heavenly bodies that simulate His.

The "body of our humble condition" refers to the frailty of our mortal existence. Every day, followers of Jesus experience the consequences of living in a fallen world. We stumble, break bones, get sick, age, and grow inevitably weaker by the day. But when Christ returns on the clouds of heaven, in the glory of His Father and in the presence of His holy angels, He renews our frail bodies, making them victorious over the effects of the Fall.

Paul uses the Greek word *metaschematisei* (transform) to describe the work of Jesus in our resurrected bodies. It means to change the outward form of something; to remodel or transfigure.[30] It is similar to *metamorphoo*, which describes Jesus' glorious transfiguration (Matt. 17:2; Mark 9:2), as well as the spiritual transformation that believers experience on this side of heaven (Rom. 12:2; 2 Cor. 3:18).

Our future glorification is not a change in identification, but in form. As Christ's glorified body is physical and identifiable, so is ours. Yet, His resurrected body exhibits astonishing characteristics that serve as the template for our glorified selves.

CSB	KJV	NIV	NASB	ESV
Transform	Change	Transform	Transform	Transform

Comparing English translations of *metaschematisei* in Phil. 3:21

1 John 3:2 - "Dear friends, we are God's children now, and what we will be has not yet been revealed (*ephanerothe*). We know that when he appears, we will be like him because we will see him as he is."

The world may not think much of Christians. That's because unbelievers don't know God, nor can they fathom the love the Father has lavished on those who trust in Him, calling them His children (v. 1). As adopted sons and daughters of God, we should look beyond the hardships that naturally come with bearing the name of Christ and catch a glimpse of the glorious inheritance that is ours.

Living in the light of eternity should prompt us to consider four truths John shares with us. First, God finishes what He starts, even though He hasn't revealed all the details of our glorification. Second, Jesus is returning for us; John doesn't say "if," but "when he appears." Third, we become like Jesus in our resurrected bodies — transformed, clothed in His immortality, free of the weight of sin's curse. Fourth, we are going to see Him as He is. Just as Peter, James, and John catch a glimpse of Christ's radiance on the Mount of Transfiguration (Matt. 17:1-7; Mark 9:2-8), we have all eternity to bask in His unveiled glory.

John writes, "what we will be has not yet been revealed." The word "revealed" comes from the Greek verb *phaneroo*. It denotes the act of making visible or disclosing something not readily seen. In several places, it refers to the appearing of Jesus — in the Incarnation (1 Tim. 3:16; 1 John 1:2; 3:8), after His resurrection (Mark 16:12, 14; John 21:1), and at His second coming (Col. 3:4, 1 John 2:28; 3:2).[31] In fact, John uses the word again later in verse 2: "We know that when he *appears* ..." In other words, we may take comfort in knowing that when Jesus returns, we both understand His resurrection power and experience it ourselves.

But the apostle doesn't stop here. He has told us what we *are* and what we *will be*. Before moving on, he tells us what we *should be*: "And everyone who has this hope in him purifies himself just as he is pure" (v. 3).

CSB	KJV	NIV	NASB	ESV
Revealed	Yet appear	Made known	Appeared	Appeared

Comparing English translations of *ephanerothe* in 1 John 3:2

Summary

The writer of Hebrews exhorts Christians to "run with endurance the race that lies before us, keeping our eyes on Jesus, the source and perfecter of our faith" (Heb. 12:1b-2a). Just as Jesus "endured the cross, despising the shame, and sat down at the right hand of the throne of God" (v. 2b), we should live our often-grueling earthly race with a heavenly perspective. The world was not always fallen, nor will it always be. Despite the constant struggle against Satan's temptations, the world's charms, and the shadow of encroaching mortality, followers of Jesus should live in joyful anticipation of a victorious and never-ending future when we see Jesus as He is and are made like Him.

The finish line of our faith looms glowingly before our eyes, and the God who has known us throughout eternity has promised to finish the work He began in us. Future glorification is as certain as the other elements of salvation. It is the completion of God's gracious work of redeeming us from the slave market of sin, breathing new life into our dead human spirits, declaring us in right standing before Him, and adopting us as His children. Just as God's creation of all things was "very good indeed" (Gen. 1:31), His redemption of fallen humans, and His restoration of the sin-stained universe to innocence one day, stand forevermore as a testimony to His goodness, faithfulness, and love.

For now, Christians are not promised an earthly walk in the park, but an arduous race through enemy territory. If we're living faithfully, we may expect hardship, shunning, persecution, and pain — not health, riches, fame, and ease. Christ is not the means to an end; He is the end Himself, accessed through a narrow gate (Matt. 7:13) and pursued down a path of good works He laid out for us ahead of time (Eph. 2:10). He walks with us, however, urging our faithfulness to Him while we "go through many hardships to enter the kingdom of God" (Acts 14:22).

In the end, we may rejoice with the apostle Paul that "the sufferings of this present time are not worth comparing with the glory that is going to be revealed in us" (Rom. 8:18).

Consider these summary statements on glorification:

- Glorification is the final act of God's redemptive work, in which He raises our lifeless bodies from the grave and restores us to a state that's better than the original because we have incorruptible bodies that never again suffer the ravages of sin or experience death.
- Glorification is multidimensional. It involves time and eternity, individuals and the believing community, saints and their Savior, resurrection of people and the regeneration of earth.
- There is glory now. As we honor the Father, Son, and Holy Spirit for their divine attributes and redemptive work, God enables us to share in the divine nature (2 Peter 1:3-4). This does not mean we become little gods. Rather, we participate in God's moral excellence, knowing that one day we will be morally perfected.
- There is glory in death. When we breathe our last, followers of Jesus leave our earthly bodies behind. Our souls and spirits pass into the presence of God in heaven, where we glorify God in ways previously unknown as He endows us with moral and spiritual perfection.
- There is glory in resurrection. Full glorification for followers of Jesus takes place when He calls our bodies from the grave and gives us incorruptible bodies similar to the body He bore when He rose from the dead.
- There is glory in restoration. Jesus refers to this as "the renewal of all things, when the Son of Man sits on his glorious throne" (Matt. 19:28). Peter urges us to wait for "new heavens and a new earth, where righteousness dwells" (2 Peter 3:13). And in John's vision of the world to come, he sees "a new heaven and a new earth" (Rev. 21:1). All of these passages refer to the future glorification of the created order, a world purged of sin and its stain, where the pristine innocence of all creation is restored.
- There is less in Scripture about the resurrection of the wicked than the glorification of the just. Nevertheless, the

Bible gives us enough information to know that those who reject Christ are physically resurrected one day and separated forever from God.

- Heaven is not the same for every believer, nor do all those who reject Christ experience hell identically. Everyone's final, personal, individual judgment before Christ is His way, as righteous Judge, of setting things right for all eternity.
- Every person is physically resurrected one day, summoned before Christ on His throne of glory, and ushered into eternity, either in a glorified body similar to the body Christ had when He rose from the dead, or in a physical body prepared for everlasting existence in outer darkness.

THINK
Questions for personal or group study

(1) In what ways is glorification the final act of God's redemptive work?

(2) Briefly describe how glorification works in the following stages:

- In our Christian duty now to honor the Father, Son, and Holy Spirit
- In death
- In resurrection
- In the new heavens and new earth — what Jesus calls "the renewal of all things"

(3) Read 1 Cor. 15:35-52 and consider:

- How does Paul use a seed as an analogy for our mortal bodies and for what becomes of them in resurrection (vv. 36-38)?
- What hope do we have in death that animals do not have (v. 39)?
- How does the rising of the sun, moon, and stars give us

hope of God's faithfulness to redeem our mortal bodies
(vv. 40-41)?

- How does Paul contrast our earthly bodies with our
  heavenly ones (vv. 42-44)?
- How quickly are we transformed when Christ calls us from
  the grave (vv. 51-52)?

(4) Why do you think the New Testament offers a good description of believers' resurrected bodies but says almost nothing about the
future bodies of the wicked?

(5) What are the five "crowns," or rewards, the New Testament
indicates believers may send ahead of us to heaven?

- The _____ crown (1 Cor. 9:24-27)
- The crown of _____ (1 Thess. 2:19-20)
- The crown of _____ (2 Tim. 4:7-8)
- The crown of _____ (1 Peter 5:1-4)
- The crown of _____ (James 1:12; Rev.
  2:10)

(6) Why do you think final judgment for all people follows their
resurrection rather than their death?

(7) In what ways is resurrection necessary in order for Christ to set
things right?

Notes

INTRODUCTION

1. Paul G. Humber, *400 Prophecies, Appearances, or Foreshadowings of Christ in the Tanakh (Old Testament)*, Associates for Biblical Research, http://biblearchaeology.org, 2012.
2. Earl D. Radmacher, "Part VII: Salvation," in *Understanding Christian Theology*, ed. Charles R. Swindoll and Roy B. Zuck (Nashville, TN: Thomas Nelson Publishers, 2003), 805.
3. Robert A. Morey, *Studies in the Atonement* (Las Vegas, NV: Christian Scholars Press, 2007), 121-128.

CHAPTER ONE: YOU ARE FOREKNOWN

1. Frederick L. Godet, *Commentary on St. Paul's Epistle to the Romans* (Grand Rapids, MI: Zondervan, n.d.), 324.
2. Robert E. Picirilli, *Grace, Faith, Free Will: Contrasting Views of Salvation: Calvinism and Arminianism* (Nashville, TN: Randall House, 2002), 38.
3. Eugene E. Carpenter and Philip W. Comfort, *Holman*

    Treasury of Key Bible Words: 200 Greek and 200 Hebrew Words Defined and Explained (Nashville, TN; Broadman & Holman Publishers, 2000), 283.

4. *Hebrew-Greek Key Word Study Bible: Key Insights Into God's Word* (Chattanooga, TN: AMG Publishers, 2013), 2256.

5. John M. Frame, *Systematic Theology: An Introduction to Christian Belief* (Phillipsburg, NJ: P&R Publishing Company, 2013), 311.

6. *Hebrew-Greek Key Word Study Bible*, 2256.

7. "What is the purpose of life?" http://mormon.org/beliefs/purpose-of-life.

8. Frame, 310.

9. Ibid.

10. Robert James Utley, *The Gospel according to Paul: Romans, Vol. 5*, Study Guide Commentary Series (Marshall, Texas: Bible Lessons International, 1998), Rom. 11:2.

11. Carpenter and Comfort, *Holman Treasury of Key Bible Words*, 283.

12. Ibid.

CHAPTER TWO: YOU ARE ELECTED

1. Included among the resources I have found most helpful are: *Chosen But Free: A Balanced View of Divine Election* by Norman Geisler; *What Is Reformed Theology? Understanding the Basics* by R.C. Sproul; *Grace, Faith, Free Will: Contrasting Views of Salvation: Calvinism and Arminianism* by Robert E. Picirilli; *Perspectives on Election: Five Views*, edited by Chad Owen Brand; and *Salvation and Sovereignty: A Molinist Approach* by Kenneth Keathley.

2. *The Baptist Faith & Message* (Nashville, TN: LifeWay Press, 2000), 12.

3. Picirilli, *Grace, Faith, Free Will*, 10-11.

4. James (Jacobus) Arminius, *The Writings of James Arminius*, tr. James Nichols and W.R. Bagnall (Grand Rapids, MI: Baker, 1956), 1:254.

5. Kenneth Keathley, *Salvation and Sovereignty: A Molinist*

Approach (Nashville, TN: B&H Publishing Group, 2010), 5.

6. Picirilli, *Grace, Faith, Free Will*, 50-51.

7. Charles Spurgeon, "Sovereign Grace and Man's Responsibility," http://www.spurgeon.org/resource-library/sermons/sovereign-grace-and-mans-responsibility#flipbook/.

8. "Exposition of the Doctrines of Grace," http://www.spurgeon.org/sermons/0385.htm.

9. Wayne Grudem, *Systematic Theology* (Grand Rapids, MI: Zondervan, 1994), 685.

10. "What is hyper-Calvinism and is it biblical?" https://gotquestions.org/hyper-calvinism.html.

11. Grudem, *Systematic Theology*, 686-687.

12. William D. Mounce, *Mounce's Complete Expository Dictionary of Old & New Testament Words* (Grand Rapids, MI: Zondervan, 2006), 107.

13. Ibid., 108.

14. Ibid.

15. *Hebrew-Greek Key Word Study Bible*, 1638.

16. *CSB Study Bible* (Nashville, TN: Holman Bible Publishers, 2017), 1796.

17. Picirilli, *Grace, Faith, Free Will*, 73-74.

18. Thomas R. Schreiner, *Baker Exegetical Commentary on the New Testament: Romans* (Grand Rapids, MI: Baker Academic, 2005), 624.

19. Pelagius (c. A.D. 360-418) was a theologian of British origin who advocated free will and asceticism. He argued that humans are able to fulfill the law without divine aid. The Council of Carthage (A.D. 418) declared him a heretic. His interpretation of free will became known as Pelagianism.

CHAPTER THREE: YOU ARE PREDESTINED

1. "10 Lucky Celebrities Who Escaped Disaster," http://smithsonianmag.com/history/10-lucky-celebrities-

who-escaped-disaster-180947668/.

2. A better answer is that God sovereignly spared McQueen's life that night, drawing the actor to faith in Christ under the preaching of Billy Graham. See Greg Laurie, "Steve McQueen: The salvation of an American icon," http://foxnews.com/opinion/2017/07/08/steve-mcqueen-salvation-american-icon.html.

3. Mounce, *Complete Expository Dictionary*, 534.

4. *CSB Study Bible*, 1794, 1870.

5. Grudem, *Systematic Theology*, 670.

6. Chad Brand, "Predestination," *Holman Illustrated Bible Dictionary*, ed. Charles Draper et al. (Nashville, TN: Holman Bible Publishers, 2003), 1323-1325.

7. Greg Bailey, "Conformed to His Image," http://ligonier.org/learn/articles/conformed-his-image/.

8. Warren W. Wiersbe, *The Bible Exposition Commentary, Vol. 1* (Wheaton, IL: Victor Books, 1996), 574–575.

9. https://biblegateway.com/passage/?search=Ephesians+1%3A1%2D11&version=NIV.

CHAPTER FOUR: YOU ARE CALLED

1. Mounce, *Complete Expository Dictionary*, 92. He cites several uses in the Hebrew Scriptures, including: (1) To call, or name. God calls the light "day" and the darkness "night" (Gen. 1:5). Adam names the animals, and he calls Eve "woman" (Gen. 2:19-20, 23). (2) God's call to service. For example, God calls Abraham (Isa. 51:2) and Cyrus (Isa. 45:3). "And when he calls someone, he expects that person to answer to his call; anything less is disobedience." (3) Man's call to God. About the time of the birth of Seth, people "began to call on the name of the Lord" (Gen. 4:26). Abraham builds an altar and calls on the name of the Lord (Gen. 12:8). The psalmist calls on Yahweh (Ps. 17:6; 18:3, 6; 30:8). (4) Servants of the Lord proclaim His will (1 Kings 13:32; Isa. 40:2; Jer. 2:2). God calls

Jonah to travel to Nineveh and "preach" against it
(Jonah 1:2).

2. Ibid., 93.
3. Ibid.
4. Ibid., 94.
5. Mark uses the verb *boao* in a parallel passage, Mark 15:34.
6. I.H. Marshall, "Predestination in the New Testament," in *Grace Unlimited*, ed. C.H. Pinnock (Minneapolis, MN: Bethany Fellowship, Inc., 1975), 127-143.
7. Keathley, *Salvation and Sovereignty*, 118.
8. *Easton's Bible Dictionary*, http://eastonsbibledictionary.org/694-Call.php.
9. *CSB Study Bible*, 1743.
10. James Oliver Buswell, Jr., *A Systematic Theology of the Christian Religion, Vol. II* (Grand Rapids, MI: Zondervan, 1962-63), 152-153.
11. Norman Geisler, *Chosen But Free: A Balanced View of Divine Election* (Minneapolis, MN: Bethany House Publishers, 2001), 41.
12. "Christ Alone," *The Valley of Vision: A Collection of Puritan Prayers & Devotions*, ed. Arthur Bennett (Edinburgh, UK: The Banner of Truth Trust, 1975), 40.
13. *CSB Study Bible*, 1794.
14. Geisler, *Chosen But Free*, 69.
15. Ibid., 74.
16. Keathley, *Salvation and Sovereignty*, 106.
17. *CSB Study Bible*, 1977-1978.

CHAPTER FIVE: YOU ARE REGENERATED

1. Kenneth S. Wuest, *Word Studies in the Greek New Testament, Vol. II, The Pastoral Epistles* (Grand Rapids, MI: Wm. B. Eerdmans Publishing Co., 1973), 199.
2. *Expository Dictionary of Bible Words*, ed. Stephen D. Renn (Peabody, MA: Hendrickson Publishers Marketing, LLC, 2005), 797.
3. Frame, *Systematic Theology*, 166.

4. Ibid.
5. I do not wish to be dogmatic about the so-called "trichotomous" view of humanity. There are good arguments in favor of the "dichotomous" view, which understands the Bible to describe people as both physical (body) and non-physical (soul/spirit). I simply prefer the trichotomous view because I believe it better fits the biblical narrative of creation, fall, and redemption.
6. *CSB Study Bible*, 1536.
7. Matthew Henry, *Matthew Henry's Commentary on the Whole Bible: Complete and Unabridged in One Volume* (Peabody, MA: Hendrickson, 1994), 2374.
8. Wiersbe, *The Bible Exposition Commentary, Vol. 2,* 267-268.
9. David K. Lowery, "2 Corinthians," *The Bible Knowledge Commentary: An Exposition of the Scriptures, Vol. 2*, ed. J.F. Walvoord and R.B. Zuck, (Wheaton, IL: Victor Books, 1985), 567-568.
10. Robert James Utley, *Paul's Letters to a Troubled Church: I and II Corinthians, Vol. 6*, Study Guide Commentary Series (Marshall, TX: Bible Lessons International, 2002), 241.
11. Marvin Richardson Vincent, *Word Studies in the New Testament, Vol. 3* (New York: Charles Scribner's Sons, 1887), 320.
12. Henry, *Matthew Henry's Commentary*, 2306.
13. Robert E. Olson, *The Story of Christian Theology: Twenty Centuries of Tradition & Reform* (Downers Grove, IL: IVP Academic, 1999), 118.
14. "What is baptismal regeneration?" https://gotquestions.org/baptismal-regeneration.html.
15. "Manuscript evidence indicates that this Gospel probably did not originally include any of vv. 9-20. Either Mark ended his Gospel here, he never wrote an intended ending, or his original ending has been lost." *CSB Apologetics Study Bible* (Nashville, TN: 2017), 1254.
16. "Does Mark 16:16 teach that baptism is necessary for

salvation?" https://gotquestions.org/baptism-Mark-16-16.html.

17. H. E. Dana and Julius R. Mantey, *A Manual Grammar of the Greek New Testament* (New York: Macmillan, 1955), 103-104; A. T. Robertson, *A Grammar of the Greek New Testament in the Light of Historical Research* (Nashville: Broadman Press, 1934), 389; Kenneth S. Wuest, *Word Studies in the Greek New Testament* (Grand Rapids: Wm. B. Eerdmans Publishing Co., 1966), 3:76-77. Robertson comments, "My view is decidedly against the idea that Peter, Paul, or any one in the New Testament taught baptism as essential to the remission of sins or the means of securing such remission. So I understand Peter to be urging baptism on each of them who had already turned (repented)." *Word Pictures in the New Testament: Concise Edition,* ed. James A. Swanson (Nashville, TN: Holman Bible Publishers, 2000), 68.

18. "Does Acts 22:16 teach that baptism is necessary for salvation?" https://gotquestions.org/baptism-Acts-22-16.html.

19. Ibid.

20. Robertson, *Word Pictures*, 332.

21. Wuest, *Word Studies in the Greek New Testament, Vol. II, First Peter in the Greek New Testament*, 108-109.

22. R.C. Sproul, *What Is Reformed Theology? Understanding the Basics* (Grand Rapids, MI: Baker Books, 1997), 213.

23. Ibid., 216.

24. The five points of Calvinism are spelled out in the acrostic TULIP: T=total depravity; U=unconditional election; L=limited atonement; I=irresistible grace; and P=perseverance of the saints. While there are many excellent resources that fully explain the so-called "doctrines of grace," a good start is *What Is Reformed Theology? Understanding the Basics* by R.C. Sproul.

25. For a more complete understanding of Arminianism, see *Grace, Faith, Free Will: Contrasting Views of Salvation: Calvinism & Arminianism* by Robert E. Picirilli. For an

even more detailed view of the life and teachings of Arminius, see *Arminius: A Study in the Dutch Reformation* by Carl Bangs.

26. Geisler, *Chosen But Free*, 237-238.
27. Ibid., 242-243.
28. Keathley, *Salvation and Sovereignty*, 101.

CHAPTER SIX: YOU ARE JUSTIFIED

1. John Murray, *Redemption Accomplished and Applied* (Grand Rapids, MI: Wm. B. Eerdmans, 1955), 121.
2. J.I. Packer, "Justification," in *New Bible Dictionary*, ed. D.R.W. Wood et al. (Leicester, England; Downers Grove, IL: InterVarsity Press, 1996), 636-640.
3. Ibid.
4. Carpenter and Comfort, *Holman Treasury of Key Bible Words,* 315.
5. Wiersbe, *The Bible Exposition Commentary, Vol. 1,* 695.
6. Packer, *New Bible Dictionary*, 636-640.
7. Ibid.
8. Morey, *Studies in the Atonement*, 232.
9. Ibid., 244-245.
10. Millard J. Erickson, *Christian Theology*, Third Edition (Grand Rapids, MI: Baker Academic, 2013), 887.
11. Vincent, *Word Studies in the New Testament*, 42.
12. Robert Jamieson, A. R. Fausset, and David Brown, *Commentary Critical and Explanatory on the Whole Bible, Vol. 2* (Oak Harbor, WA: Logos Research Systems, Inc., 1997), 228.
13. John A. Witmer, "Romans," in *The Bible Knowledge Commentary: An Exposition of the Scriptures, Vol. 2*, ed. J. F. Walvoord and R. B. Zuck (Wheaton, IL: Victor Books, 1985), 451.
14. Wiersbe, *The Bible Exposition Commentary, Vol. 1*, 524.
15. Dwight L. Hunt, "The Second Epistle of Paul the Apostle to the Corinthians," in *The Grace New Testament*

Commentary, ed. Robert N. Wilkin (Denton, TX: Grace Evangelical Society, 2010), 789.

16. Renn, *Expository Dictionary of Bible Words*, 547.

CHAPTER SEVEN: YOU ARE INDWELT

1. See E. Randolph Richards and Brandon J. O'Brien, *Misreading Scripture with Western Eyes* (Downers Grove, IL: InterVarsity Press, 2012), 120-128.

2. Charles C. Ryrie, *Basic Theology: A Popular Systematic Guide To Understanding Biblical Truth* (Wheaton, IL: Victor Books, 1986), 356.

3. Frame, *Systematic Theology*, 675.

4. *CSB Study Bible*, 1696.

5. Bruce Metzger, on behalf of the Editorial Committee of the United Bible Societies' Greek New Testament, *A Textual Commentary on the Greek New Testament*, Second Edition (Germany, 1994), 208.

6. *CSB Study Bible*, 1820.

7. "A Sermon (No. 1004) Delivered on Lord's-day Morning, August 6th, 1871, by C.H. Spurgeon, At the Metropolitan Tabernacle, Newington," Blue Letter Bible, https://www.blueletterbible.org/Comm/spurgeon_charles/sermons/1004.cfm.

8. Wiersbe, *The Bible Exposition Commentary, Vol. 2*, 520.

9. Although it's difficult to find anyone who promotes the "complete discontinuity" view. James M. Hamilton, Jr., *God's Indwelling Presence: The Holy Spirit in the Old & New Testaments* (Nashville, TN: B&H Academic, 2006), 9-24.

10. Ibid., 3.

11. Ibid., 27.

12. It should be clear that no unbeliever has ever been regenerated, indwelt, or filled — although these redemptive acts of God could occur in the future if he or she responds in faith to the gospel.

13. Robert G. Gromacki, "Part IV: The Holy Spirit," in *Understanding Christian Theology*, 501-502.

CHAPTER EIGHT: YOU ARE BAPTIZED IN THE SPIRIT

1. "10 Bizarre Rites of Passage," http://listverse.com/2009/12/28/10-bizarre-rites-of-passage/.
2. Charles Stanley, *Charles Stanley's Handbook for Christian Living: Biblical Answers to Life's Tough Questions* (Nashville, TN: Thomas Nelson Publishers, 1996), 145.
3. Ibid., 145-146.
4. Frame, *Systematic Theology*, 926-927.
5. Stanley, *Charles Stanley's Handbook for Christian Living*, 149.
6. Grudem, *Systematic Theology*, 774-775.
7. Hamilton, *God's Indwelling Presence*, 94.
8. *CSB Study Bible*, 1709.
9. See, for example, *Perspectives on Spirit Baptism: Five Views*, ed. Chad Owen Brand (Nashville, TN: Broadman & Holman Publishers, 2004).
10. Ibid., 9-14.
11. Hamilton, *God's Indwelling Presence*, 96.
12. Ibid., 183.
13. Ibid., 96.
14. "Our 16 Fundamental Truths," https://ag.org/Beliefs/Statement-of-Fundamental-Truths.
15. For more on different levels of theological urgency, see Rob Phillips, *The Last Apologist: A Commentary on Jude for Defenders of the Christian Faith* (Jefferson City, MO: MBC Press, 2017), 53-68.
16. Ryrie, *Basic Theology*, 365.
17. Henry, *Matthew Henry's Commentary*, 2062.
18. Wiersbe, *The Bible Exposition Commentary, Vol. 1*, 448.
19. Grudem, *Systematic Theology*, 767-768.

CHAPTER NINE: YOU ARE SANCTIFIED

1. Erickson, *Christian Theology*, 897.
2. Some Bible commentators avoid using the term "positional

sanctification." For example, Robert Morey writes, "It is a mistake to identify the past tense meaning of sanctification (in passages such as 1 Cor. 1:2) as referring to some sort of 'positional sanctification' because: (1) this confuses sanctification with justification, and (2) this is in direct violation of the basic meaning of ethical sanctification, which is to *make* sinners righteous." Morey, *Studies in the Atonement*, 295-296.

3. Frame, *Systematic Theology*, 986.

4. Morey, *Studies in the Atonement*, 292-293.

5. Some commentators prefer the term *progressive sanctification*.

6. "What did Jesus mean when He said, 'Take up your cross and follow me'?" https://gotquestions.org/take-up-your-cross.html.

7. Frame, *Systematic Theology*, 987-988.

8. Erickson, *Christian Theology*, 898-899.

9. Morey, *Studies in the Atonement*, 295.

10. Grudem, *Systematic Theology*, 754.

11. John Wesley, *A Plain Account of Christian Perfection* (London: Epworth, 1952), 28.

12. Georgios I. Mantzaridis, *The Deification of Man*, trans. Liadain Sherrard (Crestwood, NY: St. Vladimir's Seminary Press, 1984), 112.

13. John D. Zizioulasl, *Being as Communion: Studies in Personhood and the Church* (Crestwood, NY: St. Vladimir's Seminary Press, 1985), 50.

14. Grudem, *Systematic Theology*, 751.

15. Henry, *Matthew Henry's Commentary*, 2032.

16. Wiersbe, *The Bible Exposition Commentary, Vol. 1*, 370.

17. James Emery White, "John," in *Holman Concise Bible Commentary*, ed. David S. Dockery (Nashville, TN: Broadman & Holman Publishers, 1998), 485.

18. Royce Gordon Gruenler, "Romans," in *Evangelical Commentary on the Bible, Vol. 3*, Baker Reference Library (Grand Rapids, MI: Baker Book House, 1995), 937–938.

19. *CSB Study Bible*, 1791.

20. William D. Mounce, *Interlinear For The Rest of Us* (Grand Rapids, MI: Zondervan, 2006), 789.
21. Wiersbe, *The Bible Exposition Commentary, Vol. 1*, 568.
22. Mounce, *Interlinear For The Rest of Us,* 898.
23. Ibid., 800.
24. Ibid., 831.
25. Roger Ellsworth, *Opening up Philippians*, Opening Up Commentary (Leominster: Day One Publications, 2004), 18–19.
26. Tim Shenton, *Opening up 1 Thessalonians*, Opening Up Commentary (Leominster: Day One Publications, 2006), 114–115.
27. Roger M. Raymer, "1 Peter," in *The Bible Knowledge Commentary: An Exposition of the Scriptures, Vol. 2*, 840.
28. Robert James Utley, *The Gospel according to Peter: Mark and I & II Peter, Vol. 2*, Study Guide Commentary Series (Marshall, Texas: Bible Lessons International, 2000), 244.

CHAPTER TEN: YOU ARE ADOPTED

1. "9 Unbelievable Adoption Stories," https://oddee.com/item_99400.aspx.
2. Radmacher, *Understanding Christian Theology*, 882.
3. Carpenter and Comfort, *Holman Treasury of Key Bible Words*, 221.
4. Grudem, *Systematic Theology*, 738.
5. Ibid.
6. Ibid.
7. For more on this issue, see Rob Phillips, *The Last Apologist*, 53-68.
8. Gerald Cowen, *Salvation: Word Studies from the Greek New Testament* (Nashville, TN: Broadman Press, 1990), 129.
9. Francis Lyall, *Slaves, Citizens, Sons: Legal Metaphors in the Epistles*, quoted in David Neff, "Biblical Adoption Is Not What You Think It Is," http://christianitytoday.com/ct/2013/december/heirs-biblicaliblical-take-on-adoption.html?start=2.

10. Utley, *The Gospel according to Peter: Mark and I & II Peter, Vol. 2*, 215–216.
11. Vincent, *Word Studies in the New Testament, Vol. 1*, 630.
12. Utley, *The Gospel according to Peter: Mark and I & II Peter, Vol. 2*, 216.
13. "What does it mean to be co-heirs/joint-heirs with Christ?" https://gotquestions.org/co-heirs-with-Christ.html.
14. Read more about this in Phillips, *The Last Apologist*, 101-115.
15. For more on the errors of the Word of Faith movement, see Phillips, *The Apologist's Toolkit: Resources to Help You Defend the Christian Faith* (Jefferson City, MO: MBC Press, 2016), 243-277.
16. Wiersbe, *The Bible Exposition Commentary, Vol. 1*, 540.
17. *CSB Study Bible*, 1794.
18. Other passages on God as Israel's Father include Deut. 32:6; Isa. 1:2; Jer. 31:9; Hosea 11:1; and Mal. 1:6.
19. *CSB Study Bible*, 95.
20. Wiersbe, *The Bible Exposition Commentary, Vol. 1*, 543.
21. *HCSB Study Bible* (Nashville, TN: Holman Bible Publishers, 2010), 1961.
22. Robert James Utley, *Paul Bound, the Gospel Unbound: Letters from Prison (Colossians, Ephesians and Philemon, Then Later, Philippians), Vol. 8*, Study Guide Commentary Series (Marshall, TX: Bible Lessons International, 1997), 74.

CHAPTER ELEVEN: YOU ARE SEALED

1. See also *Bel and the Dragon* 14.
2. Cowen, *Salvation*, 130-133.
3. Theologian Leon Wood argues that since Old Testament saints are both secure and indwelt, they must also be sealed. See *The Holy Spirit in the Old Testament* (Grand Rapids, MI: Zondervan, 1976), 70-71.
4. Ryrie, *Basic Theology*, 359-360.

5. James D.G. Dunn, *Baptism in the Holy Spirit* (Philadelphia, PA: The Westminster Press, 1970), 158-159.
6. Harold W. Hoehner, "Ephesians," in *The Bible Knowledge Commentary: An Exposition of the Scriptures, Vol. 2*, 619.
7. Frame, *Systematic Theology*, 1001.
8. Ibid., 1002.
9. Consider, for example, *Four Views on Eternal Security*, ed. J. Matthew Pinson (Grand Rapids, MI: Zondervan, 2002).
10. Daniel B. Wallace, "Perseverance of the Saints," *CSB Study Bible*, 1871.
11. Ibid.
12. Geisler, *Systematic Theology, Vol. 3: Sin, Salvation* (Minneapolis, MN: Bethany House, 2004), 301-302.
13. Ibid., 314-317.
14. Ryrie, *Basic Theology*, 360.
15. Mounce, *Complete Expository Dictionary*, 24.
16. Ibid., 520.
17. Ibid.
18. Jamieson, Fausset, and Brown, *Commentary Critical and Explanatory on the Whole Bible, Vol. 2*, 343.
19. Grudem, *Systematic Theology*, 791.
20. Hoehner, *The Bible Knowledge Commentary*, 619.
21. Wiersbe, *The Bible Exposition Commentary, Vol. 2*, 12–13.
22. Henry, *Matthew Henry's Commentary*, 2315.
23. Ralph Earle, *Word Meanings in the New Testament* (Peabody, MA: Hendrickson Publishers, 1986), 293.

CHAPTER TWELVE: YOU ARE GLORIFIED

1. Barrie Barber, "Memphis Belle to go on display at Air Force Museum in 2018," Dayton Daily News, March 9, 2017, http://www.daytondailynews.com/news/local/memphis-belle-display-air-force-museum-2018/xkJg6sCmeIi4qYR4Nk96WI/.
2. Grudem, *Systematic Theology*, 828.
3. Francis Brown, S.R. Driver, and Charles A. Briggs, *Hebrew*

and English Concordance of the Old Testament (New York: Oxford University Press, 1955), 458-459.

4. Mounce, *Complete Expository Dictionary*, 290.
5. Ibid. See also Rom. 11:33-36; 1 Cor. 10:31; 2 Cor. 4:15; Gal. 1:5; Eph. 3:21; 2 Peter 3:18; Rev. 5:12-13.
6. *ESV Study Bible* (Wheaton, IL: Crossway Bibles, 2008), 2418.
7. While Evangelicals are united in their belief in future resurrection and glorification of the saints, they view the order of events surrounding Christ's return in various ways. Stanley J. Grentz offers a historical, biblical, and theological perspective on the four major positions held by Evangelicals — postmillennialism, dispensational premillennialism, historic premillennialism, and amillennialism — in *The Millennial Maze* (Downers Grove, IL: InterVarsity Press, 1992).
8. *CSB Study Bible*, 1888.
9. *ESV Study Bible*, 2229.
10. Kenneth E. Bailey, *Paul Through Mediterranean Eyes: Cultural Studies in 1 Corinthians* (Downers Grove, IL: IVP Academic, 2011), 464.
11. Ibid., 458.
12. John Crysostom, quoted in *1 Corinthians: Interpreted by Early Christian Commentators*, trans. and ed. Judith L. Kovacs (Grand Rapids, MI: Eerdmans, 2005), 272.
13. Bailey, *Paul Through Mediterranean Eyes*, 467.
14. Gen. 6:1-4; 2 Peter 2:4; Jude 6. One interpretation of these passages is that they record the first demonic possession in human history, with great consequences for people — and for some demons, who are consigned to Tartarus. See Phillips, *The Last Apologist*, 101-115.
15. Erickson, *Christian Theology*, 928.
16. See Phillips, *What Everyone Should Know About the Afterlife* (Jefferson City, MO: MBC Press, 2017), 63-69.
17. Don Stewart, "What about the Unbelievers? What Will Their Raised Bodies Be Like?" https://blueletterbible.org/faq/don_stewart/don_stewart_135.cfm.

18. Robert Jeffress, *A Place Called Heaven: 10 Surprising Truths About Your Eternal Home* (Grand Rapids, MI: Baker Books, 2017), 184-185.
19. Ibid., 185-187.
20. *Dictionary of Biblical Prophecy and End Times* (Grand Rapids, MI: Zondervan, 2007), 236.
21. Joseph Seiss, *The Apocalypse: An Exposition of the Book of Revelation* (Grand Rapids, MI: Kregel Publications, 1900), 479.
22. Ibid.
23. Charles Swindoll, *Insights on Revelation* (Grand Rapids MI: Zondervan, 2011), 266-267.
24. Mounce, *Complete Expository Dictionary*, 558.
25. Utley, *The Gospel according to Paul: Romans*, Rom. 8:11.
26. Wiersbe, *The Bible Exposition Commentary, Vol. 1*, 540–541.
27. Mounce, *Interlinear For The Rest of Us*, 817.
28. Witmer, *The Bible Knowledge Commentary*, 474.
29. Vincent, *Word Studies in the New Testament, Vol. 3*, 285–286.
30. Mounce, *Interlinear For The Rest of Us*, 859.
31. Mounce, *Complete Expository Dictionary*, 28.

Additional Resources

Other Apologetics Resources Available from the
Missouri Baptist Convention

Order printed copies at mobaptist.org/apologetics
Print and Kindle editions available from Amazon

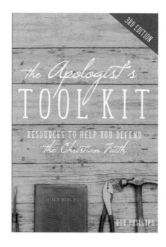

The Apologist's Tool Kit:
Resources to Help You Defend the Christian Faith

The Last Apologist:
A Commentary on Jude for Defenders of the Christian Faith

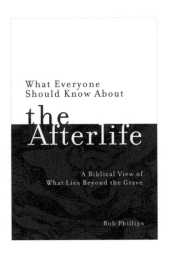

What Everyone Should Know about the Afterlife:
A Biblical View of What Lies Beyond the Grave

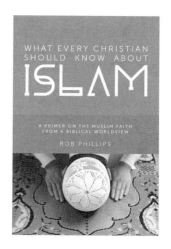

What Every Christian Should Know about Islam:
A Primer on the Muslim Faith from a Biblical Perspective

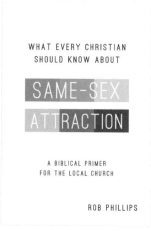

What Every Christian Should Know about Same-sex Attraction:
A Biblical Primer for the Local Church